THE **dragon's**war

THE **dragon's**war

ALLIED OPERATIONS
AND THE FATE OF CHINA
1937–1947

Maochun Yu

NAVAL INSTITUTE PRESS
Annapolis, Maryland

Naval Institute Press
291 Wood Road
Annapolis, MD 21402

Library of Congress Cataloging-in-Publication Data

Yu, Maochun, 1962–
    The dragon's war : allied operations and the fate of China, 1937–1947 / Maochun Yu.
        p. cm.
    Includes bibliographical references and index.
    ISBN 1-59114-946-0 (alk. paper)
    1. Sino-Japanese Conflict, 1937–1945—Participation, Foreign. I. Title. II. Title: Allied operations and the fate of China, 1937–1947.
    DS777.532.Y8 2006
    951.04'2—dc22

                                                                    2006015599

Printed in the United States of America on acid-free paper ∞

13 12 11 10 09 08 07 06   9 8 7 6 5 4 3 2
First printing

CONTENTS

Preface   vii

Chapter 1.   The East Meets the West: Military
             Aid to China from Western Europe   1

Chapter 2.   The Russians Are Coming: The Soviet
             Union's Military Aid to China   10

Chapter 3.   The Flying Tigers with Sharks' Teeth   24

Chapter 4.   The China Commando Group: A British Albatross   46

Chapter 5.   Miles Away in China: The U.S. Navy's Chinese Dragon   68

Chapter 6.   Uncle Sam's Carbine: Military and Financial Aid
             from the United States in Wartime China   88

Chapter 7.   The Curse That Was SACO   104

Chapter 8.   Reading Others' Mail: Cryptology in Wartime China   143

Chapter 9.   Black Propaganda and Morale Operation   155

Chapter 10. An Army of One: Stilwell's Chinese Vinegar   164

Chapter 11. Mission Impossible: Last Chance for the
             U.S. Military Operations in China,
             from Wedemeyer to Marshall   177

Epilogue   194

Notes   199

Bibliography   223

Index   233

PREFACE

MILITARY HOSTILITY BETWEEN CHINA AND JAPAN famously started on 18 September 1931, when the Japanese army invaded and quickly occupied the Chinese northeastern region of Manchuria. Since the Manchuria Incident, the Chinese and Japanese had engaged each other in frequent military skirmishes along the North China and Manchuria border regions, which eventually escalated into an all-out war nearly six years later. On 7 July 1937, the Marco Polo Bridge Incident ignited a full-scale war between China and Japan, which, in the opinion of many, marked the real beginning of World War II in Asia.[1] During this period, against overwhelming odds, China was fighting for its own survival against a formidable military force that had no match in East Asia. Despite China's determination to defeat the invading enemy, the glaring lack of parity in modern weaponry and defense industry between China and Japan created a dire need for China to acquire foreign military aid and defense assistance of various forms. These ranged from massive acquisition of weapons, to substantial financial loans to buttress a wartime economy, to readiness training, and to political reassurance of support from allies. It was obvious that China could not carry out a war against Japan alone. Acquiring foreign support became a vital factor in China's strategy of winning the war.

Conversely, the belligerence between China and Japan was not simply a war between two regional powers. Over the years, the conflict created a powerful impetus for virtually all the major powers in Western Europe to get involved one way or another in the fighting in China. Throughout the prolonged conflict between China and Japan, all major Western powers conducted significant military and intelligence operations inside China.

This is a book about military and intelligence operations in China and foreign aid conducted or sponsored by various countries (the USSR, the United States,

Britain, and France, in particular) during China's long war against Japan. It deals with the extraordinary intrigue, command, and operational manipulations, international espionage, high and low politics, and generally peculiar circumstances surrounding military and intelligence operations in wartime China among the Allies. Topics include various military aid programs to China by Germany, the Soviet Union, Great Britain, and the United States; special intelligence initiatives conducted by the British, the Free French, and the Americans; the massive joint intelligence organization of the Chinese secret police and the U.S. Navy; The secret cooperation of British and American intelligence organizations with the Chinese Communists; America's first covert overseas military operation (the Flying Tigers); and the command and control issues surrounding British, Soviet, and American military personnel in the China theater. It also illustrates the remarkable ramifications of these foreign operations in the Chinese theater of military campaigns and political drama, as well as how these operations exerted a profound influence on China's nationalism, wartime politics, and overall military campaigns.

In essence, this book attempts to illustrate how these foreign operations served to challenge the authority and legitimacy of the Chinese Nationalist government and how the failure of the Nationalist government under Chiang Kai-shek to successfully handle and control foreign operations during World War II greatly contributed to its own demise four years after the war ended.

Scattered accounts about foreign military and intelligence exploits in wartime China have been written. But most of these accounts exist in the form of memoirs, interviews, and newspaper accounts about an isolated nation's experience with the China theater. A single-volume, research-based scholarly monograph covering all major countries' operations and the remarkable ramifications of these foreign operations in the Chinese theater of military campaigns and political drama has been needed.

An overwhelming majority of the existing body of works on wartime military and intelligence in Western languages suffers from a severe lack of any meaningful Chinese-language materials. In the past several years, voluminous new sources have appeared in Chinese about wartime China. A large portion of these new sources deals with foreign military and intelligence operations, a topic that has been previously considered so partisan in nature that little scholarly value could be found in it, or in many cases it has been a taboo or restricted area in the Chinese scholarly world. As readers will see, I have used a significant amount of newly available sources in Chinese.

In the past several years, I have written articles and essays for conferences and journals in the general neighborhood of the subject covere by this book. These articles and essays deal with military and intelligence operations in wartime China by such countries as the Soviet Union, Great Britain, and the United States. I have incorporated some relevant portions of these short pieces into this book. These short pieces include "In God We Trusted, In China We Busted—the China Commando Group of the British SOE," and "The Chinese Code-Breakers, 1927–1945," both of which were published by the journal *Intelligence and National Security* (March 2002 and Spring 1999, respectively), which is a Frank Cass publication (www.frank-cass.com). A conference paper under the aegis of Harvard University's Asia Center, which was delivered in January 2004 in Maui, Hawaii, dealt with some aspects of foreign military and financial aid to wartime China. I have used portions of that paper in the text. In November 2003, I delivered a short paper at Waseda University in Tokyo on the role of media in the China theater during World War II. Some of the findings were published in the Japanese journal *Intelligence* in its April 2004 issue. Portions of that piece are incorporated into the text as well.

To conform to popular practice, I have used the Pinyin Romanization system for Chinese and Japanese characters throughout this book. However, personal and place names of historical significance remain in the Wade-Giles style. For example, the wartime capital of China is Chungking, not Chongqing; the wartime Chinese leader's name is Chiang Kai-shek instead of Jiang Jieshi.

Being a historian is a blessing. Yet, being a professor of history at the United States Naval Academy has been truly delightful. At Annapolis, I often teach a course on the military history of World War II in Asia and have been keenly aware of the glaring need for such a book as this. I should thank many of my students who provided me with the primary motivation to write this book and who have encouraged me throughout the years to actually work on it. My colleagues in the History Department are overwhelmingly helpful and generous in supplying good humor and constructive criticism of many portions of the draft through such worthy venues as the department's heralded monthly "Works-in-Progress" group. To my students, past and current, and to my colleagues goes my profound gratitude.

The editors and staff at the Naval Institute Press are an impressive bunch. I sincerely thank them for their faith in me and in this project. Without their enthusiasm, timely support and encouragement, this project would not have been possible. I would also like to express my gratitude to Tony Meisel and

Gary Kessler, who were assigned by the press as my copy editors for this project. An accomplished author himself, Tony provided great insight on book publishing and other vital issues in modern life. Experienced in the realm of intelligence as well as literary editing, Gary offered invaluable suggestions and grammatical embellishments. I am lucky to have them for this project.

My wife, Angela, was the first critic of my first draft. Her skillful and methodic copyediting feat constantly inspired me to be a better writer during the entire process. I am deeply indebted to her for her emotional support, her great understanding of a writer's occasional crankiness, and the grace with which she handled even the most glaring errors in the text. Of course, I am equally blessed to be the recipient of endless entertainment, persistent harassment, and constant cries for play during most sessions of my writing provided by our rascal beagle, the incorrigible Lou.

THE dragon's war

Chapter 1

THE EAST MEETS THE WEST
Military Aid to China from Western Europe

THE PROLONGED STATE OF WAR IN CHINA in the 1930s and 1940s meant many different things to many different nations. In post-Versailles Germany, arms industrialists saw great opportunities in exporting weapons to China and making their millions. For Great Britain and France, the military rise of Japan posed a serious concern to the security of their vast colonial empires in East and Southeast Asia. So, the Battle of China, as it was once gallantly called, assumed international significance in the major capitals in Europe. Various foreign military aid programs and operations, open or disguised, were created to sustain China's military efforts to defeat the invading Japanese military.

At the start of the conflict, the Chinese military forces under the overall command of Generalissimo Chiang Kai-shek were equipped with weapons from multiple sources, chief of which was Germany. Restricted by the Versailles Treaty, post–World War I Germany was eager to export its military expertise and weapons overseas. Large numbers of unemployed German military strategists and tacticians were on the market for grabs by anyone who needed them. Unable to rearm Germany, the industrialists in various defense businesses set their eyes on China, a nation that, until Chiang Kai-shek unified it in 1928, was ruled by a group of military strongmen who vigorously vied for the control of the titular central government by way of raising and using large provincial warlord armies. This created a significant Chinese market for German arms, considered to be the best by most Chinese warlords. Between 1924 and 1928, a whopping 42 percent of all the arms imports to China came from Germany, far ahead of any other country in this regard.[1]

Furthermore, it is not without irony to note that there was a strong sentimental reason for the affinity felt for each other between the Chinese and the Germans after World War I, because both deeply resented the postbellum settlements and regarded themselves as the justly grieved victims. Although China was on the side of the victors over Germany during World War I, all the high hopes to elevate China's status among the powers at the victors' table were dashed when the Versailles system failed to uphold China's demands for the abolition of the "unequal treaties" between China and the West. A widespread discontent among the Chinese in the immediate aftermath of the Paris Conference further stimulated a surging nationalism across the country. This sense of deep wound in China, however, coincided with the fact that Germany, on account of the Versailles Treaty, was the only Western power that was completely stripped of its privileges and unequal treaties with China. In the meantime, postwar Germany also witnessed a growing sense of being victimized by the Versailles system, as was the case in China, albeit for significantly different reasons.

In the summer of 1927, Chiang Kai-shek, the Nationalist leader, was well on his way to unifying China, wiping out one warlord after another during his victorious Northern Expedition. He fancied himself as China's Otto von Bismarck, shouldering the historic onus of national unification through "Iron and Blood."[2] For this, Chiang had prepared to approach Germany for major initiatives in the areas of military aid and cooperation. As a result, Chinese scholars who had studied at German institutions were organized to map out specific plans and asked to come up with a list of prominent German military experts to be employed by the Chinese government.[3] Top on the list recommended to Chiang was Max Bauer, a former colonel in the kaiser's army, who, upon being offered the job as military adviser, immediately accepted Chiang's invitation and came to China to serve. In March 1928, Bauer accompanied a Chinese military purchase delegation with deep pockets to Germany; they ended up signing arms deals worth more than one million German marks.

Yet, within months, Bauer contracted a disease in China and died in May 1929. Succeeding Bauer was Georg Wetzell, who served as Chiang Kai-shek's chief foreign military adviser from 1930 to 1935.[4] During that tenure, Wetzell developed a rapport with the Chinese general staff, embarking on an ambitious military reconstruction program for the Nationalist leader. Expanding Bauer's small units of training personnel, Wetzell created an "exemplary division" as a seed unit to systematically indoctrinate China's military with the German system. With Chiang's approval, Wetzell became the instructor general for the Chinese Central Military Academy, which was dedicated to the idea of professionalism and military specialization in such areas as training, coastal defense, antiaircraft artillery, and defense industry.[5]

Since the Manchurian Incident of 1931, Japan had adopted a policy of attrition, inching in on China proper. Serious military confrontations occurred from time to time. Wetzell participated in the campaign against the Japanese in the December 1932 battle of Shanghai, as well as the spring 1933 campaign with the Japanese in North China along the Great Wall.[6]

But, with Adolf Hitler's coming to power in early 1933, Japan gradually became more important in Hitler's diplomacy. Although Germany publicly declared neutrality in the increasingly tense Chinese-Japanese military confrontations in China, German advisers inside the Chinese government felt increasing pressure from Berlin to disengage. Wetzell was willing to stay on in this new situation, but he lacked clout in Berlin to support his continuing service to the Chinese government, and in May 1935, he quit his job in China.

However, the lucrative arms market in China prevented German industries from cutting off ties completely. Faced with Hitler's increasing unwillingness to risk his growing friendship with the Japanese, Chiang Kai-shek stepped up his lobbying efforts in Germany in search of a replacement for Wetzell, preferably someone with more eminence and clout to preclude another untimely resignation. Indeed, Chiang soon found such a German military adviser in the venerable strategist, former army marshal Hans von Seeckt. Seeckt carried with him a vast network of connections with the arms industry in Germany. Within months in China, however, Seeckt found himself ill at ease with the Chinese physical environment and became chronically sick. He left China merely ten months later, leaving his assistant, General Alexander von Falkenhausen, as his successor in the same capacity to serve the Chinese government.

Falkenhausen became the most devoted and influential German participant in China's undeclared war against Japan in various major campaigns, until being forcibly recalled to Berlin by Hitler in 1938.[7] During his tenure in China, Falkenhausen stressed the importance of China having a sizeable air force and a unified, well-trained army of one hundred thousand, playing down the urgency of spending any big money on maintaining a strong Chinese navy.[8] His advice that China reduce its current size of two hundred army divisions to sixty, making it better managed and better trained and with a unified chain of command, was instrumental in prompting Chiang to take actions in streamlining China's army.[9]

While Nazi Germany was fast approaching a military and ideological alliance with Japan soon after Hitler came to power, Berlin was also keenly aware of a dilemma: that militarization and rearmament of Germany required sources of raw materials. In this regard, China provided an appealing opportunity, and Hitler was willing to take the risk of irking his friends in Tokyo. As the German industrialist Hans Klein wrote to a Chinese government official on 29 October 1935, "Germany's needs for mineral materials and agricultural products are now enormous, which will include almost all the exports China could gather together in its current capacity."[10]

In light of this, Falkenhausen became an enthusiastic promoter of Sino-German trade, with Chinese raw materials and agricultural goods going to Germany, and German arms going to China. Newly uncovered archival documents indicate that between August 1934 and October 1937, China signed trade deals with Germany, mostly in arms and arms-making equipment, totaling 389 million German marks.[11] After the all-out war broke out in July 1937, China made additional rush orders in November to Berlin requesting urgent arms shipments to China. The Germans responded rapidly and shipped another 50 million German marks worth of arms to China in that month.

In December, in the aftermath of Shanghai's fall to the advancing Japanese, Germany sent two shipments of arms worth another 44 million German marks to China, including more than a dozen dive-bombers.[12] In the early days of the all-out war with Japan, Germany was estimated to have shipped arms worth a total of 144 million German marks to China, or slightly more than $58 million at the contemporary exchange rate.[13]

However, robust trade deals and key military advisers in China notwithstanding, Sino-German relations were destined to tilt toward an ultimate split. To Hitler, there was a larger picture here he must face: Nazi Germany had much more in common with a militaristic Japan in global strategic calculations, especially with regard to the Soviet Union and Western democracies. In 1936 Nazi Germany and Imperial Japan signed a military alliance in the form of the Anti-Comintern Pact. When war broke out in China in July 1937, the Japanese vociferously protested the veiled German presence in the Chinese high command. The German Foreign Ministry frequently issued weak denials of any German participation in the battlefield. By early January 1938, Hitler decided to completely cut off any German ties with China by fiat.

The death knell came when, on 20 February 1938, Hitler announced Germany's diplomatic recognition of the Japanese puppet state of Manchukuo and subsequently issued orders to recall all German military personnel from China and to stop all exports of arms to China at once. Falkenhausen and other German advisers acted slowly in abiding by Berlin's order to return home, to which the Nazi government responded with the threat of revocation of their German citizenship, confiscation of their personal assets, and putting them on trial for treason.[14] On 5 July 1938, the entire German military delegation to China left for home, vowing to their Chinese counterparts never to disclose any Chinese military secrets to Japan, now Hitler's ally in Asia.[15]

With Germany now allied with Japan, China turned to other major powers for help. At the time, four countries—Great Britain, France, the United States, and the Soviet Union—had good reasons to aid China's war efforts. Great Britain and France had vast colonial possessions in Asia that were directly threatened by the Japanese military advances in China and elsewhere, and it was in their own colonial interests to see Japan bogged down in China or even defeated by the Chinese army. As a result, a rationale existed for both countries to provide aid to China's war efforts.

On 5 September 1937, two months after the war broke out in China, the Japanese announced that a total naval blockade had been imposed along the entire Chinese coast. China's arms inflow faced a serious challenge now that the only meaningful sea lines of arms transportation into China would be the southern ports of British Hong Kong and French Haiphong. The Burma route was a possibility, but the Burma Road would not be completed until December 1938. Therefore, securing the passing rights of China's wartime materials from Hong Kong and French Indochina became a matter of life and death. Since China bordered on French Indochina, British Burma, Hong Kong, and India, the Chinese government depended on the British and the French to keep the land lines for weapons transportation into China via these colonial territories open. Therefore, throughout the war, the most significant help China needed from the British and the French was not only military hardware or financial loans, but also open land routes from their colonial territories.

Consequently, China's dealings with the British and the French mainly involved negotiating the right to use British colonies and French Indochina as arms shipment gateways. However, this proved to be an arduous task for the Chinese. Neither the British nor the French were willing to offend the Japanese by granting China the passing right for fear of a Japanese attack on their colonies. Chinese diplomats did their utmost to pressure the British and French to allow China's large quantity of foreign arms to go through. On 6 August 1937, Chiang Kai-shek dispatched his special envoy, H. H. Kung, to Paris to meet the French prime minister on this matter. The Japanese immediately advised the French of the dire consequences if the French gave China the passing right. For weeks, the French cabinet could not decide what to do, and on 17 October 1937, Paris caved in to the Japanese threat. The French cabinet decided that all arms exports to China would be allowed, provided that none of the arms should be transported to China via French Indochina.

The official reason given to Wellington Koo, the Chinese ambassador to Paris, was that the French had to take such action to prevent Japanese bombing of transportation facilities in French Indochina.[16]

The Chinese violently protested this French action. A week later, the French agreed to reconsider this issue at an international conference to be held in Brussels. The French position was to seek promises from the British and the Americans that, in the event of Japanese attacks on French assets in connection with the passing right issue, joint military retaliations would be taken by the French, British, and Americans. London and Washington had no appetite for taking such risks and refused the French proposal.[17]

While the diplomatic wrangling went on for months, the French quietly agreed that before this matter could be finalized, the port facilities and land route would be open for the Chinese to use, albeit on a temporary basis. Wary of French prevarication, Chiang Kai-shek sent his point man, Yang Jie, who was the coordinator of the European military aid, to Paris to firm up the French commitment. When war in Europe suddenly erupted in September 1939, the French could spare no energy dealing with complications in Asia and ordered the halt of all Chinese arms shipments via French Indochina. The Chinese reacted strongly. The French authorities then wobbled for a while, facing protests from both the Japanese and the Chinese on the passing right issue. The fickle state of the matter finally came to a definite end on 18 June 1940, four days after the fall of Paris to the Germans. The Japanese government issued an ultimatum to the French authorities demanding an immediate ban of all Chinese arms-shipping endeavors in French Indochina. The Japanese insisted they be allowed to send in monitoring teams to implement such a ban and threatened to resort to military attacks. Two days later, the government of Philippe Pétain accepted the Japanese terms completely as specified in the ultimatum. China's military assistance program was dealt a major blow.

China's loss of the Hong Kong–Canton route for arms shipment added to this agony. In October 1938, the Japanese launched a major offensive on the southern Chinese coast and took the strategic metropolis of Guangzhou (Canton), located just a short distance north of the British Crown Colony of Hong Kong. This effectively sealed off any possible arms traffic from Hong Kong to unoccupied parts of China.

After the loss of the French Indochinese route and the Hong Kong–Canton route, China became particularly dependent on the Burma route, which had just been completed. Yet, the British had always been wary of the Japanese reaction if the Burma Road remained open for China to transport arms from the sea. So, in July 1940, soon after the French surrendered to

Japan on its ultimatum demanding the ban of passing rights to China via Indochina, Winston Churchill caved in to Japanese threats and closed down the Burma Road. Although it was not to be closed permanently—long before the Americans arrived in China as the primary wartime ally and regarded the control of Burma Road as crucial to the war effort—Chiang Kai-shek had viewed the Burma Road as unreliable. He therefore had already developed the thought of finding alternative routes for delivering arms to China. Throughout the war, while working with the Americans on controlling the Burma Road, Chiang worked tirelessly to secure such land routes.

Even before the Pearl Harbor attack, China had decided to construct a highway from what is today's Sichuan Province to India via Tibet. This would be a monumental undertaking, of course, revealing the desperate situation China faced at the time. By January 1942, the construction survey for the highway to Tibet was progressing in earnest.[18] To even begin this highway project, however, China needed to solve two thorny issues.

The first roadblock was the Tibetans, who adamantly opposed this idea of a Chinese-controlled and operated highway for the shipment of arms going through their territory. Even though there was a titular official office in Lhasa representing the Nationalist government, the Tibetans viewed themselves as independent and were even closer to the British in India than to the Chinese government in Chungking. The Tibetans sent envoys to Chungking to protest this project. This enraged Chiang Kai-shek, who decided to move troops into Tibet if the Tibetans continued to oppose Chungking's wartime efforts. In fact, Chiang had already developed a plan of military action in Tibet to be carried out in October 1943.[19] Churchill and his ambassador to China, Horace Seymour, steadfastly opposed Chiang's hardball approach to the Tibetan issue. To counter British meddling in the Tibetan affairs and to coordinate the India side of the highway project, Chiang made a historic visit to India in February 1942. Mindful of the British threat to play the Tibetan card to upset China, Chiang took great delight in playing the India card to embarrass the British. While in India, Chiang declared his open sympathy for Mahatma Gandhi's and Motilal Nehru's aspirations for Indian independence and personally met with Gandhi against the wishes of the British governor.

But far more important than the realpolitik of mutually annoying each other, the volatile and unstable political situation in India genuinely concerned Chiang Kai-shek a great deal. He feared that if the British continued their harsh colonial stance against making any concession to the Indian nationalists, India might either go up in flames or Gandhi's nationalists might sign a separate peace with Japan. The prospect of losing India to the pro-Japanese forces was most frightening, because it would mean that China would be completely blocked from the outside world and China's war efforts would most likely be finished. To preserve India as a rear echelon of China's war efforts, Chiang, after utterly alienating the British while in India, appealed to President Franklin Roosevelt to intervene immediately in the India affair and pleaded with him to change the mind of the recalcitrant Churchill. Roosevelt expressed great appreciation and sympathy for Chiang's sentiments but nevertheless declined to directly confront his counterpart in London, the very imperial prime minister.[20]

As a result of Chiang Kai-shek's hardball politics in India, the British did indeed adjust their stance a little and help Chiang by trying to convince the Tibetans to grant China the right to build a highway through Tibet. However, the British were violently against China's intention to station troops in Tibet. The tension between London and Chungking on this matter persisted during much of the war years, and eventually, and quite grudgingly, Chiang Kai-shek was forced to scrap the idea of building the Tibet-India highway altogether.[21]

Even though the Chinese had given up on such an idea, the Americans suddenly decided that it would be worthwhile to explore the possibility of building an India-Tibet-China arms delivery route. Months after Chiang Kai-shek's India trip, Roosevelt dispatched two Office of Strategic Services (OSS) agents, Ilia Tolstoy and Brooke Dolan, to Tibet to investigate the situation. The two agents met with the young Dalai Lama and became sentimentally involved with the Tibetan cause. Alarmed by this, Chiang ordered his intelligence chief, General Tai Li of the Military Bureau of Investigation and Statistics, who had just formed a joint intelligence and special operations alliance with the U.S. Navy, to rapidly summon these two OSS agents to Chungking and place them under the watchful eye of the Sino-American intelligence apparatus called the Sino-American Special Technical Cooperative Organization (SACO). Roosevelt never gave any further thought to the matter after this.[22]

By the spring of 1941, therefore, after all the desired arms shipment routes in the South and Southwest that involved the French, British, and Tibetans were out of the question for the Chinese, the situation became dangerous and dire for Chungking. The land route via the Soviet Union resurfaced as the only remaining and viable possibility. But by now Joseph Stalin had greatly shifted his strategy and stunned the world by signing a nonaggression pact with Germany and a neutrality pact with Japan. Afraid of provoking the Japanese to attack the USSR from its Asian flank, Stalin doggedly stuck to the Soviet-Japanese Neutrality Pact and steadfastly refused to use Soviet territory to deliver military assistance to China. In the years to follow, the issue of a land route via the Soviet Union to China for the delivery of American Lend-Lease materials would remain the predominant issue in the Sino-Soviet relationship.[23]

All in all, for the first several years of the Sino-Japanese war, the British and the French proved far less helpful to China's war effort than what the logical rationale might have indicated. Prevalent throughout official circles in London and Paris before 1939 was the spirit of appeasement to aggressors, the futile hope for "peace in our time." In Asia, appeasement to Japan's aggression in China muffled the voices of support for China in both countries. In fact, not only did the British and French fail to provide meaningful military aid to China for the war effort, but they also created numerous crises for the Chinese cause by unilaterally closing down the land routes that had become China's life lines after the Japanese successfully blockaded the entire Chinese coastline. Yet, unlike Germany and Italy, Great Britain and France always kept the Chinese tantalized about the possibility of support. The effort to solicit British help never stopped throughout the war, and in the French case, it ceased only with the fall of Paris in June 1940.

The United States offered the biggest hope to China for military aid and assistance at the outbreak of the war. By far the largest industrial and financial country in the world, the United States had strong sentimental ties with China through its throngs of China-bound missionaries, traders, journalists, adventurers, industrialists, and other roving individuals of high energy and influence. Indeed, there had been much talk in Washington of giving aid to China's war efforts. Yet, in a fundamental way, the America of the late 1930s remained deeply isolationist. It had sympathy for the suffering outside world, but was determined to keep itself free of any entanglements in war-wracked China or Europe. As a result, for the first four years of the Sino-Japanese war, American aid to China was difficult to obtain and remained highly inadequate.

Chapter 2

THE RUSSIANS ARE COMING
The Soviet Union's
Military Aid to China

WHILE CHINA'S PLEAS to the governments of the United States Great Britain, and France for help received little promising or substantial response, the country that took immediate action on a massive scale to help China's war efforts was the one Chiang Kai-shek wished to have the least to do with—the Soviet Union.

The Soviet Union over the years had invested heavily in China in the hope of establishing a pro-Soviet nation, if not an outright Communist Chinese government. Moscow's approach toward this strategic objective was two-pronged. The Comintern, after its founding in 1919, sent agents to China to establish a China branch, leading to the creation of the Chinese Communist Party (CCP) in July 1921, with Mao Zedong being one of the initial participants of CCP meetings. Yet the prevailing and overwhelming force at play in China's political stage at the time was not Communism but nationalism, whose spiritual leader was Dr. Sun Yat-sen. Moscow was keenly aware of this while buttressing the fledgling development of the small, albeit loyal, Chinese Communist Party.

Soviet leader Vladimir Lenin recognized the prevailing wisdom of adopting a pragmatic approach to the China situation. In 1923 he approached Sun Yat-sen for an agreement. Desperate for any foreign help to unify the warlord-ruled China under Sun's Nationalist Party, the Kuomintang (KMT), Sun agreed to form a United Front with the fledgling Chinese Communist Party, in return for the Soviet Union's political and military help. For this purpose, Sun sent his lieutenant, Chiang Kai-shek, to Moscow to arrange a cooperative project. In 1924, with an initial budget of 2 million rubles directly appropriated by Lenin, Moscow set up a military academy near Canton, China, for Sun Yat-sen. Heading the Soviet-backed military training project, famously known as the Whampoa Military Academy, was Sun's right-hand man, Chiang Kai-shek.

But the Soviets had overwhelming control over the training and indoc-trination programs at Whampoa. Mikhail Borodin was the powerful political adviser for Chiang's academy, with Vasily Konstantinovich Blücher (Galen) as Whampoa's overall training coordinator.[1] As a result, the Communist-dominated political wing within this KMT-CCP united front became a heav-ily polarizing factor for rapidly escalating the tension between the Nationalists and the Communists, especially after the deaths of Lenin in 1924 and Sun Yat-sen in 1925. Chiang, now the inheritor of Sun's political fame and legitimacy, grew steadily impatient with his Soviet handlers and their CCP followers.

In April 1927, on his way to a complete elimination of warlord fiefdoms in China, Chiang conducted a bloody purge of the Communists. Subsequently, all Soviet personnel were forced to withdraw from China, thus marking the total failure of the Soviet's adventure in the East Asian country. In 1929 the now-unified Nationalist government of China under Chiang Kai-shek clashed with the Soviets over Moscow's handling of the Soviet-owned Chinese Eastern Railway in Manchuria. As a result, the USSR and China broke off diplomatic relations.

Yet, on 18 September 1931, the Japanese invaded and conquered Chinese Manchuria, fundamentally changing the international situation in East Asia. Both the Soviet Union and China felt the direct threat from Japan. Consequently, the frigid Sino-Soviet relationship soon began to be thawed by a common concern over Japan, even though China and the USSR were based on vastly different ideological grounds. On 12 December 1932, the Soviet Union and China resumed diplomatic relations despite the fact that China was not particularly amused by the Soviet decision to sell the Eastern Chinese Railway to the Japanese in 1933.[2]

The turning point finally came in the summer of 1935, when Stalin made a major switch in foreign and defense policy. He decided that the most imme-diate danger and threat to the Soviet Union and the worldwide Communist movement came not from the Western capitalist democracies any more but from the fascist regimes in Europe and Asia. Thus, suddenly Moscow's obses-sion became to coordinate a worldwide, all-out resistance against the fascist powers of Germany, Italy, and Japan, a policy known as the Popular Front, the first manifestation of which, of course, was the Soviet Union's remarkably substantial military and political involvement in the Spanish Civil War that broke out in the Summer of 1936.

In the overall scheme of this Popular Front strategy, China assumed an unambiguously important role. But China was still embroiled in nasty politi-cal strife between the Chinese Communists led by Mao Zedong in North

China and the Nationalist government in Nanking led by Chiang Kai-shek, a situation far from ideal for Stalin to carry out a popular front by the entire nation to fight the menacing Japanese in Asia.

In December 1936, the Xian Incident, whereby Chiang Kai-shek was kidnapped by his pro-Communist subordinates, provided an impetus for Chiang to give up his pursuit of the Chinese Communists and instead form an anti-Japanese "united front"with the Soviet-backed Chinese Communists. The key role the Soviets played in the ultimate release of Chiang Kai-shek helped put a positive spin on the thawing relationship between Chiang's government and Moscow.

Sensing the imminent outbreak of war between China and Japan, which might further endanger the Soviet Union by a Japanese victory in China, Stalin authorized his ambassador to China, Dimitri Bogomoloff, to inform Chiang Kai-shek on 1 April 1937 that the Soviet Union would provide China with military hardware should a war with Japan break out.[3] Three months later, the Marco Polo Bridge Incident touched off the all-out war.

With the war in China in earnest after 7 July1937, Stalin offered immediate support. On 8 July 1937, Chiang and Stalin agreed to sign a "Sino-Soviet Nonaggression Pact." This pact was tantamount to a military alliance directly aimed at Japan. China received a major morale boost from this unequivocal political and diplomatic support from Moscow. The pact was signed on 21 August 1937, one week after the fierce battle in Shanghai had begun. Although the pact did not specifically include provisions for direct military aid, Article 2 postulated that if either country was under attack by a third country and its allies, neither the Soviet Union nor China would provide any direct or indirect help to the third country or its allies.[4]

But the Soviets went much further than a diplomatic alliance with China after the fighting started. What China needed most at the time was military hardware, and Stalin spared no time in providing help by ordering a large-scale weapons supply. Thus began a massive military aid program to China, which would involve weapons inflow, substantial financial loan packages, dispatch of Soviet military advisers to the China theater, and direct combat participation in various campaigns in the China theater.

In mid-August 1937, soon after the war broke out, the Chinese gave Bogomoloff a list of arms the Soviets could provide. It included 350 airplanes, 200 tanks, and 236 field cannons, along with a sizeable Soviet training crew to be dispatched to China to instruct the Chinese military personnel how to use those weapons.[5] To follow up on this request, Chiang Kai-shek two weeks later dispatched a military delegation to Moscow led by General Yang Jie, the deputy chief of staff of the Chinese army and a resident Soviet expert within the Nationalist government. The instructions given to Yang were to quickly seek a Soviet declaration of war on Japan, which would be the best scenario; to obtain a steady supply of arms from the Soviets to China; and to make sure such supply would go on "uninterrupted."[6]

In late September 1937, the first wave of Soviet weapons began to arrive in China. The delivery lasted about four months, and the items given were impressive, because they included 62 heavy bombers, 101 fighters, 62 fighter-bombers, 82 tanks, 400 trucks, 2,000 antitank canons, antiaircraft batteries, machine guns, ammunition, and other materiel, totaling more than $485 million.[7] By the standards of the time, this was an extraordinarily generous package of military aid. This initial Soviet package alone surpassed the total amount of arms imported from Germany in all the previous years.[8] A cursory look at the items the Chinese requested from Moscow reveals that the priority in Chiang Kai-shek's weapons acquisition was clearly airpower. This strategic priority would last throughout the eight-year war and would play an important role in China's overall foreign aid programs, especially those involving the United States after the Pearl Harbor attacks.

How much military hardware did the Soviet Union supply the Chinese during the entire war? Statistics vary. By the Soviet count, between late September 1937, when the first Soviet armaments arrived in China, and June 1941, when all Soviet military aid to China finally stopped, the Soviet Union provided the Chinese with the following items: 900 aircraft, of which 318 were heavy bombers; 1,140 artillery sets; 82 tanks; close to 10,000 machine guns; 50,000 rifles; 2,000 trucks; 2 million hand grenades; 31,160 airborne bombs; 2 million shells; 180 million bullets; and other materiel.[9]

Not only were the Soviets extraordinarily generous in providing military hardware to China in the first bitter years of war with Japan, especially compared with the far less meaningful support coming from the United States, Great Britain, and France during this period, but they were also unhesitant in giving China much-needed financial loans with which to stabilize China's wartime economy and to purchase weapons at a nominal price.[10] Before the Pearl Harbor attack in December 1941, no other country was more at ease with giving China financial support than the Soviet Union was. By the end of 1941, the Soviet Union had granted China three major loan packages, totaling $250 million, at the request of the Chinese government. Unlike the $120 million loaned to China by the United States before the Pearl Harbor attack, which had an interest rate between 4 and 4.5 percent and was specifically prohibited from being used to purchase armaments, the Soviet loans, with a low flat interest rate of 3 percent, were not restricted to purchase military hardware.[11]

The first Soviet loan of $50 million was approved in Moscow in March 1938; the second for an additional $50 million in July of the same year. More interesting is the third and largest loan signed in Moscow on 13 June 1939. The amount agreed to was a whopping $150 million, by far the largest of any loan China had ever received from any foreign government. The Chinese government had used up the first two loans, totaling $100 million, by September 1939. Stalin decided that the third loan should be given in four installments between 1 September 1939 and 1942. This schedule of loan delivery is of particular interest because it coincides with the signing of the Nazi-Soviet pact. It meant that Japan had become an indirect Soviet ally by virtue of being an ally of Nazi Germany, yet the Soviets continued to provide China with a $150 million loan package specifically designated to purchase Soviet weapons to be used in the China theater against the Japanese. However, this peculiar arrangement by Moscow should not be mistaken as a mitigating factor in calculating the impact of the Nazi-Soviet pact, which was for all its practical purposes a treacherous one for the Chinese, because soon after the pact was implemented, the essential Soviet arms supply and military involvement in China dramatically declined and remained in name only.

To keep the illusion that the USSR was still on the side of the Chinese cause, Stalin replaced arms supply and combat support with an enlarged financial loan package. But the conditions for this new loan were much harsher, and the actual release of the installments was deliberately made slow and difficult. This chilling effect of the Nazi-Soviet pact on the Chinese was immediate and apparent, because China would not receive the promised $150 million in total. By the time Moscow and Tokyo made their increasingly cozy relationship official in April 1941 by virtue of the neutrality pact, China had received far less. When the Nazis betrayed Stalin in June 1941 by invading the Soviet Union, Stalin abruptly stopped all military aid to China to focus on his own war against a fierce enemy in Europe. As a result, the actual amount China used from this loan was $73.175 million.[12] All told, of the entire Soviet loan packages of $250 million between September 1939 and the summer of 1941, China was able to use $173 million, about two-thirds of the total amount stipulated by the agreements.[13]

During the Sino-Japanese war, as in all other wars, troop combat capability was a major factor in deciding the outcome of battles. Most of the Chinese forces were disorganized, having been hastily put together under the overall command of Chiang Kai-shek. China badly needed trained personnel and able operators of sophisticated modern military machines such as aircraft and electronic communication gear. Soviet assistance in this regard came in two ways. First, Stalin dispatched a sizeable contingent of military advisers and technical experts to the China theater to start various ambitious training programs for the Chinese army. These Soviet military advisers and experts were under the overall command of senior Red Army general officers sent to China as Chiang's top foreign advisers.

The first such top adviser, General M. I. Dkatwin, came to China in November 1937, in the guise of the Soviet Military attaché to Chiang. General Alexander Ivanovich Cherepanov assumed the position of Chiang's military adviser in August 1938 until August 1939; General K. M. Kachanov served in China in the same capacity from September 1939 to February 1941; Stalin's star general, B. I. Chuikov (Chyikov), served as Chiang's top foreign military adviser beginning in February 1941. Chuikov was recalled a year later when the American general, Joseph Stilwell, replaced him as Chiang's top foreign adviser.[14]

All of these four top military advisers to China had advanced to important posts in the Soviet Red Army, and all of them had previously served in China under Field Marshal Blücher (Galen) during the Guangdong and Whampoa years and were therefore old acquaintances of Chiang Kai-shek.[15] Beneath these top Red Army generals were a whole list of Soviet military personnel and weapons experts, totaling 140 by January 1941, who were assigned to various Chinese field commands as specialists in such fields as air force, artillery, and tank warfare.[16] These Red Army advisers participated in key battles in the early years of China's war against the Japanese, including the Taierzhuang and Wuhan campaigns. Liu Zhiqing, China's foremost authority on the Sino-Soviet military relations, who is well versed in Russian and CCP archival materials, writes, "[Before the Pearl Harbor attack,] almost every major and minor campaign and battle involved the participation of the Soviet military advisers."[17]

Initially, the Soviets sent Red Army personnel to Lanzhou, Gansu Province, to train Chinese pilots and mechanics to operate the Soviet aircraft. In early 1938, Stalin ordered the Red Army pilots inside China to directly participate in air combat against the Japanese air forces stationed in China. To avoid any diplomatic blowup with Japan, these Soviet pilots acted as "volunteers" for the Chinese government. In the battle of Wuhan in the spring of 1938, Soviet pilots fought with valor and gallantry alongside the Chinese pilots, downing forty-seven Japanese planes. All told, the Soviets claimed about two hundred downed Japanese planes. A total of seven hundred Soviet "voluntary" pilots and aircraft mechanics were sent to China to fight the Japanese, of whom more than two hundred were killed in combat.[18]

With such a large-scale military aid program, China had a dire need to train capable operators of various weapons and equipment. During this period the Soviets provided substantial training programs for China. More than ninety thousand Chinese military personnel received various kinds of Soviet training. By 1939 the Soviets had trained a total of 1,045 combat pilots, 81 air navigators, 198 air gunner and radio operators, and 8,354 other aviation technicians.[19]

As noted before, a major hindrance in wartime military aid to China was the seemingly insurmountable task of delivery, which was the second major area in which the Soviets provided assistance. The most direct and meaningful arms delivery route from the Soviet Union to China was the Chinese Northwest. The road conditions in this area were primitive and hazardous. In the first months of the war, at the request of Chiang Kai-shek, Stalin ordered the construction of a truck road stretching from Soviet Kazakhstan through Dihua (Urumqi), Xinjiang, to Lanzhou, Gansu, a total length of 2,925 kilometers, or 1,816 miles. This was a tremendous undertaking by any standard. Much of the Soviet military hardware bound for China came to the China theater through this route. A single truck delivery mission of weapons would take eighteen days, passing through some of the most hazardous terrain and road conditions.[20]

From the beginning, Stalin was keenly aware of the enormity of the task of supporting the war in China. In addition to the large amount of weaponry required in the war, a major problem was China's lack of any essential industrial capability to produce modern weapons and the lack of energy sources to fuel the imported military machinery. Therefore, on 11 November 1937, Stalin summoned Chiang Kai-shek's ambassador to Moscow, General Yang Jie, for a talk. Essentially, Stalin offered to build an aircraft manufacturing facility in Xinjiang, where the Soviets would provide the engine blocks and the Chinese would provide everything else to build China's own combat aircraft. Stalin also offered to drill oil inside China to solve the fuel problem. Consequently, the Soviets chose the Dihua Farming Tool Machine Factory and remodeled it as an aircraft plant. The Soviets also established an oil field at Du San Zi in Xinjiang.[21]

Yet, not all of these military aid programs were a one-way street. There was much reciprocity in the Sino-Soviet relationship. In addition to international and national security considerations, the Soviet Union's massive military aid program to China, much like Germany's previously, was also motivated by another factor—China's strategic materials such as minerals and agricultural goods were urgently needed in the USSR. The Chinese appreciated this situation and readily accepted the Soviets' requests for a robust wartime trade. During this period of Sino-Soviet wartime cooperation, China supplied the Soviet Union with the strategic materials needed by the vast Soviet defense complex. During the eight years of war, 43 percent of China's entire strategic minerals trade, such as tungsten (31,177 tons), tin (13,162 tons), zinc (600 tons), and mercury (560 tons), totaling $48.5 million, went to the Soviet Union in exchange for weapons. In comparison, China's trade with the United States in these strategic materials during the same period amounted to $47.78 million, less than the sum of the Sino-Soviet trade.[22]

It would be a mistake, however, to believe that Stalin put all his eggs in Chiang's basket. The large-scale military aid programs the Soviets delivered to China were predicated on remarkably shaky ground. During the entire course of robust wartime military cooperation, Chiang Kai-shek and Stalin failed to resolve several fundamental issues, which gradually led to the demise of all Soviet-sponsored programs of military aid and assistance to China.

The first issue that gravely disappointed Chiang Kai-shek was Stalin's steadfast refusal to declare war on Japan despite Chiang's repeated appeals to do so. While appreciative of the timely and substantial military aid from Moscow, Chiang was never happy about the furtive and secretive way in which the Soviets demanded the military aid programs be handled. Virtually all the military advisers in China had to be disguised as diplomats; Soviet combat personnel in various China campaigns were provided with extra cover stories to avoid being recognized by the Japanese. Moscow made great efforts to conceal the Soviets' direct involvement in combat. By 1941, in addition to the hundreds of Soviet Red Army air force combat personnel, 140 Soviet senior military advisers were in China, all of them using the diplomatic cover of working for the Soviet embassy. The U.S. naval attaché dutifully reported to Washington that the Soviet embassy had become "by far the largest staff of any diplomatic mission in Chungking. . . . The Soviet need for these people for their embassy is more than a diplomatic mission."[23]

In the famous battle of Taierzhuang in 1938, the Chinese resoundingly routed the Japanese army. The Japanese suspected Soviet participation in the battle and protested to Moscow, but both the Chinese and the Soviets vehemently denied any Soviet involvement. It would be naïve, however, to believe that the Japanese had no inkling whatsoever about the Soviet support for China's war efforts.[24] What Stalin expected was not Japanese ignorance of Soviet activities in the China theater but a plausible deniability should Japan openly accuse the Soviet Red Army of direct combat participation. Needless to say, this Soviet furtiveness and reluctance to declare war on Japan was interpreted by the Chinese as a fence-sitting act of opportunism. In other words, China did not trust Soviet intentions in aiding China and feared the Soviet Union might seek an opportunity to abandon the Chinese cause and make peace separately with the Japanese at any moment.

One particularly odious act on the part of the Soviets that appalled Chiang Kai-shek was the signing of the Nazi-Soviet Nonaggression Pact in late August 1938, which was particularly pernicious to China on two grounds. First, since Japan had already become an ally with Nazi Germany, the pact would naturally qualify Japan as an indirect ally of the Soviet Union, because an ally's ally would become one's ally as well. Second, the Nazi-Soviet pact was most boisterously celebrated by the CCP's powerful propaganda machines in China and was hailed by Mao Zedong and the Chinese Communist Party headquartered in Yenan as the battle cry for worldwide Communist upsurge against the global bourgeoisie.

Mao instructed his deputy, Zhou Enlai, who was in Moscow at the time, to maximize the CCP's voice of support for the pact and for the subsequent Nazi-Soviet partition of Poland. Mao's enthusiastic call to arms against the worldwide bourgeoisie became such a marked event in Moscow that the Comintern mouthpiece, the *Communist International,* put out a special issue for Mao, in which the super comrade in China praised the Soviet invasion of Poland as "a socialist peace effort" to "liberate the 11 million ethnic Ukrainians and White Russians oppressed by the reactionary ruling class in Poland."[25]

On 9 September 1939, the Comintern's executive body issued instructions to the Chinese Communist Party in Yenan that no effort should be spared in attacking the "imperial block."[26] Chiang Kai-shek was greatly alarmed that the CCP would be so emboldened by Stalin's treacherous act and the USSR's subsequent participation in the partition of Poland. As we shall see, Chiang's fears proved to be justified.

Chiang Kai-shek was always instinctively suspicious of Soviet intentions in East Asia. This, in turn, caused Moscow to increasingly view Chiang as an ingrate. The two major military campaigns the Soviets fought against the Japanese in 1938 and 1939 particularly soured Chiang's relationship with Stalin. In July 1938, the Soviet Union and Japan fought an extraordinarily nasty battle over a large territory near Zhang Gu Feng Peak (Changkufeng/ Khasan), which is within the boundary of the Japanese puppet state of Manchukuo. Over the course of ten days, the Soviets deployed more than fifteen thousand troops with mechanized weaponry and routed the seven

thousand Japanese defense troops.[27] The peace treaty between the victorious Soviets and the defeated Japanese allocated this large chunk of land to
the USSR. Since China never conceded to give up its sovereign claim over
Manchukuo, Chiang Kai-shek was not amused and remained cynically silent,
while the Chinese Communist Party's propaganda machines vociferously
supported the Soviet action and condemned the Japanese.[28]

One year later, a more serious territorial issue concerned Chiang Kai-
shek, and Stalin grew furious over Chiang's lack of support. The territory was
Outer Mongolia, over which the Chinese government claimed jurisdiction,
but which in reality had been under Soviet control for many years. In May
1939, troops of the Japanese-controlled Manchukuo clashed with troops of
the Soviet-controlled Outer Mongolia at Nomonhan inside Outer Mongolia.
A large military campaign ensued. The battle of Nomonhan remains a fasci-
nating military campaign that has been greatly understudied. The battle lasted
from late May to early September 1939 and involved several hundred thousands of troops from each side as well as thousands of aircraft and tanks. In
the end, the Red Army soundly routed the Japanese.

The smashing defeat of the Japanese by the Soviet Red Army handed the
Soviets another territorial gain in the Chinese border province of Helongjiang,
an area totaling about two thousand square kilometers. Stalin expected Chiang
Kai-shek to support both the Soviet action at Nomonhan and his subsequent annexation of Chinese territory, but Chiang thwarted Stalin's wish and
remained agonizingly quiet. Both the Zhang Gu Feng Peak and Nomonhan
affairs took place at the height of Soviet military aid to China. Stalin clearly
expected China's political support for both actions. The failure of Chiang Kai-
shek's government to provide any political and diplomatic support for Stalin
at this juncture greatly displeased Moscow and soured the otherwise mutually
beneficial Sino-Soviet wartime relationship.[29]

In a similar vein, the issue of Xinjiang also became a contentious issue
between Stalin and Chiang. This vast Central Asian area connecting the
USSR and China had long been under the de facto control of the Chinese
warlord Sheng Shicai, who was a master of opportunism. Chiang Kai-shek
was grateful to Stalin for providing timely military aid to China at a most
critical juncture. But Chiang was also aware of the Soviet desire to create pro-
Soviet buffer zones in China's northwestern backyard. In fact, while the Soviets
were extraordinarily generous in offering to build various large construction
projects inside Xinjiang, Chiang was wary of Soviet political penetration into
this territory. While the Northwest passage provided the most practical and
useful land route for delivering Soviet military hardware, Chiang Kai-shek

preferred a southern route, fearing further Soviet influence in Xinjiang and the Northwest, and engaged in strenuous negotiations with the French and British to obtain passing rights for the Soviet weapons to travel via sea through Burma, Hong Kong, and French Indochina.

When the war first began in 1937, China was in the most critical and difficult stage of its resistance against the Japanese, and Chiang Kai-shek was in no position to object to Stalin's suggestion of the construction by the Soviets of an aircraft plant in Dihua and an oil field in Du San Zi, both inside Xinjiang. When both projects were completed, Stalin dispatched large numbers of Soviet personnel to exert effective control over these facilities. This irked Chiang greatly, and Stalin reciprocated with the same acrimonious sentiment. Eventually, Chiang ordered the unconditional evacuation of the Soviets from these two Chinese facilities when Soviet aid altogether ceased after the Nazi-Soviet war started in the summer of 1941.[30]

The ill feeling between Stalin and Chiang was further aggravated by the New Fourth Army incident of early 1941. While the Soviets believed Chiang Kai-shek was the only capable national leader in a war against Japan, Stalin did not abandon his Chinese Communist comrades on political and ideological grounds. He persistently pressured the KMT government to leave the CCP forces alone, giving them the liberty to develop their guerrilla bases regardless of Chiang's overall strategy and command, and to refrain from attacking the Communists in order to buttress the "United Front" against the Japanese.

The New Fourth Army was under the control of the Chinese Communist Party and had been actively expanding its area of control in violation of the mutually agreed domain of operations. According to the agreed principles of the United Front forged in late 1936 between the Chinese central government and the CCP, all Chinese armed forces, including those commanded by the CCP, should be under the overall command of Chiang Kai-shek. The New Fourth Army had been ordered to move north of the Yangtze River by Chiang's headquarters. When the order was not carried out effectively, Nationalist troops ambushed the New Fourth Army in January 1941, creating the first crisis between the Nationalists and the Communists since the formation of the United Front in 1936 and the most serious one of the entire war. Stalin protested loudly to Chiang and condemned him for the military attack, threatening to end all Soviet aid for such an ambush.[31] As Stalin's military envoy to China, General Chuikov was instructed to lodge a "most serious" protest to the Chinese Nationalist military authorities in Chungking, which he did.[32]

The invasion of Finland by the USSR further deepened the mutual suspicion between Stalin and Chiang and profoundly affected the Soviets' military aid program to China. In late November 1939, Stalin launched a blitzkrieg against Finland, forcing Finland to concede large areas of its territory to the Soviets. The League of Nations was appalled by this blatant violation of international law and condemned the USSR as an aggressor, deciding to punish Moscow by expelling the USSR from the League. This would be a most humiliating diplomatic defeat for Stalin. At the time, China held a crucial vote in the League of Nations and could save Stalin from this humiliation. Naturally, Moscow requested that China vote against the League's decision to expel the USSR. Chiang Kai-shek was torn. On the one hand, China needed Soviet military aid for its war efforts. On the other hand, China would be soundly condemned by the majority of the world's major powers if China cast its vote to keep the Soviet Union in the League. In the end, Chiang instructed his ambassador to abstain.[33]

Since this was at the height of Soviet military and financial assistance to China, Stalin was furious with Chiang Kai-shek and blamed him for the USSR's ultimate expulsion from the League of Nations.[34] Marshal K. E. Voroshilov, Stalin's defense minister, summoned the Chinese ambassador, Yang Jie, to the Kremlin for an explosive conference, lecturing the envoy that "If China had voted against the motion to expel the USSR from the League of Nations, the result would definitely have been different. What China has done undoubtedly helped the British and French scheme to harm the Soviet Union!"[35]

On 13 April 1941, the event Chiang Kai-shek had dreaded for years finally befell Chungking. On that day, the USSR and Japan signed a neutrality pact. This shocking agreement nullified the 1937 Sino-Soviet Nonaggression Pact, guaranteed mutual recognition of territorial control of Outer Mongolia by the Soviets and Manchukuo by the Japanese, and essentially ended all Soviet military and financial aid to China. But it also confirmed beyond any doubt all the suspicions of opportunism Chiang Kai-shek had held against Stalin's motives in aiding China since the beginning of the Sino-Soviet rapprochement in the summer of 1937.

It had become abundantly clear to Chiang and his inner sanctum by now that Stalin's strategy had always been to help the Chinese pin down as many Japanese in China as possible, not for the sake of an ultimate victory, but for a protracted war to make Japan stuck in China so that it could not attack the Soviet Union. In so doing, Stalin had to walk a tightrope carefully balancing his center of strategic gravity—he would aid the Chinese just so much that the Japanese could not win a decisive victory in China; but if he aided China by openly declaring war with Japan, the Japanese would surely attack the Soviet Union; yet, if he failed to support Chinese resistance against the Japanese, and Chiang Kai-shek capitulated to the Japanese, then the Japanese would be freed from their entanglement in China and would most likely move north to attack the Soviet Union, using the vast resources an occupied China could provide. In either case, Stalin's ultimate objective was not for a Chinese victory over Japan but for a protracted military imbroglio in China to wear off Japan's aggressiveness, lest Japan attack the Soviet Union.

Thus, Stalin's motive to send military aid to Chiang was essentially based on cold geopolitical calculation, not on sentimental affinity for China's nationalist ideals. As Stalin instructed his envoy to China, General Chuikov, in the fall of 1940, "Ideally, we should be much closer to the Chinese Communist Party than to Chiang Kai-shek. Ideally, our military aid should be given to our Chinese comrades . . . but . . . the Chinese Communist Party and the Chinese proletariat are too weak at this particular point in time to assume the leadership of China's anti-imperialism movement. . . . In addition, the imperialists will never allow the Chinese Communists to replace Chiang Kai-shek. . . . With our help to Chiang, and possibly help to him from the British and the Americans, Chiang Kai-shek may not be able to defeat the Japanese aggression but at least he could pin down the Japanese in China for a long time."[36]

In the meantime, Stalin, in unmistakably clear terms, revealed to Chuikov his ultimate objective in providing military aid to China, that is, "to tightly tie up Japan's hands and feet in China, and only when Japan's hands and feet are tied up can we [the USSR] avoid a two-front war once the German aggressors attack us."[37]

The Japanese of course were clearly aware of such a Soviet intention. Thus, another possibility of geopolitical realignment had always existed there: when the Japanese were indeed tied up and pinned down in China partially as a result of foreign military aid, they could always find a conduit to assure the Soviet Union that Japan might not attack the Soviet Union after all, thus removing Stalin's incentive to aid China altogether. In fact, with the Nazi-Soviet pact in 1939, Moscow's aid to China had been steadily in decline in volume and vigor, thus accordingly reducing the likelihood of a Japanese attack on the Soviet Union for aiding China. Yet, in the meantime, the likelihood of massive military aid from the United States and Great Britain began to increase dramatically in 1939, thus increasing Japan's likelihood of going after the United States and Great Britain, which had vast colonial interests in the western Pacific and Southeast Asia. Therefore, the moment Japan's intention to direct its military advance southward in Southeast Asia instead of the Soviet Union to the north became clear to Moscow, Stalin was willing at once to abandon China militarily and politically. By the spring of 1941, Stalin's spies in the inner circle of the Japanese imperial court had reliably informed him of Japan's decision to attack Southeast Asia instead of the Soviet Union. Hence the Moscow-Tokyo Neutrality Pact of April 1941.

A little more than two months later, Stalin's great strategic miscalculation of two years before bore grave consequences when the Nazi army poured into the Soviet defense line. With Japan a nonthreat to the Soviet Union in the East by virtue of the Soviet-Japanese Neutrality Pact, Operation Barbarossa brought a complete end to all Soviet military programs to China. The weapons shipments to China were abruptly halted and the remaining installment payments of the 1939 loan of $150 million were summarily canceled by Moscow, with a total of $76.8 million unpaid. All the military advisers, combat personnel, and technical experts were evacuated from China immediately.

In the agonizing years between the Japanese invasion of Manchuria in September 1931 and the outbreak of an all-out war between China and Japan in July 1937, Germany was China's major supplier of armaments on various private, industry-based initiatives. Hitler's rise to power and the rapid growth of a Berlin-Tokyo politico-ideological and military alliance soon ended all those initiatives. In the first couple of years of the all-out war, for reasons of mostly realpolitik and self-interest, the Soviet Union was the only foreign country to have provided substantial military and financial aid to China; the three leading Western nations, the United States, Great Britain, and France, failed to make helping China's war efforts their national policy. Despite this unfortunate reality, however, China was aware of the overwhelming moral and public opinion support for China's cause in those countries, and therefore conducted arduous lobbying acts in those nations despite powerful bureaucratic resistance.

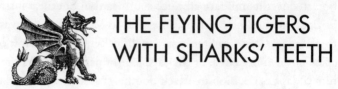

Chapter 3

THE FLYING TIGERS
WITH SHARKS' TEETH

TIGERS AND SHARKS are different animals, but both are known for their ferocity and destructive prowess. Such is the hallmark of a group of American fighter pilots who went to war-torn China as the American Volunteers' Group (AVG). Yet, throughout the war and the world, they are more famously known as the Flying Tigers, with sharks' teeth painted on all their airplanes. In the end, with the combined strength and tenacity of tigers and sharks, they created a legend for Sino-American cooperation and a spectacular air combat record.

It all started on a wintry day in sunny Miami, Florida, in January 1936. The U.S. Army's Air Corps allowed three of its best fighter pilots to stage an acrobatic air show at the Pan-American air maneuvers. Led by a stocky southerner with Cajun gallantry named Claire Lee Chennault, the three-man team, including John "Luke" Williamson and Billy MacDonald, was known as the Flying Trapeze and went on to awe the spectators with great showmanship. Unbeknownst to the Flying Trapeze a Chinese air force general was mingling in the crowd. General Mao Bangchu had been informed by his American friends of the Flying Trapeze's great fame and specifically came to Miami on an unusual mission: to persuade the three to quit the U.S. Army and go to China to serve the Chinese air force. Luke Williamson and Billy MacDonald were greatly impressed by the Chinese general's eagerness and generous offer and decided to follow General Mao to China on this grand adventure.[1]

However, the person—Captain Claire Lee Chennault—the Chinese general really came to Miami for, decided to decline the Chinese offer, as he was already on an even more adventurous mission and he could only accomplish it by staying within the U.S. Army as an air fighter pilot. Chennault's mission was a simple but revolutionary one, which was to change American armed forces' air strategy and put fighters, not bombers, at the center of the Army Air

Corps. For years, this mission had become Chennault's obsession. His determination was quite apparent. As he explains it, "As senior instructor in fighter tactics, I plunged into the job of modernizing fighter techniques with the greatest enthusiasm. Wheeling heavy bombers around never held any attraction for me. I was a fighter pilot for as long as I could fly."[2]

The problem was that virtually no other senior officers within the U.S. Army Air Corps agreed with Chennault. In his memoir, he bitterly ruminates on his dilemma: "It became apparent that, just as the Navy was dominated by the 'battleship admirals,' so the Air Corps would be run from the bias of 'bomber generals.' These bomber generals had an inflexible orthodoxy all their own and were just as ruthless and unfair in squelching opposition within the Air Corps as the Army and Navy were in attempting to smother the development of all airpower."[3] General H. H. Arnold, the chief of the Air Corps openly declared that "frankly, fighters have been allowed to drift in the doldrums."[4] One of Chennault's classmates at the Army's tactical school years earlier, Clayton Bissell, was another legendary fighter pilot, but in 1931, Bissell was still indoctrinating young trainees with the obsolete fighter tactics of World War I.[5]

Such bomber-centric air strategy had its theology too. And it had been written by the Italian general Giulio Douhet in a book called *The War of 194–*. In it, Douhet stressed the supremacy of bombers, and claimed that with little or no fighter escort, bombers could effectively finish the war by massive bombardment of enemy targets and quickly force the enemy to sue for peace.[6] The Douhet Theory, as it was called by its fanatical admirers, served as the guideline for air development in many countries during the interwar years, and the United States was particularly vandalized by it.

Chennault was the U.S. Army Air Corps' chief opponent to Douhet's pitch for bombers. His tireless efforts to debunk the Douhet Theory throughout his stint in the Army made him a world-famous innovator in fighter tactics. By meticulously studying air combat records of World War I, and by voracious reading of German and other literature on air war, Chennault developed a system of his own air tactics, all of which would assume strategic importance in his later years. The first tactical innovation attributed to Chennault was the two-plane formation. Inspired by the German air ace Oswald von Boelcke, Chennault put the two-plane team combat into doctrine through the rest of his military career. To put it simply, Chennault believed that a two-plane team attacking a single enemy plane would enjoy "odds not of 2 to 1 in its favor, but of 4 to 1," because "the difference between the firepower of two opposing forces—all other factors being equal—is not the difference in the number of fire units but the square of the difference of the number of fire units."[7]

The second contribution by Chennault to air tactics—the necessity for establishing an air-warning ground intelligence system—was even more significant, because it would become the major characteristic of Chennault's command throughout his military career. "Without a continuous stream of accurate information keeping the fighters posted on exactly where the high-speed bombers were," Chennault argues, "attempts at interception were like hunting needles in a limitless haystack."[8]

Chennault's third tactical innovation involved his advocacy for long-range fighters with bigger firepower. He argued that it was entirely fit and possible to add multiple synchronized high-caliber cannons and machine guns behind the propellers. Years later, facing Japanese planes that had superior maneuverability, yet generally less firepower, Chennault would make this tactical priority one of his winning practices.

Fourthly, Chennault stressed the importance of teamwork in either paratrooper transporting or formation fights. This tactic made him particularly renowned outside of the United States.

In an effort to make all these innovations permanent and actionable, Chennault proceeded to write one of the most influential books on air combat. Published in 1935 as *The Role of Defensive Pursuit*, the tome systematically analyzes the fallacy of the Douhet Theory, and it would serve as a bible for all of Chennault's combat command in future operations. In a nutshell, Chennault in the book summarizes his innovations as two major principles:

1. Defending pursuit could make interception of attacking bombardment before the bombers reached their target if furnished timely information and if the interception area had sufficient depth to allow for necessary time factors.
2. Bombardment, flying deep into enemy territory, required friendly fighter protection to prevent heavy losses if not utter failure of the mission.[9]

Yet, whatever Chennault was trying to sell to the Army high command, it was considered heresy. Adding to the problem was Chennault's blunt style of advocacy. When "Hap" Arnold, the World War II commanding general of the U.S. Army Air Corps, was dogmatically practicing formation according to the Douhet Theory in the early 1930s, Chennault, who was much lower ranked, once wrote a scathing criticism of Arnold's tactics. Incensed, Arnold made a round of inquiry by asking, "Who is this damned fellow Chennault?"[10] When Chennault's book, *The Role of Defensive Pursuit*, came out in 1935, the Army generals paid little attention to it.

But Chennault was determined to stay in the Army to make his revolution in air combat. To him, nothing else could be more important than accomplishing this mission. His international fame as a superb fighter commander and instructor had only earned him admirers from abroad. Even the Soviet Union once tried to lure him to serve the Red Army on a five-year contract and "$1,000 a month, plus expenses, rank of colonel, and the right to fly any plane in the Red Air Force." Chennault refused the offer, because his primary interest was in reforming the U.S. air strategy.[11] Similarly, it was this sense of duty to his country and his service that made Chennault decline Chinese general Mao Bangchu's invitation to serve the Chinese air force, for he hoped that, despite his lack of popularity with the "bomber generals," he could still somehow be given a chance to implement his innovations in fighter tactics within the U.S. Army Air Corps.

But his last hope was brutally dashed in the winter of 1936 when the fearless Chennault fell seriously ill. He was grounded by flight surgeons and confined to the hospital. Physical illness tremendously affected his mental spirit. Frustrated at not being able to have his innovations accepted by the Army brass, Chennault unleashed his melancholy, "Lying on a hospital bed in Hot Springs during the winter of 1936 and spring of 1937 there was ample time to look back over my forty-seven years and think about the future. It was obvious that I was going round and round and getting nowhere."[12] The lamentation reached a conclusion. "Several times I have felt myself swirling in one of life's eddies and struck out desperately for open water and the main current of my ambitions. This time I knew that I would have to find something that would give me a chance to keep flying, to fight, and to prove my theories on tactics." Since the U.S. Army Air Corps had snubbed him outrageously over the years, Chennault finally decided to leave the Army and resigned his commission in the spring of 1937.[13]

Meanwhile, correspondence from his old friends Billy MacDonald, Luke Williamson, and Roy Holbrook, who had already gone to China, sparked new interest in Chennault. He suddenly decided China might just be the place where he could test and implement his fighter tactics. So, he made preliminary inquiries to his contacts in China. Immediately, the Chinese renewed General Mao's earlier offer, and Chennault accepted a three-month mission from none other than Madame Chiang Kai-shek to survey the Chinese air force. The terms were "$1,000 a month, plus expenses, a car, chauffeur and interpreter, and the right to fly any plane in the Chinese air force"—almost exactly the same terms the Soviet Union had offered him several years before, except this time, with nowhere else to go, Chennault enthusiastically agreed to them. Hours after he officially retired from the U.S. Army, Chennault embarked on a journey to China on the morning of 1 May 1937, a journey that was to last not three months, but more than eight years.

Awaiting Chennault in China were Madame Chiang Kai-shek and an enigmatic Australian, William Henry Donald, two of the most powerful persons in the inner circle of the Chinese national government. Madame Chiang was an elegant, American-educated, English-speaking powerhouse within the Chinese power elite. Petite and resolute, she completely captivated Chennault. "This was an encounter from which I never recovered," Chennault confessed, describing their first meeting, and wrote in his diary that "She will always be a princess to me."[14] But far more important than personal rapport is the fact that Madame Chiang was Chennault's real patron in China. She was in charge of China's entire budding air force, with the title of the secretary general of National Aviation Council, functioning as proxy controller over national military and civilian aviation for her husband, Generalissimo Chiang Kai-shek. In fact, it was Madame Chiang who initiated the letter of invitation to Chennault in which he was instructed to report directly to her on the current condition of China's air force.[15]

But Madame Chiang's intense interest in airpower had been inspired by the Australian, William Henry Donald, who, in turn, had developed an equally fanatic belief in air force as a potent instrument of modern warfare. Initially working as an unknown journalist in China in the beginning years of the twentieth century, Donald soon became one of the most powerful foreigners living in China, with a vast network of political informants within the Chinese political circle. By the time Chennault arrived in China, Donald had been in China for more than thirty years, with a reputation as "China's First Adviser," who also simultaneously served as Madame Chiang's English embellisher.[16]

But Donald's most famous stint in China was his long-time association with the Manchurian warlord Zhang Xueliang.[17] Zhang had been a firm believer in airpower and was the foremost promoter of air war in China. Since 1921, he had been the man in charge of building and maintaining the largest and strongest warlord air force in the country, with a total of more than 100 aircraft.[18] Even after Chiang Kai-shek unified China and placed Zhang Xueliang under the central government, the Manchurian strongman still controlled his former military forces, including his prized air force. But in September 1931, Zhang's entire air force, China's strongest, was wiped out by a Japanese blitzkrieg, and Zhang and his troops were driven out of Manchuria.[19] As Zhang Xueliang's top foreign adviser, William Henry Donald was keenly aware of the importance of air force in Chinese military and political affairs, and had been the strongest advocate for acquiring such military instruments. Donald's contagious air mindedness fundamentally influenced Madame Chiang Kai-shek, who had sent her agents to the United States and found Chennault.

Donald demonstrated not only ample air mindedness but also savvy wisdom on Chinese political intrigues. Chennault immediately found his Moses in the vast desert of the Chinese cultural, political, and military landscape. Chennault expresses his eternal gratitude to Donald for mentoring and supporting him this way:

> Donald readily grasped the decisive significance of airpower in modern warfare. He became one of my strongest supporters, because he felt that urgent need to build a strong Chinese Air Force while there was still time. It was Donald who introduced me to the inner circles of the Chinese government where the intricate wheels within wheels revolved. It was Donald who, through his ready access to the Generalissimo, carried my problems directly to the supreme authority, and it was Donald who mediated between Madame Chiang and myself during those nerve-racking prewar weeks when two short-tempers flared. Without Donald's unstinting help and understanding I could have accomplished little in China and no doubt would have sailed home in disgust with a superficial Occidental contempt for the East.[20]

With such high-level support, Chennault went in earnest to investigate the state of readiness of the Chinese air force. On paper, China had about five hundred combat airplanes in the summer of 1937. In reality, only about ninety of them were combat ready.[21] Yet, the most worrisome aspect of the Chinese air force at the time, as Chennault found out, was its severely inadequate training of pilots, mostly by the faulty methods used by incompetent Italian instructors, who were "in complete control of the Chinese Air Force and had cornered the Chinese aviation market."[22] Most of the Italian-trained graduates from the air force schools were not able to master the basic flight skills.[23] On 7 July 1937, toward the end of the three-month investigation and as he was concluding in his report that the Chinese air force under Italian control was totally unready for war, Chennault heard the news that an all-out war had broken out between China and Japan, triggered by the Marco Polo Bridge Incident.

Suddenly, Chennault saw new opportunities to revitalize his military career in the China theater. But mostly, he enthused, "after all the years of classroom argument and theoretical debate over my theories of air warfare, I wanted a chance to give them an acid test in combat."[24] Immediately, Chennault cabled Chiang Kai-shek to offer his service in fighting the invading Japanese. Wasting no time and none of Chennault's talent, Chiang quickly accepted the offer and ordered him to train China's fighter groups.[25]

Facing Japan's overwhelming numerical superiority in airpower, China's airplanes fought well in such campaigns as the Battle of Shanghai in the summer and fall of 1937, and the Battle of JianQiao in mid-August 1937. Without sufficient fighter escort, Japanese bombers were shot down in great numbers by Chennault's small fighter groups. During the second month of the Battle of Shanghai, for example, more than sixty Japanese planes, mostly bombers, were shot down.[26] Yet, the reality was grim for the nascent, ill-trained, and poorly equipped Chinese air force. Although Chennault carried out his two-plane formation tactics, the result normally was not satisfactory. China simply could not match Japan in the number of planes available, and planes were rapidly dwindling because of the frequent combat missions. By October 1937, there were only a little more than a dozen combat-ready airplanes left in the Chinese air force.[27]

Under such adverse circumstances, Chennault was greatly vindicated by the great success of establishing an efficient air-warning ground intelligence system for China, which lay at the core of the fighter combat tactic he had developed in the United States before coming to China. In the early months and years of experience in China, he saw the great benefits of such an intelligence system. In close cooperation with the Chinese military intelligence, Chennault placed multiple agents in vast areas of China to monitor and spot Japanese air activities. These instantaneous air-warning reports provided precious time for the dwindling air force to adopt appropriate tactics to either take off to intercept the incoming Japanese bombers at pinpoint location, or to effectuate an orderly evacuation to avoid direct hits by the aerial bombardment.

Even though Chennault was generally disappointed by the rapidly disappearing Chinese airpower, he was greatly delighted to find ample downed Japanese aircraft to conduct meticulous studies of the enemy's advanced design and specifications. Within two years, Chennault had amassed a large volume of notes and study reports on major Japanese planes in service in China, which enabled him to become the foremost expert on Japanese planes, the Japanese pilots' combat doctrines, formation charts, and general pattern of target missions. This encyclopedic knowledge would prove to be crucial in later years when Chennault organized and commanded larger and stronger air forces in China.

Chiang Kai-shek's response to the rapidly shrinking number of airplanes was to acquire more planes from foreign countries. Despite China's desperate purchase missions in major aircraft producing nations, however, the Japanese far outstripped the Chinese in airpower and became so emboldened by their numerical superiority that ferocious bombing sorties were increasingly flown over such heavily populated civilian cities as Chungking (ChongQing) and wreaked devastating havoc. The bombing was so horrendous that Chennault, the ultimate fighter advocate, began to develop a burning idea of acquiring long-range bombers to bomb the Japanese homeland to exert revenge.

Facing such adversity, Chiang Kai-shek decided to appeal to the Americans for help in airpower. The only person readily available to pitch for China in Washington was Claire Lee Chennault, now a staunch supporter of China's war against Japan. On 20 May 1940, Chiang summoned Chennault to his headquarters and instructed him to proceed to Washington to lobby for the sale of American airplanes to China for immediate relief from Japanese bombing runs. Chennault's point of contact would be Dr. T. V. Soong, Chiang's brother-in-law, who permanently lived in Washington, where he ran a military hardware acquisitions entity called China Defense Supplies, Inc.[28]

Three years had passed since Chennault left the U.S. Army Air Corps in great disappointment. Antagonism toward him from the Army brass had not died down a bit, however. Especially because the lowly former captain returned to Washington with the halo of the Chinese high command on an acquisition mission, jealousy, contempt, and outright hostility were clearly demonstrated from General Arnold on down. After arriving in Washington, Chennault found himself squandering his time for several weeks in T. V. Soong's office building without a clear direction as to where his lobby mission was going.

Then, during this rare period of idle time, Chennault was able to pull out the thick volumes of notes and study papers he had accumulated while in China since 1937. Particularly refreshing was the data he had collected or was given to him by the Chinese military intelligence on the more than two hundred and fifty Japanese airbases inside China and the forty Japanese bases in Thailand. He had not had time to carefully study them until now. Also, during his China years, Chennault developed useful insight into Japanese air combat tactics. He noticed that the Japanese pilots were extraordinarily rigid about combat formation and would rarely break any predetermined flight path or formation patterns, despite the fact that the Japanese air force had one big advantage in hardware because their planes were better built and very maneuverable. While sitting in T. V. Soong's empty office on V Street in Washington, D.C., Chennault was hit with a powerful idea: the Japanese air force could be beaten in China if there were decent number of decent airplanes and if these planes were flown by American pilots.[29]

With this, he could draw up an air strategy to establish a brand new air force to be deployed in China, and this air force would be equipped with American planes and operated by American pilots. T. V. Soong was greatly elated by such a bold strategy and immediately gave Chennault a carte blanche. "Buy what you need and send me the bill," Chennault was told by Soong.[30] With this approval, Chennault drew up a to-buy list that included 350 fighter (pursuit) planes and 150 long-range bombers.

Chennault's plan of building an American-led air force in the service of a foreign government immediately drew fire in Washington. General Arnold scolded such a plan as ludicrous. Even many officials who were sympathetic to the Chinese cause became openly convinced that 500 planes were way too much to ask at a time when the "Arsenal of Democracy" was primarily feeding England with most of America's war supplies.[31] The "desperate situation in England," Chennault observed, "gave the Royal Air Force a share of top priority with the Air Corps on the few planes trickling off the lines."[32] Undaunted, armed with T. V. Soong's deep pockets, Chennault began to visit various aircraft plants around the country to plead for his 500-plane purchase. But these visits resulted in nothing encouraging, except for one case where at the Curtiss-Wright factory in Buffalo, New York, Chennault hit on a rare opportunity. As he reports, "they had six assembly lines turning out P-40's for the British, who had taken over a French order after the fall of France. If the British would waive their priority on 100 P-40B's then rolling off one line, Curtiss would add a seventh assembly line and make 100 later-model P-40's for the British. The British were glad to exchange the P-40B for a model more suitable for combat."[33] These 100 Curtiss P-40B fighters were to become world famous for their service in China in the years to come.

This was far short of the 500 planes Chennault had originally demanded to build his air force in China. But it was better than nothing under the circumstances. In comparison, the extraordinary difficulty with which Chennault proceeded to get his 100 fighter planes was not nearly as noticeable as that associated with accomplishing the second part of his strategy—to enlist approval from the American government to allow American pilots to operate these planes in China to fight the Japanese. "Personnel proved a tougher nut to crack," Chennault offered in his classic understatement. "The military were violently opposed to the whole idea of American volunteers in China... [General Arnold] was 100% opposed to the project."[34]

The opposition was not merely motivated by turf rivalry and interservice jealousy. What Chennault proposed to accomplish in China bore severe foreign policy implications. For one, while China and Japan were actively at war with each other, the United States was officially neutral. That American war planes were to be flown by American pilots in the China theater and engaging in combat with the Japanese air force would be considered an act of belligerence and might evoke a Japanese attack on American interests in Asia and thus drag the still-isolationist nation into a foreign war in Asia.

But the timing was excellent for Chennault. And this had much to do with the Soviet Union and its China policy. From the beginning of the war in July 1937, the Soviet Union took a great stand in providing military support for China's war efforts against Japan. It was a necessary measure for Stalin, because if Japan were to win in China, its next target of attack would surely be the Soviet Union. Of all the military support the Soviets provided to the Chinese, airplanes were the most important and most significant items. Yet, starting from the summer of 1939, the Soviet Union suddenly and deliberately halted its robust military support for China, as the war ravaged Central and Western Europe. While Stalin wanted to focus his attention on Europe, by forging an alliance with Nazi Germany and by invading countries such Poland and Finland, Stalin was also keenly aware of the importance of pinning down Japan's aggressive military forces inside China, lest the Japanese invade the Soviet Far East, thus forcing Moscow to confront a two-front war. The Soviet withdrawal of air support to China meant that the Soviet Union would prefer to have another country pick up the onus of providing China with airplanes to keep Japan in a quagmire in China; and no country at the time could serve this function better than the United States.

The person who stepped in at this juncture to vigorously push the United States to fill the airpower vacuum in China as a result of the Soviet withdrawal was none other than Lauchlin Currie, a Canadian-born man of international mystery, with extensive ties to the Soviet Union, a devoted agent of the Soviet intelligence, and at the time a powerful administrative aide to the president of the United States, Franklin Delano Roosevelt. Currie was specifically in charge of China affairs.[35]

In fact, President Roosevelt was so impressed with Currie's interest in China's war that he dispatched Currie to Chungking in February 1941 to conduct a comprehensive survey of the situation there. Currie's lengthy report to Roosevelt at the conclusion of the trip was an important document that had great influence on Roosevelt's policy toward China. In the report, Currie lambasted the reactionary nature of the Chiang Kai-shek Nationalist government and promoted a progressive image of the Chinese Communists: "[whose] introduction of progressive taxation on landlords, of local village democracy, their anti-Japanese propaganda, and their ardent advocacy of a rapid carrying out of Dr. Sun's Three Principles, have all proved popular with the peasants," it says.[36]

In light of this understanding, Currie in his report recommended to Roosevelt that an American political adviser be sent to Chiang Kai-shek to influence China's political developments. Within weeks, Currie would hand pick Owen Lattimore, the foremost pro-Soviet Union academic in the United States at the time, to Chungking as Chiang's political adviser, representing the U.S. government. In the meantime, Currie lauded the Soviet Union's benign intentions about China, trying to convince Roosevelt that Stalin "regarded the National Government's dispute with the Chinese Communists as a purely internal affair," and believed China was not "ready or would be for a long time for the Russian type of Communism;" and that "Russia had no territorial ambitions in China, and that just as soon as the National Government was in a position to assert adequate authority in outer Mongolia the Russians would give up their tutelage," and the Soviet Union's dispatching two Red Army divisions to China's Sinkiang (Xinjiang) in 1935 was not an act of malice.[37]

Having tied a political noose on Chiang Kai-shek, Currie made a special appeal to Roosevelt to give China massive military aid to buttress Chiang's war efforts. On giving the Chinese large number of American aircraft, Currie informed FDR of China's affinity for Russian planes and pilots that both essentially were gone and that the Chinese were building large airfields in strategically important places without any aircraft in sight. Finally, Currie told the president, "I questioned the Generalissimo and the various generals I met closely on the specific need for airplanes. It developed that the most pressing need is for pursuit ships [fighter planes] and a few very long-range bombers. . . . Pursuit ships are essential to protect troop concentration in an offensive and to machine gun opposite troops."[38] Why would this matter?

Because, Currie told the president, "the Chinese will not assume the offensive [against the Japanese] until they have more pursuit ships, more artillery, and more small arms ammunition."[39]

Thus, to Chennault's complete surprise, while for months he had been tirelessly pedaling for his air force plan alone in Washington, D.C., without any progress, he suddenly received an invitation from the powerful White House aide to the president, who had just come back from China. "Dr. Currie," Chennault recalled, "was sent to China as President Roosevelt's special adviser and returned a strong backer of increased aid to China in general and my air plans in particular."[40] Chennault had no inkling about Currie's background and intentions, but was quite taken by Currie's being "shrewd and scholarly, adept at threading projects through the maze of prewar Washington."[41] With Currie's White House blessing and T. V. Soong's intimate friendship with Secretary of the Navy Frank Knox and Secretary of the Treasury Henry Morganthau, the lowly Chennault proceeded to recruit his American pilots from the armed forces and to battle the Army and Navy brass who were opposed vehemently to an American air force operating in China.

With the acquisition of 100 Curtiss P-40s, Chennault needed at least 100 qualified fighter pilots from the Army and the Navy. General Arnold and many Navy commanders were incensed by Chennault's efforts to lure active-duty pilots and aviators to join Chennault's enterprise, now officially called the American Volunteers' Group (AVG). But with Currie's influence in the White House, the commander-in-chief was in full support of Chennault's plans, and on 15 April 1941, President Roosevelt issued a secret executive order "authorizing reserve officers and enlisted men to resign from the Army Air Corps, Naval and Marine Air Services for the purpose of joining the American Volunteers' Group in China."[42]

With this presidential order, Chennault went around the nation's Army and Navy bases to recruit. John "Dick" Rossi, a young Navy pilot and a prominent Flying Tiger later on, recalls the process, "[I] reported to Pensacola the last week of December 1939, and we started our flight training in January 1940 as class 134-C. After getting my commission and wings, I was ordered to the newly opened Saufly Field as an instructor at Squadron 1-C. I remained there until August 1941 when, in the old San Carlos Hotel, I signed up to go to China [with the AVG]. . . . We were required to resign our commissions due to the covert nature of the job and the relations with Japan. The contract was for one year with assurance that we could return to the Navy in our old slot with no loss of seniority."[43]

The recruiting efforts in the United States would continue for months.

The plan was to first recruit a fighter group, then a bomber group to follow, with yet another fighter group in the horizon. Although there were lofty goals and grand plans in the minds of Chennault, Currie, Roosevelt, Knox, T. V. Soong, and Morganthau, to the young recruits, the sense of purpose for this adventure was not all that clear. As recruit Dick Rossi recounts, "I have been asked many times why I volunteered. There are several reasons, here are some: I had been instructing at Pensacola [at the Navy's flight school] for over a year and I wanted to get into flying fighters; I felt that it would further my career in the Navy to go out to China and fly for the one year of the contract; the pay they offered was good; it seemed like a good thing to do for the U.S. and China; and the adventure of it appealed to me." Such was the feeling of Rossi's seventeen other Navy buddies from Pensacola who signed up for Chennault at the same recruiting session.[44]

On 8 July 1941, "confident for the first time in [his] battle against the Japanese that [he] had everything [he] needed to defeat them," Chennault boarded a Pan American Airways Clipper for China. He was accompanied by an odd fellow traveler, Owen Lattimore, who had been chosen by Lauchlin Currie, and endorsed by President Roosevelt as special political adviser to Chiang Kai-shek.[45]

8 December 1941 was a beautiful day in Toungoo, Burma, where Chennault had set up a temporary training base for his American Volunteers' Group pilots, who, after a few months of initial training, would be transferred to Kunming, the capital city of China's Yunnan Province, some six hundred miles northward. John "Dick" Rossi, one of Chennault's recruits, hailing all the way from Northern California, remembers what transpired in his mind at the time, "On Monday morning, 8 December [local time], as we were showing up at the flight line, first came rumors and then confirmation of the attack on Pearl Harbor. We were both shocked and excited. We were aware of the danger of a Japanese attack on the United States, but it was a big surprise that the first U.S. target was Pearl Harbor. Now our presence had a much bigger purpose. We would be fighting directly for the United States as well as our allies."[46]

The next day, Chennault sent a few scout planes to nearby Thailand, and the report came back that a large number of Japanese troops were busily landing there and there were quite a number of Japanese airplanes in the Bangkok airfield. Chennault immediately radioed Washington, D.C., requesting air bombardment of the targets in Thailand. This was an untimely request, because the nearest American air bases had all been mercilessly destroyed by well-orchestrated Japanese attacks. Bombers from Hawaii were obviously out of range and had been largely destroyed by Admiral Chuichi Nagumo's carrier-based aerial attacks anyway during the Pearl Harbor assault. General Douglas MacArthur's defense forces were also completely caught by surprise when the Japanese attacked the Philippines simultaneously. Virtually all the American airplanes under MacArthur's command were destroyed on the ground at Clarke Air Force base and other facilities by the Japanese within hours of the attack. The British were allies, but the Royal Air Force (RAF) was in terrible shape in Asia when it came to combat.

The vast British colonial empire in Southeast Asia, from Hong Kong to Burma to Singapore was also under simultaneous Japanese attacks. The British military prowess in Asia crumbled most humiliatingly under Japan's blitzkrieg. Within forty-eight hours, the crown jewels of the British Royal Navy, HMS *Prince of Wales*, and HMS *Repulse*, two of the largest battle ships in the world, were sunk by the same Japanese bombers that Chennault's scout planes had spotted in Bangkok hours earlier. Chennault had some planes at hand, but most of them were light-loaded fighters, and many of the P-40s were not yet ready to take off in the Burmese jungle. The agony of defeat and loss of opportunity for attack made Chennault and his eager AVG volunteers particularly impatient and restless.

Yet, during this period of most depressing Allied military defeat throughout the Pacific, Chennault and his AVG pilots would make history within a couple of weeks and become a legend with which they would be forever associated with glory and pride. In Chennault and the AVG, several extraordinary things were happening. First of all, Chennault's meticulous preparation for air combat and unmatched knowledge on Japanese fighter planes and tactics gave the AVG pilots great advantage over the often smug Japanese pilots. Chennault proudly recalled how he imparted his knowledge to his trainees: "I taught them all I knew about the Japanese. Day after day there were lectures from my notebooks, filled during the previous four years of combat. All of the bitter experience from Nanking to Chungking was poured out in those lectures."[47]

Of particular interest was Chennault's understanding of the mentality and behavior pattern of Japanese pilots. "They have plenty of guts," Chennault tutored his trainees, "but lack initiative and judgment. They go into battle with a set tactical plan and follow it no matter what happens. Bombers will hold their formations until they are all shot down. Fighters always try the same tricks over and over again."[48] Based on this observation, Chennault emphasized AVG's overall tactical objective as one of breaking the Japanese battle plan. "The object of our tactics," Chennault concluded, "is to break up their formations and make them fight according to our style. Once the Japanese are forced to deviate from their plan, they are in trouble. Their rigid air discipline can be used as a powerful weapon against them."[49]

Chennault's training sessions were miraculous because he could finally implement his innovative tactics that he had long developed while serving in the U.S. Army Air Corps, tactics that were ignored and jeered by his former superiors as ridiculous and impractical. Especially important in Chennault's system of fighter combat tactics was the two-plane formation groups that he had learned from Baron von Richtofen's Flying Circus. During the rigorous flight training, a two-plane team would be closely observed from a watch tower for each pilot's strengths and weaknesses and would be followed by a performance analysis afterward.[50]

Another crucial innovation Chennault had developed during his army days was the emphasis on an extensive ground-based air-warning intelligence system. In his way of thinking, a fighter group's main task was to intercept enemy bombing sorties. As such, accurate information on the enemy's flight path, strength, and attitude was supremely crucial. This became even more salient when the AVG was such a small air force in a widespread area, with a grave task of protecting Burma and China's air space from the far more formidable Japanese air force. The 100 P-40B fighters Chennault was able to assemble were divided into three squadrons, respectively named "Adams and Eves," "Panda Bears," and "Hells Angels." After being assembled in Burma, two of the three squadrons, Adams and Eves and Panda Bears, were moved to Kunming, China, within days, with the third squadron, Hells Angels, stationed in Burma to protect China's passage to the sea. With the superior and vast air-warning systems the Chinese military intelligence had already set up for Chennault, Japanese bombers were spotted and reported at the earliest moment of their bombing sorties.

On 20 December 1941, ten Japanese heavy bombers were launched to raid Kunming, where AVG's P-40s were stationed. With the excellent air-warning system, Chennault ordered all his fighter planes to take off to intercept the Japanese bombers. Within the hour, a legend was born. Of the ten invading enemy planes, six were shot down and three were damaged, while none of the AVG's P-40s was downed, with only one of them crash landed safely.[51] The citizens of Kunming affectionately gave the AVG a new name, the Flying Tigers, which has stuck in the annals of history.[52]

The Flying Tigers' victory became an instant morale booster throughout the Allied war camp. Two weeks after the Pearl Harbor attacks, when everywhere in Asia and the Pacific the Japanese were victorious over the

Chinese, the Americans, the British, and the Dutch, Chennault's pilots had become the only beacon of victory and hope in the depressing post–Pearl Harbor malaise.

The British in Rangoon were particularly impressed by Chennault's victory. They urgently requested that Chiang Kai-shek order Chennault's squadrons to move to Rangoon to join the RAF there in the defense of the port city. Concerned about the lack of an efficient air-warning system, neither Chennault nor Chiang was willing to comply, which prompted Winston Churchill and Roosevelt to get indirectly involved in the affair. Reluctantly, Chiang agreed to keep the Hells Angels in Burma. On 23 December 1941, fifty-four Japanese bombers and twenty fighters invaded Rangoon's sky. The RAF and AVG's Hells Angels took off to face the incoming enemy. At the end of the day, the Flying Tigers were able to shoot down six Japanese planes, while losing five of their own and two pilots.[53]

Chennault regrouped his fighters and stressed the importance of breaking the Japanese formation in the sky. The next day, Christmas Eve, sixty Japanese bombers and thirty fighters swarmed over Rangoon again. This time, the Flying Tigers climbed to a higher attitude to wait for the enemy and then pounced on the incoming aircraft by breaking the enemy's rigid formation. The result was yet another miracle. Over the blue sky of Rangoon on that day, a single squadron of the Flying Tigers in Burma shot down fifteen Japanese bombers and nine fighters, while losing only two P-40s and with no Flying Tiger pilots killed. The squadron leader of the Hells Angel jubilantly reported to Chennault, "It was like shooting ducks!"[54]

During the two-month stay and fighting in Burma, the third squadron of the Flying Tigers never had more than twenty aircraft, and at one time had only five P-40s. They engaged the Japanese planes thirty-one times and shot down a total of 217 enemy planes, an astonishing kill ratio that has never been exceeded in the history of the U.S. Air Force.[55]

Fame and glory brought Chennault into the world's spotlight. Suddenly, he became the media's darling at a time when the Allies were desperate for a hero. But to Chennault, far more important was the fact that he had brilliantly proved the validity of his neglected and sometimes scorned fighter tactics that he had developed years before in the U.S. Army Air Corps. The fact that he had to prove his innovations in a war far away from his homeland in the service of a foreign leader was an unfortunate reality, but it was an even more biting indictment of the Army brass and their narrow-mindedness, dog-in-the-manger backwardness, and general fallacies about modern tactics and airpower. Yet, precisely because of this detachment from home and the officialdom of Washington, there was no doubt that Chennault's many former detractors became jealous and sour. No one wants to be proven wrong, but to be proven wrong by such a flashy personality as Chennault in such an open media arena with such a public display of chutzpah and high-decibel volume of cockiness is tantamount to unceremonious international humiliation.

To add gasoline to the fire of jealousy and sour grapes, a cable was sent to the vindicated Chennault, who had been basking in flowers and honey, on 3 February 1942. It was from Madame Chiang Kai-shek, his strongest backer of the AVG endeavor. It states, among other things, that as a result of his extraordinary achievement, Chennault would be promoted to the rank of brigadier general and would be put in charge of commanding the entire air force in China and training the Chinese new air force personnel.[56] Thus, the lowly and disgruntled former captain of the U.S. Army Air Corps was now a general with great political clout.

However, unbeknownst to Chennault, Chiang Kai-shek, and Madame Chiang Kai-shek, this jubilant promotion of Chennault to general rank ignited a violent reaction and marked the beginning of a protracted internecine turf war between the U.S. Army brass and Claire Lee Chennault. The issues involved were both personal and institutional.

On the personal side, the China theater had been regarded mostly as the U.S. Army's special turf, with ground operations at the core of all the anticipated military movements against Japan. Four months before the Pearl Harbor attacks, Army Chief of Staff General George C. Marshall ordered the establishment of an American military mission to China led by the U.S. Army's Brigadier General John Magruder.[57]

This high-level U.S. military mission to Chungking was designed by the Army as a preemptive move to make sure the Army alone would play the most prominent role in the coming conflict with Japan in the China theater. At the time, the Army had three leading "China experts" with top China credentials—John Magruder, A. J. Bowley, and Joseph Stilwell, all of whom had served in China for many years and were familiar with the political, military, and economic terrains in the war-torn nation. Yet, none of these three top guns from the Army could come even close to matching Chennault's fame and popularity.

John Magruder was to stay in China until June 1942 as the leading U.S. military official. But Magruder was far outshone by Chennault and became constantly marginalized by the dashy air force cowboy from Louisiana. As a result, the Army brass in Washington from Generals Marshall and Arnold on down became quite resentful of Chennault's popularity both in China and in the United States. Immediately after the Pearl Harbor attacks, the War Department began to take advantage of China's request for a more comprehensive joint war planning and cooperation arrangement in the China theater and decided to replace the melancholy and low-key General Magruder in China with someone more media savvy and charismatic to match and check Chennault's run-away popularity with the Chinese and the American people. In January 1942, at the height of Chennault's fame and glory, General Marshall managed to pick his protégé, Brigadier General Joseph Stilwell, to replace Magruder as the head of the American Military Mission to China, aka AMMISCA. Not only that, Stilwell would come to China with much more clout. He was to be the most senior and commanding American military officer in what was then hastily designated the China-Burma-India theater of war (CBI theater), as well as the chief of staff to Chiang Kai-shek, and the lone controller of all American Lend-Lease materials destined for China.

To counter Chennault's media stardom, Stilwell was the Army's matching choice to head the American military's China mission. Already a legendary figure in the U.S. Army for his colorful and often vulgar "army talk," for his blunt and undiplomatic straightforwardness, for his romantic image as a tenacious infantry commander, and for his bravery under fire, Stilwell was also media savvy and a public relations genius. Lieutenant General Albert Wedemeyer of the U.S. Army, a close colleague of Stilwell's, who was also General George Marshall's protégé, observed that while in China, Stilwell had an "acute sense of public relations insofar as the press was concerned as contrasted with his lack of diplomatic qualifications in his dealings with the British and the Chinese. . . . Everywhere Stilwell went a newspaper correspondent or newspaper photographer was present to catch him in brave poses: peering between leaves at the enemy, or snuggling close to a gun, always giving the appearance of being a field soldier, which was the role in which he so loved to be presented."[58]

Chennault was stunned by the Stilwell appointment, because he believed "Stilwell brought with him three things that served him ill during his difficult assignment in Asia: a strong prejudice against airpower, coupled with a faint suspicion of any weapon more complicated than a rifle and bayonet; a 'treaty port' attitude toward the Chinese, regarding them as inferiors incapable of managing their own affairs without foreign direction; and a complete disregard of the diplomatic facets of a top military post in a coalition war."[59]

All signs indicated that a Chennault-Stilwell struggle for command and prominence was inevitable. This struggle was soon manifested in several major aspects of America's tangled involvement in China during World War II. The first clash was hidden, but fundamental, for it was related to the basic strategy for victory over Japan in the China theater. For Chennault, airpower was the most important implement of war against Japan in the China theater. In his strategy, Chennault unambiguously promoted an offensive strategy through airpower against Japan. Airpower would be used to launch an offensive campaign to destroy the enemy's shipping lines along the China coast; it would be used to pound the Japanese ground troops and military facilities, it would be used to bomb key infrastructure in Japanese-occupied Northern and Eastern China; and eventually, but not long in the future, long-range aircraft would be organized to bomb even the Japanese homeland. This aggressive and offensive air-centered strategy was in sharp contrast with the U.S. Army's overall war plan for the China theater.

Wrapped in pessimism and defensiveness, the Army's general approach to war in China was first formulated by Stilwell's predecessor, Brigadier General John Magruder. As America's top military official in China in the fall of 1941, Magruder, under instruction from the War Department in Washington, D.C., proceeded to map out a war plan in the China theater. His conclusion was that the role the United States military could play in the China theater in a war against Japan would be remarkably limited by distance, personnel, and transportation shortages. As a result, the best the United States could help China fight the war was not through any offensive campaigns, air, sea, or ground, but rather through playing a distant role primarily limited to providing arsenal, not direct troop, participation. In other words, the War Department's war plan for China was that "the United States furnishes the guns and the Chinese do the fighting."[60]

As such, in the Army's thinking, how to transport sufficient American weapons to China became a paramount concern, which placed the Burma campaign at the top of all the military priorities, because Burma was China's only meaningful connection to the outside supplies of military hardware, while for Chennault, using the existing resources to launch offensive air attacks on the Japanese was the top priority of all war moves. As it would turn out, for Stilwell and the U.S. Army, the preponderance of the Burma campaign would violently clash with Chennault and Chiang Kai-shek, who placed airpower at the center of their strategy. This Burma vs. airpower debate would form the core of the epic Stilwell-Chennault-Chiang imbroglio.

In addition to this schism on strategy, the Chennault-Stilwell struggle was also a result of the Army's personnel policies. With undeterred adamancy, General Marshall, since taking over as the Army's chief of staff in 1939, had implemented a policy of "command unity," which required absolutely no U.S. military personnel under foreign command. This policy, which had been implemented by Marshall with absolute insistence, met serious challenge when it was applied to Chennault and his Flying Tigers, who, on paper, were retired American private citizens on the payroll of a foreign government and were classically a force of mercenaries, thus falling outside the official military authority.

In fact, Chennault was promoted to brigadier general in early February 1942 by his Chinese commander, Chiang Kai-shek. At the time, Chennault was expected to rejoin the U.S. military as an active duty officer, but he only took orders from Chiang Kai-shek, so technically he was a brigadier general only in the Chinese army. In fact, the War Department never fully recognized the legitimacy of such promotion authority and regarded Chennault's promotion to general rank by Chiang as a not-so-subtle challenge to Stilwell's authority in China. This ambiguity of command chain quickly promptly the Army brass to step up their efforts to break up the Chennault group and their command relationship with the Chinese and to make it totally subject to American commander's authority, via Stilwell, of course.

The Army's first step was to dismantle the AVG and reinduct all the Flying Tigers into the U.S. Army Air Corps under an Arnold crony. The new designation would be called the 23rd Fighter Group of the Army Air Corps and the commanding officer would be Chennault's old nemesis back in the training days of 1931, Clayton Bissell, with Chennault still in operational control of his pilots.

With Chiang Kai-shek's support, Chennault vehemently objected to the induction of the AVG. He passionately argued that "The AVG had a combat record that was never equaled by a Regular Army or Navy fighter group of similar size. . . . It was criminal to sacrifice the spirit and experience of the group for a mere change in uniform. The AVG was a unique organization, specially trained for a task it had performed with unbelievable success. Its combat record had proved the soundness of my theories to the satisfaction of everybody except some of my Air Corps colleagues."[61]

But the Army excelled at playing hardball in those days. Chennault's protest went nowhere. On 13 February 1941, the enigmatic and powerful Lauchlin Currie at the White House, the man most directly responsible for a presidential clearance in the creation of AVG in the first place, cabled Chennault, informing him that General Hap Arnold wanted Bissell to be Chennault's boss and Chennault had better cooperate with such an arrangement. In return, Currie promised Chennault that the U.S. Army would soon officially recognize his promotion to brigadier general, only this time in the U.S. Army Air

Corps.[62] Chennault felt betrayed by Currie, but there was nothing he could do at the time because Stilwell now was in total control of all American war materiel for China. On 29 March 1941, Stilwell and Bissell arranged a meeting with Chennault and Chiang Kai-shek, during which Stilwell and Bissell told Chennault in no unambiguous terms that if the AVG continued to fly, no further supplies from the United States would be provided.[63]

Sensing the futility of fighting the Army, with solemn promises from Stilwell that the new fighter group would be given equal strength, Chennault most reluctantly accepted induction of AVG into the regular U.S. Army, upon which the Army promptly and officially promoted Chennault to brigadier general, but one day after Bissell's promotion to the same rank so that Bissell would be technically senior to him.[64]

But for the rank and file of the Flying Tigers, the induction, scheduled to take place on 4 July 1942, was an affront to their fighting spirit. Bissell was equally blunt in his threat to those with the Flying Tigers who were not enthusiastic about going back to the U.S. Army. In an open forum in front of a general assembly, Bissell threatened, "and for those of you who don't join the Army, I can guarantee to have your draft boards waiting for you when you step down a gangplank onto the United States soil."[65] In the end, of the total of 250 personnel in the Flying Tigers, only 5 pilots and 22 ground crew members, signed up for induction, and the rest left with defiance and resentment of the first degree.[66]

Chennault would never get his promises from Stilwell fulfilled, because the stubborn Army general was obsessed with his Burma campaign and saw airpower as at best a support element, at worst useless. Bissell would continue to become Stilwell's overall commander of airpower, suppressing Chennault's numerous ambitious plans to enhance the air elements of the war efforts. This "air vacuum" in China under Stilwell's command was finally changed for the better when President Roosevelt and Chiang Kai-shek directly intervened soon after the Casablanca Conference and got Chennault out of the zealous watch of Bissell to become the commander of a Kunming-based independent air force, with a presidential promotion to the rank of major general. Thus was born the legendary 14th Air Force.

During its seven months in existence, the Flying Tigers fought more than fifty air battles with the Japanese. Not once did it lose in battle. It destroyed 299 enemy planes and damaged another 150 or so. During all these air battles over Burma, China, Thailand, and French Indochina, Chennault lost only twelve P-40s in combat, with sixty-one planes destroyed by the Japanese on the ground. Only ten Flying Tiger pilots were killed in the air by enemy fire, three on the ground by enemy bombs, with ten killed in accidents.[67]

Chennault's personal assessment of his experience with the Flying Tigers was a moving testament to a fighting man's pride: "The AVG gave me the greatest opportunity an air officer ever had. . . . It afforded me enormous satisfaction. Not only was I able to prove my methods sound, but in so doing I made a significant contribution to the common cause against the enemy I hated so bitterly. My twin regrets were that circumstances had prevented me from ever throwing the entire group at the Japanese in a single battle and that the Army had forced the group to disband."[68]

For the Chinese, the Flying Tigers remained the finest episode of working with Americans during the entire World War II. T. V. Soong, China's wartime foreign minister and the person largely responsible for backing the grand enterprise, summed it up this way: "The AVG was the soundest investment China ever made."[69]

Yet, the saga of the Flying Tigers from its inception to its untimely demise foretells a stormy wartime experience of military cooperation between China and foreign governments. Several months before his death in 1958, Chennault provided the best perspective on his time in China: "I always found the Chinese friendly and cooperative. The Japanese gave me a little trouble at times, but not very much. The British in Burma were quite difficult sometimes. But Washington gave me trouble night and day throughout the whole war!"[70]

Chapter 4

THE CHINA COMMANDO GROUP
A British Albatross

OF ALL THE FOREIGN MILITARY AND INTELLIGENCE in wartime China, the most intriguing was Britain's grandiose project called the China Commando Group. Its rise and demise was symbolic of all the major contentious issues encountered by all other major similar initiatives by various countries.

By the time Japan launched an all-out war against China on 7 July 1937, Britain still regarded Japan as a local bully primarily interested in Northern and Central China, where the British maintained little colonial interest. Yet, London was given good reasons to end its lethargic reaction to Japanese aggression in China on 21 October 1938, when the Japanese army marched into Canton (Guangzhou), the southern Chinese metropolis adjacent to the British Crown Colony, Hong Kong. This event seriously threatened British colonial interests in East Asia.

The fall of Canton in October made Chiang Kai-shek desperate. For China, Canton had been the crucial port to receive munitions supply from outside via Hong Kong. Now Canton was lost, and the nearby Hong Kong faced a serious threat from Japan. This was a devastating blow to China's war effort. If Hong Kong fell, China would be most seriously hampered. Since the Japanese capture of Canton, however, the British had shown little sign of strong reaction. This frustrated Chiang, and on 4 November 1938, the British ambassador, Sir Archibald Clark Kerr, was hurriedly summoned to Chiang's command post in Changsha to hear the most direct challenge to Britain's China policy by far.

The 4 November meeting between Chiang and Kerr presented the first of many Sino-British diplomatic dramas during World War II. Chiang opened the meeting by bluntly challenging Kerr, "What will be Great Britain's Far Eastern policy in view of this latest move on Japan's part? Will Great Britain view the occupation of Canton in the same light as she viewed the occupation of Manchuria, North China, and Shanghai?" Chiang's outburst continued:

China has been fighting lone-handedly for the past sixteen months. We have looked to Great Britain and hoped for help, but up to the present we have received nothing tangible. We appreciate that we secured munitions through Hong Kong, and upon a mutually advantageous basis, but that avenue has now been closed.

As long as South China was not attacked, we made allowances for Britain's hesitancy to extend practical aid to us, but now that Japan has cut off British trade there is no reason why Britain should hesitate to extend help to us.

For the past sixteen months we have been hearing a lot of discussion about loans, and we have been put off from time to time with excuses that loans were impossible because of Parliamentary complications. But the whole world witnessed the granting almost overnight to Czechoslovakia of a loan similar in nature to that asked for by China.

Clark Kerr listened to Chiang, while the generalissimo made a harsh announcement: "Now the moment has come when we must have definite knowledge of Great Britain's intentions. If Great Britain turns her back alike upon us and her principles, then I shall never bring up this question again. Nor shall I ever mention anything concerning Great Britain's Far Eastern policy. Nor shall I consult Great Britain as to China's future policy or attitude, or anything concerning the Far East."

Finally, Chiang Kai-shek pointed the finger of scorn at the British leadership under Neville Chamberlain: "I can hardly believe that an Empire which produced such statesmen as Disraeli and Gladstone could fail to see the significance of the repercussions of the occupation of Canton, and the inactivity of Great Britain upon her future in the whole of Asia."[1]

Chiang Kai-shek's hardball politics found sympathetic ears in Sir Clark Kerr, who, unlike his counterpart, the British ambassador to Tokyo, believed China should be adequately aided by Britain. He had appealed most strongly to London for such aid. But the official British policy in East Asia had been one of Chamberlainesque appeasement designed not to offend the militarily strong Japan. The Japanese knew this; so did all the British officials in China at the time.[2]

Exactly what effect Chiang Kai-shek's harangue had on the British is not clear. But the Japanese robust southward advance relentlessly continued. On 10

February 1939, the Japanese navy occupied Hainan Island, directly challenging Britain's Southeast Asian colonial interest as well as the Pacific naval equi-
librium of the Washington Conference of 1922. Chiang warned that Japan's
landing on Hainan meant the beginning of Japanese naval dominance in the
Pacific.[3] The fall of Hainan prompted London to take Chiang's plea more seriously this time. On 8 March 1939, London made history by announcing a five
million pound credit to China to purchase military equipment.

But the vigor of this new China policy did not last very long. In early June
1939, a Japanese spy named Cheng Xi-geng was assassinated in the British
Concession in Tianjin, possibly by the Japanese themselves. Thus, a pretext was
set. In a manner that epitomizes Japanese international behavior as substanti-
ated in the pretexts for their invasions of Manchuria in 1931 and of North
China in 1937, Japan on 14 June "retaliated" against Britain by blockading the
British concession in Tianjin and openly demanding that Britain relinquish
any form of support to the Chinese Nationalist government and cooperate
fully with Japan in creating a Japanese-dominated "new order" in East Asia.[4]
This action was tantamount to a de facto declaration of war on the British in
East Asia and was the most serious military challenge by Japan so far.

But by this time, Britain already had too much to handle in Europe with
an increasingly aggressive Nazi Germany. The failed policy of Chamberlain's
wondrous "peace for our time" miraculously found its Asian echo: China's
worst nightmare was realized on 23 July 1939, when an Anglo-Japanese agreement was signed. Chiang Kai-shek's outcry was heard throughout the world
the next day, when he least subtly denounced it as a "Far Eastern Munich."[5]

On 1 September Germany invaded Poland; two days later, Britain
declared war on Germany. Busy with its lone fighting with Japan, China felt
little impact of the war in Europe. Assured of nonintervention by big powers,
Japan expanded its scope of war effort rapidly. In June 1940 France surrendered to Hitler. Within days, the Japanese warships showed up along the coast
of French Indochina and seized effective control. Less than one month later,
the Japanese scored another victory: Winston Churchill, the new prime minister of Britain, responded to Japanese demands and closed the Burma Road
for three months starting from 18 July 1940. China's vital supply line was thus
cut off at one of the most critical moments of the war. During these three
months, the Japanese attack on China devastatingly accelerated. Three weeks
later, The Japanese forced London to withdraw garrison troops in British concessions in Shanghai and North China. On 26 September, the Japanese army
marched into French Indochina from Canton and further entered China from

there. The next day, on 27 September, Japan signed a tripartite military pact with Germany and Italy.

Only now did Britain finally take serious action. Churchill rather remorsefully reopened the Burma Road at the end of the three-month closure terms. But by this time, China's deep distrust of the British policy in East Asia was already in firm shape. With all the major powers in Europe at each other's throats, the United States became the only industrial power capable of supporting China's lone fight against Japan. Chiang Kai-shek would still need British help, but he would no longer beg for it. The terms of discourse were now changed, for it was the British's turn to plea for cooperation from Chiang to defend their endangered colonial empire in East Asia. But the plea must be subtle and diplomatically face-saving. Most important, any military cooperation between Britain and China must be covert so that an open declaration of war from Japan could still be avoided.

Already at war with Germany and Italy in Europe and threatened by a vigorous Japanese southward advance, the British military command was now eager to seek help from the Chinese. In early 1941, the British initiated a series of high-level talks with the Chinese on how China and Britain could provide "mutual assistance" in the case of a Japanese declaration of war on Britain, or vice versa. Major General L. E. Dennys, Churchill's military attaché in Chungking, became the chief organizer of these meetings. Chiang Kai-shek believed that the change of attitude on Britain's part was caused by London's desire to drag China into a grand military defense line for the British colonial empire in Asia ranging from Singapore and Malaya to Hong Kong, Burma, Siam (Thailand), and India.

But China could benefit from this scheme as well. There was one region vital to China in the British Empire in Asia: Burma. With the fall of Hainan and Canton, the only meaningful defense supply line from outside to China was the Rangoon-Lashio-Kunming road. Chiang agreed to Britain's request and designated General He Yaozhu (Ho Yao-tsu) as his deputy to participate in these talks. These "unobtrusive discussions with Generalissimo Chiang Kai-shek and General Ho Yao-tsu . . . [were conducted] with the greatest frankness," General Dennys confided.[6] A wide range of issues was discussed, with the opening and maintenance of a smooth transportation route between Burma and China holding a prominent place.

As a result, a joint military inspection team was formed to explore the extent to which "mutual assistance" could be effectuated in the near future between Britain and China. In February 1941, accompanied by General L. E.

Dennys, Chiang's general, Shang Zhen, chief of the Foreign Affairs Bureau of the National Military Council, led a military inspection mission to visit India, Burma, and Malaya. The mission included General Du Yuming (Tu Yu-ming), the commander of the Chinese Fifth Army; Lin Wei, Chiang's powerful chief secretary; and about another dozen Chinese army, navy, and air force generals.[7] Shang Zhen paid little attention to affairs in India and Malaya but insisted on joint actions in Burma. As a result of this mission, a joint Sino-British defense plan was drawn. The core of the plan pertains to the defense of Burma. It was agreed that China would have ten armies ready at any time to enter Burma.[8]

But the most meaningful result of these talks was a plan for a joint Anglo-Chinese sabotage team. It was brought to the table by the British. On 7 February 1941, in the fourth meeting held between General Dennys and the Chinese, the British general proposed a rather earnest scheme that caught the Chinese by surprise. In his secret report to the War Office, General Dennys described in full his scheme and the Chinese reaction:

The Chinese would welcome experts to advise them in guerilla warfare. The M.A. [Dennys] outlined very broadly a plan which he had in mind and which went rather further than the mere provision of experts. It envisaged making the fullest use of the existing Chinese guerilla bodies and forming a sort of guerilla "corps d'elite." This would consist of companies commanded by selected British officers who would have a small staff of expert soldiers, drawn probably from the Indian Army, and who would be given special training in demolitions, etc. and provided with explosives. The Chinese guerillas would have to be trained and tried men of the very best type. Controlling the work of two or more companies would be a more senior British officer. He might be stationed at the Headquarters of the nearest [Chinese] Army or Zone Commander and would have a small staff and some reserves of supplies and explosives. One of his duties might be liaison to coordinate action between his guerilla companies and the Chinese regular forces.

These companies would as far as possible be employed in areas where the Japanese lines of communication were weak. Their object would be to contain as many Japanese forces as possible and the best way of doing this would be to cut their lines of communications, inflict as many casualties as possible on the parties sent out to repair them and so make the Japanese stage large expeditions to deal with the guerilla menace. All this would require a lot of previous investigation and reconnaissance. If the idea was approved in principle both by the Generalissimo and the by H.M.G [British government], the M.A. would work out a scheme in some detail for discussion with the Chinese.

General Ho was obviously pleased with this scheme and said there should be no difficulty in providing the right type of man for these guerilla companies out of the enormous numbers of guerillas in China. The idea was, however, a new one, for the Chinese had not expected us to offer more than expert advice, and he would therefore have to refer it to the Generalissimo.[9]

Chiang Kai-shek agreed on Dennys's proposal for such a special force. Dennys also received permission from London to start organizing the British commandos and training experts in Burma and elsewhere in the British colonies in East Asia. This was the beginning of British special operations for guerrilla warfare in China. This program was code named by the British as Detachment 204.[10] The objective of this unit was twofold: training of Chinese regular army officers by the British in guerilla warfare and training of British commando units in northern Burma that would move into China to operate "as soon as war broke out between Britain and Japan."[11] The mission was under the direct control of General Dennys and was composed entirely of British army personnel, many of whom had previous experience in commando work in Norway, France, Crete, Libya, and Abyssinia (Ethiopia).[12]

But the policy implication of Detachment 204 was enormous to London, because it touched a sensitive nerve of the British government: open and provocative military actions against Japan should be strictly prohibited for the time being. Consequently, the order came down from London immediately: no one or action of Detachment 204 could be used to engage in any military operations against the Japanese inside China, because Britain was still trying not to provoke Japan to declare war. Although it was organized to fight in China, this group could not be used "until actual war was declared between Great Britain and Japan."[13]

General Dennys pleaded to London to change this policy only to meet constant opposition. For the time being, he seemed only to be supported by the sympathetic Ambassador Clark Kerr in Chungking. Yet that support remained spiritual rather than material. As a result, Detachment 204 was forced to minimize its scope of operation and remain low key in the vicious jungle of Burma, with many of its members dying off from tropical diseases. The situation was so grave that in March 1941, Brooke-Popham, the British commander in chief in East Asia, tried again to plea to London with a proposal that a British-led corps d'elite of Chinese guerrillas be organized to operate in occupied China. Once again, London vetoed it.[14] Ambassador Kerr was most distressed by the sorrow state of affairs related to the absence of any British military actions in China. New ways had to be found to render British assistance to the Chinese in the fight against the Japanese. Thus entered the China Commando Group.[15]

On 22 July 1940, Winston Churchill officially proclaimed the creation of the Special Operations Executive (SOE) "to create and foster the spirit of resistance" in occupied countries and "to establish a nucleus of trained men who would be able to assist as a 'fifth column' in the liberation of the country concerned."[16] It was further decided that the Ministry of Economic Warfare would be the umbrella for the new organization. For the Asian theaters, the SOE specifically created the Oriental Mission, to be headed by Valentine Killery, who had been a businessman and the president of Imperial Chemical Industries (China), Ltd.[17]

Arriving in Singapore in May 1941, Valentine Killery established the headquarters there for the Oriental Mission.[18] Killery's plan was ambitious. He hoped to operate in China, French Indochina, Siam, the Philippines, the Dutch East Indies, Burma, Malaya, Hong Kong, and Borneo.[19] However, he had one problem to deal with before he could get anything done: despite his direct mandate from London, the British regular army's theater commanders in Asia did not welcome Killery's SOE contingent. Killery was barred from Malaya by Lieutenant General A. E. Percival, the British military governor. Killery was not welcomed by the British governor in Burma either. By September 1941, the role of Killery's people in Burma was virtually nonexistent. The same fate was also awaiting Killery in Siam, where the official British policy was to take absolutely no "provocative action." In Indochina, a secret agreement between Britain and the French Vichy government ensured that Britain would not support the Free French in Indochina so long as the French navy took no hostile actions in the China Sea. As a result, Killery's operatives in that area were closely watched by the Japanese police and accomplished virtually nothing by the end of 1941.[20]

A secret report to London by Killery's people later bitterly notes, "The opposition put forward on political grounds was allegedly based upon the risk of endangering British relations with other powers, or upon the danger of undermining local morale by encouraging the anticipation of a Japanese invasion. On military grounds, it was urged that the mission's organization would either not be required or was competing with parallel military organizations. Events proved that all this opposition was ill founded."[21]

To Killery, it became increasingly clear that his mission would accomplish nothing if no new ground could be broken. Facing frustration everywhere else in Asia, Killery turned his eyes to China, a country that had been actively at war with Japan since July 1937. Precisely because of the existence of belligerence between China and Japan, London had long established a divine rule: since Britain was not at war with Japan, no British personnel could be directly used in any military operation in China. This rule posed a dilemma to Killery and his Oriental Mission.

How to get into China without violating London's no-British-personnel rule? For this, Killery received sympathetic support from the British ambassador Kerr. In a nutshell, an ingenious scheme was worked out by Kerr, who himself also needed to show his good faith to Chiang Kai-shek. Why not, Kerr suggested to the SOE, employ some *non-British Europeans* who had lost their countries to the Nazis and send them to China on Britain's behalf? Killery was much delighted at this suggestion and quickly managed to get approval from the War Office in London.[22] The newly conceived China setup would be remote controlled by Killery in Singapore. The code name for this organization would be "Antipodes," with a main objective of "[giving] covert assistance to Chinese guerillas."[23]

In August 1941, Clark Kerr took the approved proposal to see Chiang Kai-shek. The main points of the proposal were:

a. The importation into China via Burma of a substantial quantity of the most modern explosives and demolition material
b. The establishment of training school for guerrilla demolition squads in Chungking and in Honan, Hunan, Chekiang, and Kwangtung
c. The establishment of "advance sections" in the war zones entrusted with the distribution of demolition materials for trained guerrillas for definite approved tasks and for planning commando raids
d. The establishment of a "Central Advisory Board" attached to the head quarters of the C-in-C of guerrillas with a view to unifying their activities
e. This central organization was to be divided into Training, Operations, Transport, Intelligence and Supply sections. All operations were to be carried out *under the direction of the foreign group with full coordination and cooperation with a Chinese general designated by Chiang.* All of the foreigners were, however, to be under a pledge of secrecy as to their activities both to maintain military security and to assure the Chinese of full credit for the operations

f. All expenses for the establishment of the organization, pay of both foreign personnel *and of Chinese employed by them,* explosives, rent, construction of buildings, transportation, etc., would be borne by the British Government. The Chinese would supply and pay their own men in their part of the organization to which the foreign group was attached [emphasis added].[24]

Habitual suspicion toward the British notwithstanding, Chiang Kai-shek was happy that the British finally came to him for a specific joint project. More important to Chiang was the fact that, since Dennys's Detachment 204 people had been barred from entering China to fight, this new setup could bring a joint military operation inside China finally, albeit indirectly. But key to the plan was the understanding that all the British-sponsored personnel working inside China were to be part of the Chinese army and to be under the command of the Chinese authorities. Clark Kerr was emphatic about this key provision, as SOE's own report noted, "He [Kerr] is enthusiastic about this newly planned basis of the work, namely, that we should work for and with the Chinese within their own army and there is no doubt that General Chiang Kai-shek feels the same."[25] Moreover, Chiang believed this proposal was Clark Kerr's oblique way of supporting China through material aid. What other interpretation could he have? It was materiel in-flow to China, training schools for China's guerrilla forces mostly paid for by the British, and most important of all, only a couple of dozen dislocated, stateless non-British Europeans were to be involved. Chiang Kai-shek approved Kerr's proposal— in Keswick's words—"with alacrity."[26]

The importance of the Clark Kerr proposal cannot be overestimated in that it marks the very beginning of a tragic saga of China's dealing with foreign special operations and intelligence involvement on a governmental level during the war. Kerr did not tell the Chinese that this was actually a British governmental plan directly controlled by some high-powered people in London, with the purpose of setting up in China an intelligence and special operations net. Once this scheme was exposed later, friction naturally arose.

The person Chiang Kai-shek designated to enforce the proposal was Major General Tai Li, the powerful chief of China's secret police. A native of Jiangshan County, Zhejiang Province, Tai Li attended the sixth class (1926) of the famed Soviet-backed Whampoa Military Academy, of which Chiang Kai-shek was the superintendent. After the bloody split between the Nationalists and the Communists in April 1927, Tai Li's loyalty to Chiang became even more unshakable. In 1931 Tai Li established an organization called the Revival Society (*fuxing she*), which was composed of Kuomintang (KMT) party diehards and ultraloyalists to the KMT cause. Members of the Revival Society spread out to virtually every key military agency and branch of the Central Government. The society was vital to Tai Li's rise, because it provided him with an intra-agency, horizontal connection with every part of the KMT bureaucratic mammoth. Members of the society could be found in the army, air force, finance and communications ministries, and Chiang's supreme command headquarters. They all would listen to Tai Li despite the fact that throughout his career Tai Li never reached the highest echelon of the KMT hierarchy.[27]

Tai Li was known as an ardent anti-Communist. He once penetrated into the secret circle of the Chinese Communists while at the Whampoa Military Academy in Canton and knew well the ties between Moscow and the Chinese Communists. When Chiang Kai-shek finally staged a showdown with the Comintern and Stalin, who had threatened to "squeeze" Chiang "like a lemon" in the spring of 1927, Tai Li turned in twenty of the powerful Comintern agent Mikhail Borodin's Chinese Communist comrades, thus started his upstart career as Chiang's ears and eyes.[28]

Yet, most foreigners had developed a strong sense of mystery about Tai Li. Perhaps because of Tai Li's lifestyle of phantasmal secretiveness, the American diplomatic and intelligence circle in China treated him with much suspicion, and often malice. An intelligence report by the U.S. Military Intelligence Division crystallizes the typical opinion: "Tai Li's relationship with Americans have been none too good. Superficially, he has been friendly and cooperative, but his peculiar personal brand of loyalty to Chiang, his lack of a Western education and training, his ignorance of English and other foreign languages places him at a great disadvantage and breeds with in him a strong sense of suspicion of all things he does not understand."[29]

In reality, Tai Li was no stranger to the business of dealing with foreigners in China. He disliked Russians, because he had been thoroughly convinced they were the conspirators behind the Chinese Communists. To Americans he gave a mixed feeling. He loathed the loquacious, pontifical, moralistic type of Americans living in China, many of whom he would label later as the "Old China Hands." However, Tai Li loved to deal with no-nonsense, slightly crazy, straightforward American personnel. In 1939 Tai Li granted his instant favor to Herbert Yardley when, at a dinner party in Chungking, the American code-breaking master made the following speech on the necessity of assassination during war: "In war an assassin's bullet is no more than a soldier's, to my way of thinking, and quite as patriotic. Western tradition says differently. There is an unwritten law that the leaders should go unharmed while the pawns slit each other's throats. Napoleon bled Europe for years without suffering a scratch. One assassin's bullet would have saved countless lives and untold suffering. In the American Civil War the Confederate general Robert E. Lee, by his military genius, dragged out the war for four long years. Assassination is not pleasant, but neither is war." Tai Li immediately rose up and called for another *Gan Bei*, the Chinese way of making a toast whenever strong alcohol is involved.[30]

But to Tai Li, the British were what he disliked most personally. He considered the British secret police in Shanghai and Hong Kong not only as a symbol of colonial arrogance but also an infringement on the development of his own secret empire. He was particularly bitter all his life about the collaboration between the British and the Japanese in Hong Kong and Shanghai. In 1939 the British in Hong Kong had gotten a lead from Japanese intelligence sources that Tai Li was in town. Unexpectedly, he was arrested and roughly handled by British agents and spent a humiliating night in a British jail. His release was only made possible by the personal intervention of Chiang Kai-shek.[31]

Consequently, upon receiving Chiang Kai-shek's order to deal with Clark Kerr, Tai Li decided he would not handle this project personally. Instead, he designated Zhou Weilong (Chow Wei-long), one of his unpublicized subordinates, as commander in chief of the British project. Zhou was in charge of a huge guerrilla force called the Special Operations Army (*bie dong jun*) that contained a quasi-military troop known as "the Royal Patriotic Army" (*zhongyi jiuguo jun*).

Clark Kerr was elated; so was Killery. The Oriental Mission chief was ecstatic with the unexpected success. He went to Chungking to meet Zhou Weilong and was greatly impressed by him. Killery reported back to London about Zhou having made "a most favorable impression. He is practical, thorough, determined, and experienced."[32]

The preparation got under way immediately after Chiang Kai-shek approved the Clark Kerr proposal in August 1941. The project was officially named the "China Commando Group." Killery proceeded in London and Asia simultaneously. In London, John Keswick, the Hong Kong and Shanghai-based Jardine, Matheson & Co. Ltd. business tycoon and an intimate friend to T. V. Soong and Madame Chiang Kai-shek, was chosen to be the powerhouse in the Ministry of Economic Warfare for this Oriental Mission project in China.

In the meantime, the non-British Europeans Killery was looking for were found in the United States, China, and elsewhere. They were largely Danes and other Scandinavians. Most were businessmen with China interests. There were seven or more from the China-based Danish concern East Asiatic Trading Corporation. One Swede, George Soderbaum, was recruited from Inner Mongolia, where he had been doing business for years.[33]

Killery's choice to head the China Commando Group was Erik Nyholm, a Danish contractor in China and an agent for the Madsen Arms Co. in Copenhagen, which had sold "a great deal" of ordnance to the Chinese government during the War. The second in command was a Russian, Vladimir Petropavlosky, who was never able to land in China to command because he was imprisoned in Hong Kong by the Japanese in December 1941.[34]

After a brief preparation in Malaya, the China Commando Group was transported to Lashio, Burma, for further training. Nyholm went to China in late October. He told the Chinese that since Denmark had been invaded, they were, in effect, men without a country, and that they would be willing to work for China in the training of sabotage and intelligence. Zhou Weilong apparently liked Nyholm initially and sent many young Chinese college students to work with Nyholm's people; the training program started smoothly.[35]

But in Tai Li's inner circle, there was a profound suspicion of this group of Old China Hands from the very beginning. Of particular concern was Nyholm's pompous claim that he had "limitless money" to operate in China, and his suggestion that China treat the China Commando Group with the same respect and enthusiasm as China treated the American Lend-Lease Act.[36]

Then came the attack on Pearl Harbor. Britain finally declared war with Japan. John Keswick immediately flew to Chungking from his London desk and became the representative of the Ministry of Economic Warfare in China, with the cover rank of first secretary in the British embassy.[37] Upon his arrival, Keswick informed China that they, the British SOE, had been the real backers of the China Commando Group and they, the British, would now take charge.[38]

Tai Li was taken aback by Keswick's blunt demand to take over the China Commando Group. But Keswick had the strong backing of Madam Chiang Kai-shek and her brother, T. V. Soong. He was also holding an important position in the British embassy and was one of the most influential British citizens in East Asia. "For the time being, it appeared that John Keswick was sitting on the top of the world."[39] All things considered, Tai Li said nothing.[40] Keswick then took charge of the training and added British instructors to the program. Things continued to look good for the China Commando Group.

But this calm and nicety was a grand façade. Keswick's takeover of the China Commando Group on behalf of the SOE constitutes a major change in the basis upon which the joint Anglo-Chinese project could work—the underlying principle of all British or European personnel associated with the China Commando Group must be part of the Chinese army and that they must be under operational and command control of the Chinese central authorities, as initially proposed by Sir Archibald Clark Kerr to Chiang Kai-shek in August 1941. This change made Keswick the actual commander of the China Commando Group, separating it from Chinese military control.

Naturally, the Chinese went back to the Clark Kerr proposal to thwart this change of command. But upon carefully examining the original British proposal, the Chinese found several latent loopholes regarding China Commando Group's command structure.

First of all, according to the agreement, the British would provide China with much-needed "most modern explosives and demolition material." But the question was that once these materials were in China, who was authorized to distribute them? Section C of the Kerr proposal states that it should be the "advance sections" attached to each war zone. Those advance sections were to be ultimately controlled by foreigners.

Secondly, it was nebulous on the question of operational command. Ostensibly, the Chinese would provide the "commander in chief" for this endeavor (Section D), but he was immediately supervised by a "Central Advisory Board." Section E further stipulates that China would be assured of "the full credit" for the operation, but states as well that "All operations were to be carried out under the direction of the foreign group with full coordination and cooperation" of the Chinese commander in chief. This is to say that the Chinese would have a commander in chief who might have no operational control.

Thirdly, Section F states that the foreign side could employ Chinese in their units. Under this arrangement, the nature of the relationship between the foreign employer and his Chinese employees would inevitably become mercenary. Consequently, his employees would be outside the boundary of bureaucratic and political obligation to Chiang Kai-shek's regime. The real danger, however, was this: what if the foreigners employed people the Nationalists deemed undesirable, say, the Communists?

Almost immediately after Keswick's takeover of the China Commando Group, the Chinese objections and obstructions to Britain's special operations inside China independent of Chinese central command began to mount. The future for the China Commando Group suddenly seemed ominous. To make matters worse, the months following the Pearl Harbor attack mark as the darkest hours of British military defeats in East Asia, which caused a stormy drop of the British reputation and the rapid rise of anti-British sentiment throughout China. It was this terrible blow to the Anglo reputation that soon put the China Commando Group in fatal trouble.

The outbreak of the Pacific War following the Pearl Harbor attack suddenly rendered China the great hope that an international united front among the United States, Britain, and China would be formed instantly. It seems perfectly logical—they had a common enemy and enemy's enemy should be friends. But Chiang Kai-shek realized quickly that such hope was unrealistic. On the day the Japanese attacked Pearl Harbor, Chiang proposed a joint declaration of war against Japan by the United States, China, and Britain and told Brigadier General John Magruder, head of the U.S. military mission in China handling the Lend-Lease affairs; British ambassador Kerr; and British General Dennys that he was "prepared to throw all of China's resources into support of our war effort."[41]

Unexpectedly, Chiang Kai-shek's hope of a grand Sino-British-American alliance met with Britain's stonewalling. Chiang offered three armies to help the British defend Hong Kong, but the British refused. When China insisted, the British replied that they might not provide air cover.[42] From the British point of view, "it was desirable that Hong Kong, being a British possession, should be liberated by the British, albeit using Chinese guerrillas in the first assault. There would have to be an all-British follow-up, however, either airborne, sea-borne, or both—otherwise Chiang Kai-shek might claim that the Colony, wrested by the Japanese from the British Empire, had been reconquered by the Chinese."[43]

The same logic was followed in the Burma and Malaya defense. Field Marshal Sir Archibald Wavell fiercely refused having Chinese troops enter Burma to defend Rangoon and the Burma Road, violating an earlier military agreement. He cited bad roads as reasons for his refusal and preferred Indian troops for "safety" concern.[44] Furthermore, the British, on 18 December 1941, surreptitiously took American lend-lease materiel designated for China from USS *Tulsa*. This angered General Magruder, and Chiang exploded, accusing the British of thievery and threatening that there would be great crisis if the British interfered in the future. The British demanded that Chiang send Chennault's American Volunteers' Group air force to Rangoon, and Chiang did so, "because of larger issue at stake."[45] When Chennault suffered dearly on the ground from Japanese air bombing for lack of a British air-warning system, Chiang ordered the AVG back to Kunming temporarily. The British protested. When Chiang explained, General Dennys said in scorn that "Chennault's group is probably spoiled because of the excellent warning net in China." Chiang fought back by saying he did not want his planes bombed on the ground.[46]

All these Anglo-Chinese clashes were accompanied by an avalanche of the collapse of the British empire in Asia. Hong Kong surrendered to the Japanese on 25 December 1941. In Singapore, the central pillar and the head-quarters of the British military in Asia were rendered totally nonfunction-al by an all-out strike of the native civic service. When the Japanese troops captured Singapore on 15 February 1942, a total of eighty thousand British armed forces personnel surrendered to the Japanese. On 9 March, Rangoon fell. William J. Donovan, chief of the office of Coordinator of Information for the United States, sent two of his agents to observe the British fiasco. The reports came back to Donovan, who immediately sent them to Roosevelt. The reports concluded that British military's faulty strategic conceptions and the civilian disobedience—"You can't win the war with slaves," Donovan's agent, Colonel Brink wrote—accounted for the British plight in Singapore and else-where in Asia.[47]

However, the reports that came back to Tai Li from General Zheng Jiemin (Cheng Kai-min), who was asked by Wavell to train native guerrilla groups in Singapore just before the Pearl Harbor attack, were much more devastating.[48] Zheng Jiemin was arranging to operate his training units in Singapore when the Japanese attack occurred. With awe, he witnessed the greatest military defeat he had seen. The conclusion Zheng and his people in Chungking had drawn was unequivocal: the British were not merely militarily ill managed, they also did not have the *willingness* to fight.[49] Madame Chiang Kai-shek wrote a timely article in the *New York Times*, stating that Britain's scorn of China's weakness in resisting Japan was unwarranted; that the Chinese did not have a military buildup in Shanghai when the Japanese attacked, yet the Chinese resistance went on for three months; but the British had been build-ing up a most modern military force in Singapore in the past twelve years and were defeated soundly by the Japanese within only two weeks.[50]

In the meantime, American opinions were also overwhelmingly critical of Britain's empire mentality in Asia and its subsequent military catastrophe in the hands of the Japanese. Pearl Buck made speech after speech denouncing the British intransigence. The China Commando Group field officer promptly filed a report to London, warning that the British prestige in China was rapidly declining and that "the ignorant sentimentality of the average American, encouraged by Chinese propaganda, has increased considerably the difficulty of securing the desired unity," labeling Madam Chiang's and Pearl Buck's speeches as "virulently anti-British."[51]

The sweeping British defeat by the Japanese stimulated yet more thunder: the Indian independence movement. For China, a stable situation in India was vital, because India was the springboard for recovery of Burma and for the reopening of a supply route in China's war against Japan. Yet, Donovan's agent reported that "the Hindus are incorrigible ideologists and have less fear of Japanese domination than of the present British domination."[52] To make the matter worse, after the fall of Malaya, Japanese spies tied up with the Indian nationalists in late December 1941. Instantly, the spark of Japanese agitation set a prairie ablaze. Fujiwara Iwaichi, a chief of Japanese military intelligence, successfully persuaded a group of young Indian officers led by Mohan Singh to form the Indian National Army.[53] In the meantime, Mahatma Gandhi's Congress Party demanded immediate independence from the British or it would even venture to negotiate a peace with the Japanese. This prospect of India falling to the Japanese frightened both the British and Chiang Kai-shek.

Now the British needed Chiang badly—it was really a time for an "Asia for Asians" tactic. The British earnestly invited the leader of the "Good Asians" to India to placate their agitated subjects. Chiang's chief aides opposed the British invitation, and Chiang replied, "Isn't it a wonderful thing for someone to unite 450 million Chinese with 350 million Indians? If I don't go right now, do you think the British would let me do it when the war is over ?"[54] On 10 February 1942, Chiang Kai-shek arrived in India to talk with the British and the Indian nationalists. John Keswick, the chief of the China Commando Group, was the chief arranger of all things for Chiang's trip to India.[55]

The Indians went wild for Chiang's visit, a grand military parade—the Indian army only—was held for Chiang, and the National Student Union declared 15 February as "China Day." Chiang's sympathy for the Indian aspirations, as well as his concern in the stabilization of the country until at least the war was won, was equally strong. On 21 February 1941, still in India, he urged the British to give "real political power" to the Indians and further proposed a roundtable negotiation of four sides, with China and the United States serving as monitors to make sure of the ultimate fulfillment of any British promises made to India. The British flatly rejected this proposal.[56] This deeply angered and humiliated Chiang Kai-shek. Furthermore, alarmed by

Chiang's pro-Indian remarks, the British governor-general of India, Victor Alexander John Hope, the Second Marquess of Linlithgow, tried to prevent Chiang's final meeting with Gandhi. This further displeased Chiang, and he went to see Gandhi in Calcutta anyway and talked for hours, much to Linlithgow's chagrin.[57]

Chiang's entourage, with Keswick's accompany all along, returned to China in late February, charged with furor against the intransigent British, thus providing the basic background for the ouster of the China Commando Group, the only British military setup in China at the time. As a secret report of the China Commando Group decried to London, "The military disasters suffered by the Allies, and in particular the British, in the Far East have had the anticipated effect on Chinese opinion in Chungking . . . [these military disasters] gave rise first to a sense of keen disappointment followed by a feeling of resentment, particularly strong against the British who are blamed for the loss of Hong Kong and Singapore."[58]

Against these backgrounds, the Chinese gradually found the China Commando Group operating inside China menacing and irritable. In fact, the China Commando Group had been doing something beyond the limit of tolerance of Chiang, who was extremely hostile, and fault finding toward the British after his return from India in late February 1942. Clashes soon occurred between Keswick and Tai Li. The first issue that led to an open squabble between the Chinese and British was the military value of China's cooperation.

Chiang Kai-shek had long sought an international military alliance in Asia against Japan. Before the Pearl Harbor attack, the British did not seem to have much problem with China's direct regular army involvement beyond Chinese borders should war between Britain and Japan break out. After the Pearl Harbor attack, however, the British changed their mind. Chiang's enthusiastic offer of large Chinese regular armies to help the British was cold shouldered. The British did not believe the direct involvement of the Chinese standing army was of much value. Instead, they wanted the Chinese to confine themselves to China proper and help the British *indirectly* by keeping large numbers of Japanese troops exhausted in China, thus alleviating pressure on the British elsewhere outside of China.

On 10 December 1941, Ho Yin-chin, Chiang's chief of staff, asked General Dennys what exactly the British expected in the nature of help from China. Dennys replied that *indirect* help would be of great value—it would include bringing "pressure everywhere in China to keep the Japs pinned down." He mentioned minor offensive patrols, guerrilla action, spreading rumors of a general offensive for Japanese consumption, and propaganda against the puppet troops to keep the Japanese worried about their loyalty.[59] In other words, the Chinese should be preoccupied with what the China Commando Group was supposed to do—guerilla warfare and clandestine operations. Dennys's strategic conception was construed by the Chinese as a sign of British contempt for the Chinese army. The Chinese were rightfully insulted, considering the incredible British military impotence and defeat throughout Asia at the time.

Nevertheless, this British strategy had a great influence on the new role of the China Commando Group. Following General Dennys's strategy, Keswick was endowed with an increased importance in his project. Now he must rapidly expand his operation throughout China and help the *indirect* pinning-down warfare. Under the Clark Kerr agreement of August 1941, Keswick had an enormous advantage in accomplishing his expansion into other parts of China, because it provided the British with virtual control over both materiel and operations. Keswick could also now decide by himself which war zone commanders or Chinese governors he would like to approach directly without consulting the central government and Chiang Kai-shek. In fact, the China Commando Group might have even contemplated secretly contacting the Chinese Communists in Yenan (Yanan) at this juncture.

A China Commando Group's secret report later mused that "Satisfactory contact with the Communists in Yenan may lead not only to valuable results in China, but also in Malaya where the Chinese Communist Party represented the only active militant Chinese force in that territory, which was known still to be operating in Malaya after the fall of Singapore.... The approach to Yenan is so important that every effort should be made to find means of achieving it successfully." Knowing the danger of approaching Yenan without permission from Chiang, the China Commando Group memo cautions, "Such a move will require the most careful and delicate handling and must not be in any way associated with OM [Oriental Mission] in Chungking."[60] By March and April 1942, the China Commando Group had already brought ten or twenty tons of materiel into China.[61] They were all assembled in Kweiyang (Guiyang) under the careful control of Erik Nyholm.

Keswick's expansion met instant opposition from Tai Li. Suspicion was already high. Tai Li's people firmly believed that the British only wanted to use Zhou Weilong's Special Operations Army as a cover to install secret agents in mainland China at a time when the British were being soundly defeated by the Japanese elsewhere in the Southeast Asia.[62] Starting from March 1942, Zhou Weilong was informed by Tai Li that the British were dispatching secret agents all over China without any Chinese authorization and had indeed set up clandestine radio stations at many points in China's interior.[63] Zhou was furious, because this was occurring without his knowledge.

Meanwhile, Tai Li's men immediately intensified surveillance over Keswick's people. As expected, the first blow soon came to the China Commando Group. A secret letter written by the Swedish businessman George Soderbaum, one of Keswick's "non-British Europeans," was discovered by Tai Li's men. It was addressed to General Fu Tso-yi (Fu Zuoyi) of Suiyuan Province, adjacent to Inner Mongolia. In the letter, Soderbaum offered to come up and help the general.[64] Soderbaum was widely known in China to have a longtime interest in Inner Mongolia, China's ethnically supersensitive territory. Fu Tso-yi's loyalty to Chungking had often been a major concern in the inner circle of the KMT.[65] This matter aroused serious alertness and was promptly reported to Chiang.[66]

Another political complication, suspected by the Chinese, was Keswick's support of a Kwangtung (Guangdong) Chinese guerrilla leader, Chan Chak, who had turned very pro-British. Suddenly, it was widely rumored that Chan Chak was to be named chairman of Kwangtung Province.[67] It was likely that the British were responsible for the rumor, because an important feature of the China Commando Group was rumormongering for circulation throughout China.[68] The specter of a separatist Kwangtung supported by the British was quickly haunting the KMT leadership. It was a terrifying prospect for Chungking. Moreover, Tai Li discovered that the British had also approached General Gu Zhutong, the commander of the Third War Zone, about setting up a demolition training camp there.[69]

In late February 1942, Chiang Kai-shek, returning from India and, accompanied by Keswick, stopped over in Yunnan where most of the Allied military activities were being conducted. Yet, Governor Lung Yun was running things in virtually his own way. The American naval attaché pointedly observed, "Lung Yun is treated by the Generalissimo as an ally rather than a subordinate."[70] Ignoring this Chinese sensitivity, Keswick made what he later insisted was an innocent request to call upon Lung Yun without telling Chiang Kai-shek.[71] This deepened Chiang's distrust of Keswick. The situation was so sensitive that when the remaining members of Detachment 204, the ill-fated commando unit organized by Major General Dennys in 1941, emerged from the Burmese jungle in the border region of Yunnan, Zhou Weilong firmly believed they were actually Keswick's secret agents sent into China without his consent.[72]

But Keswick's troubles did not stop here. The thorny issue of Hong Kong also came up. Before the fall of Hong Kong, the British had organized a clandestine network based in the New Territories, where the Chinese Communist guerrilla forces were organizing anti-Japanese activities and managing one of the main smuggling routes to China.[73] The British team was named Z Force and was led by F. W. Kendall. Its scope of operation was in Canton, Amoy, Swatow, and Hainan.[74] But the Japanese came rapidly, and the Z Force was rendered ineffective. Most members surrendered, while three of them fled to Chungking, where they met John Keswick, who had just arrived from London. Keswick immediately took over Kendall's project and merged it with the China Commando Group.[75]

Britain's flat refusal to accept Chinese troops to defend Hong Kong upset many Chinese officials. The unceremonious surrender of the British Crown Colony aroused a deep contempt among many Chinese for Anglo military prowess, or lack of it. The Hong Kong surrender was indeed regarded by some as a useful lesson—teaching punishment for the perceived British arrogance and military incompetence. This feeling, however, clashed with the growing belief that Keswick's overwhelming interest now was to use the China Commando Group to recapture Hong Kong, where part of his own commercial empire of Jardine and Matheson was much at stake. It was bad for the British to be suspected of such things by the Chinese. It was even worse, if not devastating, for the British that many of Keswick's people openly bragged about such ambitions, thus confirming the Chinese suspicion. In mid-March 1942, Erik Nyholm told the Chinese that the major task of the China Commando Group was not to liberate China but Hong Kong. Tai Li exploded when Eddie Liu reported this to him.[76] He immediately ordered Zhou Weilong to play tough with the British.

Already feeling deeply cheated by the British on the issue of command control, Zhou sent a curt letter to Nyholm in Kweiyang on 20 March 1942: "You will immediately turn in all of the equipment you have brought to China. Zhou Weilong." Nyholm was incensed and replied simply, "I will not turn in my equipment to you. Nyholm."[77] The stalemate prompted Zhou Weilong to write directly to Keswick, "the Honorable Representative of the British Side," demanding that "Since the Commando Group would be part of the Chinese army, it must drop its name. Radio stations set up to support it must close. Its demolition materials, trucks, petrol, and stores must be handed over to the Chinese. Its offices, storehouses, and living quarters must be built by the Chinese."[78] Keswick was calm upon receiving Zhou Weilong's message and hit him back with a powerful weapon, the August 1941 agreement approved by Chiang Kai-shek, stating that, according to his own interpretation, the Commando Group must remain independent; therefore, no material would be turned over by him. Furthermore, Keswick told Zhou that he would appeal to Chiang.

But it was too late; Chiang refused to see Keswick. On 4 April 1942, Hollington Tong (Dong Xianguang), Chiang Kai-shek's confidant and interpreter, carried a short message from the generalissimo to Ambassador Clark Kerr. It demanded the immediate withdrawal of the China Commando Group. Chiang gave the reasons for his order as "bad reports received"[79] and the Commando Group's "improperly dealing direct with Provincial Governors."[80] But in the mind of Keswick, this disastrous British fiasco was undoubtedly caused by Zhou Weilong, the man once admired by Killery, Nyholm, and Keswick himself. A list of Zhou Weilong's alleged obstructions—consisting mostly of such trivial logistical matters as quarters, water supply shortage, inadequate storage spaces for Nyholm's people—was later compiled to document the British complaints against the Chinese general. Now Keswick had every reason to curse Zhou Weilong: "He is a little man and will always remain so."[81]

The China Commando Group was Tai Li's first official cooperation in intelligence and special operations with Western Allies. It was a fiasco for both sides. To the British, it was a total loss of face and a major blow to its China penetration programs, which subsequently led to a devastating attack on Tai Li within Britain's intelligence allies. This intensified attack on Tai Li would soon thereafter have a deep impact on American intelligence's entry into China. Although the unceremonious ending of the China Commando Group did not end SOE's ambition for China altogether, it affected the quality and scope of all its future programs in China. After the China Commando Group debacle, a new partner was soon found by the SOE in the Institute of International Relations (IIR), headed by the Chinese general Wang Pengsheng. The SOE soon clung to IIR and spent money on it lavishly. A special branch called Resources Investigation Institute (RII) was set up within the IIR as a base for the British intelligence, shielded and protected by the Chinese general throughout the entire war against Japan. But that route taken by the British in China was far less important than the potential of the China Commando Group, and it would take the British a long time to rebuild an intelligence network sufficient enough to become an organization of any consequence.

Tai Li gained a new fierce enemy. The increasingly bad odor about him in the foreign press after this incident would soon force Chiang Kai-shek to restrain Tai Li's contact with foreign intelligence. This only cornered Tai Li and intensified his tenacity to struggle with his domestic competition in controlling cooperation with foreign intelligence. At this point, to both the Chinese and British intelligence, the single most important step to take after the fiasco of the China Commando Group was to look for new partners.

But this time Tai Li would find a partner on his own terms. This experience with the British had shaped Tai Li's "foreign policy" in five fundamental areas—all of which would have a crucial impact on the future intelligence operations in China by both the British and, especially, the Americans

First, since Tai Li's distrust of the British was deeply unshakable, any future attempt by, or associated with, the British to conduct clandestine activities in China would meet his strongest opposition. Second, in any future cooperation, it would be absolutely essential to have a well-thought-out, clearly defined written agreement signed and understood by both sides, lest the Clark Kerr kind of proposal be repeated. This would be Tai Li's primary motive to start his Sino-American Special Technical Cooperative Organization (SACO) Agreement with the Americans immediately after the China Commando Group fiasco. Third, to avoid any unduly foreign "intrigue" with provincial strongmen of dubious loyalty to Chiang, Tai Li must have unequivocal command and operational control over any cooperation projects. Fourth, to avoid any secret dispatch of materials by foreigners to interior China and to do away with attempts to control him through foreign aid, Tai Li must have veto power over the distribution of materiel brought in by his foreign partners. Finally, the new partner must be rich and generous.

On 1 April 1942, the Bureau of Investigation and Statistics held its annual commemoration for its birthday. Tai Li made an emotional speech to his agents about the China Commando Group in which he suddenly announced, "My comrades, don't be discouraged by the departure of the British. They have gone away, and that's all right. But the Americans have already packed their luggage and are on their way to Chungking now!"[82]

Chapter 5

MILES AWAY IN CHINA
The U.S. Navy's Chinese Dragon

"THE UNITED STATES NAVY LAUNCHED a secret weapon in China in World War Two—a two-headed dragon with a million eyes, thousands of claws and numberless stinging tails. In China dragons are understood to be powerful friends if you know their ways. They control important things like weather, river flow, and earthquakes. At first I didn't know I had a dragon by the tail."[1] Thus wrote Rear Admiral Milton Edward "Mary" Miles of the United States Navy. The name of the dragon referred to here is SACO, short for Sino-American Special Technical Cooperative Organization, a massive intelligence and special operations enterprise jointly run by the Chinese and the Americans.

Arguably the most controversial and most significant Western military and intelligence endeavor in China during the entire war, SACO started with a humble origin, germinated from a casual encounter in Washington, D.C., between a Chinese military attaché and a lowly U.S. naval commander at a social function, and grew within a few years into one of the largest paramilitary and intelligence organizations in the history of modern warfare, with Chinese and Americans "fighting together as guerillas, running weather stations, radio direction and intercept, intelligence gathering of all kinds including targets by land and sea, sabotage, anti-sabotage, location of spies, rescue of pilots . . . [operating] from the Gobi desert to Siam, from the Pacific to Burma."[2]

And all this was primarily related to one U.S. naval officer, Milton Miles, who had an illustrious track record of encountering Asia in the early part of the twentieth century. After graduating from Annapolis, Miles served in the U.S. Navy's Yangtze River patrol in China from 1922 to 1927 and went back to China eight years later for another four years of tour of duty. During these long tour periods, Miles witnessed the most dramatic political and military upheavals in the revolutionary and war-torn country, including the Northern

Expedition, the first United Front between the Chinese Communists and the Chinese Nationalists and its bitter demise, the liberation of China by Chiang Kai-shek's Nationalist army from the chaotic warlord rule, the brutal and naked Japanese aggression in China, and the internecine fight between the Chinese Communist Party (CCP) and the Kuomintang (KMT). But most strongly, Miles felt the rise of a Chinese nationalism that demanded international recognition and respect.

Milton Miles was a man of many legends. He was universally known as "Mary Miles," not for his lack of masculinity but for the jocular pun associated with Mary Miles Minter, the popular Broadway actress at the time. In 1938 Miles had risen to the number two position in the U.S. South China Squadron commanded by Captain Jack Stapler. In October of that year, the Japanese launched a sudden amphibious invasion of China's Hainan Island. Miles's ship sailed into the action to observe the Japanese invasion and was threatened by the Japanese for getting too close to the invasion site. Miles ignored Japanese warnings and hoisted a deliberately confusing pennant to respond to Japanese warning signals. Confused by the pennant, the Japanese commanding officer did not want to create an unwanted international incident such as the one that had taken place the year before in the bombing of the American gunboat the USS *Panay* on the Yangtze River and left the American ship unmolested. Many years later, the internationally famous journalist Edgar Snow wrote a story about Miles's "What the Hell" pennant in the *Saturday Evening Post* and made Miles nationally renowned for this action.[3]

After the end of his second China tour in 1939, Commander Miles was reassigned to the Navy Yard in Washington. D.C., to record and write weapons specifications. Far away from the raging flames of war in China, the relative calm of Southeast Washington provided the setting for a few like-minded salty sailors who had acquired sufficient China experience to group together in a casual fashion to chat about the war in China, to swap odd and interesting encounters with China and its people, and more important, to unleash their frustration coming out of America's vigilant isolationism toward Asian affairs. Miles belonged to this group of sailors. So did Captain Willis "Ching" Lee, who had previously served along the China coast as well.

Occasionally, Miles would bring an old Chinese acquaintance of his, Xiao Bo, or Hsin Ju Pu Hsiao, who was working in the Chinese embassy in the capacity of an assistant military attaché, to the casual chat that normally took place in the officer's club or a local bar. Amicable, charming, with quick wit and thorough understanding of American social and political etiquette, Xiao mingled nicely and seamlessly with this group of naval officers who longed to get into action in the boisterous China theater that was in the news every day. Yet, everyone understood it was simply a social occasion that bore no policy implications.

But things began to change when an active member of the group, Willis Lee, was promoted to rear admiral in charge of weapons development for the U.S. Navy. With war escalating in China, Lee announced to his staff in the summer of 1941 that "We know a lot about the German and British systems of making war, but so far as I can tell from the intelligence reports coming in, we do not know much about what precautions the Japanese are taking against the weapons that we have now. Do they know what we are planning? It seems to me that we should send someone out to China now, someone who may be able to obtain access to the Chinese Intelligence Service and who can find out about Japanese training methods. Also it may be possible to loan the Chinese some of our equipment to use so we can see how effective it is."[4] Lee chose Milton Miles to be his man for such a mission and ordered Miles to get ready.

A few months later, in the immediate aftermath of the Japanese attacks on Pearl Harbor, Willis Lee became an assistant chief of staff to Admiral Ernest J. King, the commander in chief of the entire U.S. Fleet. Forever a China enthusiast, Lee immediately put his proposal to send Miles to China for King's consideration. But nothing really could happen to the idea around the time of the Pearl Harbor attacks because of other overall strategic reshuffling and shifting priorities, until February 1942, when several new developments suddenly made the Miles mission a top priority on King's list.[5]

The first was the formation of Admiral King's Pacific strategy, which demanded substantial deviation from the Anglo-American grand strategy of "Europe First, Asia Second" approach. King's insistence on waging a major and sustained campaign against the Japanese in the Pacific region envisioned a push-back movement to enable the U.S. forces to reach the China coast of the Pacific, from where a northward drive into the Japanese inner zone of Manchuria to Korea and eventually to the Japanese home isles could be launched to ensure an ultimate victory. To do so, the U.S. Navy had to send a mission to China to cooperate with the Chinese resistance and coordinate a future amphibious landing campaign from the Chinese inland.

Secondly, as the U.S. naval operations began to reach full scale in the vast waters of the Central and South Pacific, there was a dire need for weather intelligence from the Asia mainland. As most of the weather patterns in the Pacific germinated from the mainland, weather intelligence from inland China could provide precious forecasts with which to plan naval operations. The chief of the U.S. Naval Weather Service, Captain Howard T. Orville, was "most interested in the possibility of setting up small portable weather stations in the interior of China, or any other place possible, in order to get the weather information out of China to amplify his weather setup at the time, because, during the period 1937–1941 most foreigners were pushed out of the interior of China and out of contact with Chinese military circles." Consequently, Captain Orville was delighted that there had been a plan to send Miles to China and instructed him that "if you can get even occasional weather from any series of stations in China, it will assist us in completing our Pacific weather map in order that long-range planning can be made for carrier strikes in the Far East."[6]

Finally, the lack of any meaningful preattack intelligence and intelligence analysis in the Pearl Harbor raids on 7 December 1941 shocked the entire intelligence circle in Washington. An immediate intelligence shake-up took place when the Navy most enthusiastically endorsed a plan to revamp the obsolete system of naval intelligence from China that had been based on a single source, that is, the naval attaché's office in the U.S. embassy. A quick setup in intelligence operations in China would preempt other competitors, especially the Army's Military Intelligence (G-2) and the newly established Office of the Coordinator of Information (COI), under the charismatic lawyer-turned-sleuth Colonel William "Wild Bill" Donovan. It would also free American naval intelligence in China from heavy and unduly influence of the British, who had become increasingly unpopular with the Chinese.

On 12 February 1942, Admiral King approved Willis Lee's proposal and authorized the Miles mission to China.[7] Immediately, Miles went to see his friend, Xiao Bo, at the Chinese embassy in Washington and informed Xiao of the situation. Knowing the high-level endorsement and support of the Miles mission, Xiao cabled Chungking for instructions, and within hours Chiang Kai-shek wired his approval back. Xiao then told Miles that his interlocutor in China would be Major General Tai Li, the de facto chief of China's military intelligence and that Xiao's real boss was General Tai.[8]

A great enterprise was thus born, with the initial name of "Friendship Project." As Admiral King's assistant chief of staff, Willis Lee elevated the plan to be directly commanded from Admiral King's office. Captain Jeffrey C. Metzel was designated to be the overall Washington coordinator for the Friendship Project. Vice chief of naval operations, Admiral Frederick J. Horne, signed off an initial $40,000 for the Miles-Tai Li cooperation.[9] Then Admiral King summoned Miles, who had just been promoted to commander, to his office and gave order as follows: "You are to go to China and set up some bases as soon as you can. The main idea is to prepare the China coast in any way you can for U.S. Navy landings in three or four years. In the meantime, do whatever you can to help the Navy and to heckle the Japanese."[10]

With that, Miles left for China on 6 April 1942, five days after Major General Tai Li announced that the ouster of the British intelligence group from China would be a good thing and that the Americans were soon to take the place of the British in China. Twenty-eight days later, Miles landed in Chungking and received a hearty and pompous welcome by Tai Li, who badly needed a new foreign partner on his own terms and was elated that he had finally found an ideal one in Miles.

Miles's remarkable initial success made many resident China intelligence specialists envious, especially the most senior American intelligence officer, the naval attaché and a Marine officer, James McHugh, who was Miles's classmate in the class of 1922 at the U.S. Naval Academy. With bitterness, McHugh reported to the secretary of the Navy, Frank Knox, "Commander Miles has gotten off to a flying start and has been taken completely into the confidence of the Chinese Secret Service. He has seen and done things already that I never thought any foreigner would be able to do . . . whatever the Navy gets in the way of useful information here in the future will be that which Miles digs out. . . . As for the rest of this show here, it is in the hands of the U.S. Army for better or for worse."[11]

What McHugh did not know and failed to report to his boss in Washington was that Miles's flying start with Tai Li was also full of bumps and obstacles. As we have seen, Tai Li had developed a profound dislike for the British intelligence personnel running London's Asia projects. Many of them were European businessmen who had been living in China for many years with an overbearing "treaty port" mentality. Tai Li knew that Miles was a different foreign partner who respected the Chinese and was a professional military officer. But he had to make sure Miles was not tainted by an "Anglo superiority complex." Unfortunately, several incidents in the early days of Miles's arrival in Chungking did not look good for Miles's claimed innocence and made the already supersuspicious Tai Li increasingly doubtful of his new partner's intentions and organizational background.

First of all, on his month-long journey from Washington to Chungking, Miles stopped in India for a prolonged period of time. While the real reason for this was that it was difficult for Miles to find a plane seat to Chungking and he had to wait for the next available opportunity, Tai Li suspected that Miles had to stop in India so that he could confer with British officials there.

While waiting for a plane in India, Miles quite unexpectedly encountered a number of people who Tai Li was particularly not predisposed to like. The American ambassador to China, Clarence Gauss, and the U.S. naval attaché, James McHugh, happened to be in India and met Miles in the hotel hallway. Since Miles was to be officially known in China as the U.S. naval observer attached to the embassy under Gauss, and McHugh was Miles's Annapolis classmate, the three had extensive exchanges in the open.

A career diplomat with a bureaucratic mind, Gauss was universally recognized as a turf-minded old crank in Chungking, who had developed a penchant for excessive moral lectures to his staff and his Chinese interlocutors. The White House had not been happy with Gauss's performance in Chungking and was contemplating his reassignment. As Harry Hopkins, the president's gray eminence, pointedly told China's de facto ambassador to Washington, T. V. Soong, "Our Ambassador in Chungking is no good and has not succeeded in establishing the necessary connection."[12] McHugh was known as the most pro-British American in Chungking and for a long while actually lived within the British embassy, and many of his reports to Washington had their origins inside the British intelligence circle. At the time Miles met them, Ambassador Gauss and McHugh were arranging their escape spots in India, because they both firmly believed that the Chinese government would not last very long and a Japanese takeover of entire China was imminent.[13] Chiang Kai-shek was furious at the defeatist sentiments of the American officials in China, including Ambassador Gauss, and vowed not to listen to the Americans' dire prediction and retreat any more. Tai Li's agents in India took notice of Miles's encounter with these two gentlemen and created some guilt by association for Miles.

To make matters worse, while in India, Miles also met a fellow traveler by the name of Alghan Lusey, who had been a businessman in China for many years and was now an agent for the newly established American intelligence organization called the Office of the Coordinator of Information, under Colonel William Donovan. Lusey was on his way to Chungking to set up a secret radio network for COI's propaganda operations in the China theater, but his points of contact in Chungking were the British embassy in Chungking and Wang Shijie, a known rival of Tai Li and at the time China's minister of communications. While in India, the observant Lusey realized Miles's interlocutor in Chungking was a much more powerful partner and sponsor and requested that he be allowed to go along with Miles and meet Tai Li in Chungking upon arrival, to which Miles consented. The two arrived in Chungking together. Tai Li had heard of the COI and Colonel Donovan and regarded the COI as a British SOE (Special Operation Executive) clone. Yet unbeknownst to Miles, Lusey had sent secret cables back to Donovan in Washington about his "extraordinary" hookup with Miles. Sensing the great potential of intelligence operations in China under the Miles-Tai Li establishment, Donovan used his close relationship with Frank Knox, the secretary of the Navy, and went to the Navy Yard to talk with Captain Metzel and his new superior, Admiral W. R. Purnell, to negotiate a merging of the COI's China initiative and the Friendship Project. New to his job and completely unaware of the potential conflict between Miles and Donovan, Purnell readily agreed to Donovan's plea and gave Miles a concurrent title as the chief of the COI's China project.

This new appointment was immediately known to Tai Li by cable from Washington via Xiao Bo but not to Miles. To make the matter worse, the energetic Donovan immediately began to send COI intelligence teams to China to report to Miles, who had no clue as to what was going on. One special operation team of twenty led by Donovan's "deadliest colonel," Carl Eifler, left Washington in late May for Chungking; another COI secret intelligence initiative was the Duff mission to Chungking, also to be under Miles's command. When these gung ho secret agents entered China and roamed around Chungking looking for their superior, Milton Miles, all over town, Tai Li was incensed that Miles had not given him any notification whatsoever.

Particularly worrisome to Tai Li was Arthur Duff of the COI. A Canadian businessman with long China experience, Duff was regarded by Tai Li as an Old China Hand with suspicious British connections. In fact, Duff was in the employment of Donovan but also was reporting to the British intelligence through former Shanghai business tycoon C. V. Starr. In Tai Li's mind, there was no doubt that Duff came to Chungking to pick up where the British China Commando Group had left off. Duff got himself in deeper trouble with Tai Li after he got to Chungking with his frequent contact with the left wing in China, including Madame Sun Yat-sun and Sun Fo, the most ardent pro-Soviet and pro-Communist elements in the Chinese officialdom outside the Chinese Communist Party.

It should also be noted that Duff's not-so-secret mission to China was to organize an arms smuggling route via French Indochina. Tai Li was adamantly opposed to such arms smuggling without clear distribution destinations. In addition, Donovan sent his top scholar at the COI, Dr. Joseph Hayden, formerly of the University of Michigan, to Chungking to pedal the COI's grand intelligence initiative for China, colorfully called the "Dragon Plan," to

General Joseph Stilwell and General Claire Chennault. Part of Hayden's activities in Chungking involved the Dragon Plan's key element of using Koreans in exile as COI agents to penetrate Japan's inner zone. While Hayden went around the city and mingled with the large Korean exile community, Tai Li believed major portions of the Korean community were under the control of the Nanking puppet government of Wang Jingwei. Hayden therefore became an affront to Tai Li. When Hayden was ordered by Donovan in Washington to report to his new boss, Miles, Tai Li was understandably upset.

And finally, without notifying any Chinese authorities, Donovan had also dispatched a two-men mission to Tibet. Formerly renowned global explorers, Ilia Tolstoy and Brooke Dolan, were sent to Tibet to find a possible arms transport route to China via India. While in the Himalaya Buddhist kingdom, Tolstoy and Dolan met the young fourteenth Dalai Lama but also created a political firestorm by denouncing Chinese territorial rule of Tibet and openly applauding British influence in Tibet. This caused a fury in China. Tai Li was again outraged by the meddlesome COI agents who were presumably under Miles's command.

Despite numerous clues provided by the increasingly edgy Tai Li in hopes of extracting acknowledgement from Miles of such COI groups, Miles remained growingly puzzled by Tai Li's mood swings. This initial mutual suspicion and animosity did not dissipate until Miles's appointment order in paper form as the COI's China chief finally arrived in Chungking via personal carriage on 12 October 1942. As Miles wrote with great relief, "I finally got off the hook with General Tai when Lusey returned [from Washington] October 12th, bringing my orders issued September 22nd, as Coordinator of O.S.S. [the Office of Strategic Services].[14] General Tai had the news by radio, but nobody had informed me. My orders were hand-carried by Al. Somebody in O.S.S. certainly knew how to keep a secret—at least from me."[15] Miles further elaborated, "No wonder General Tai thought I had been holding out on him. There were secret missions in his bailiwick that he was entitled to hear about. Americans arrived that he knew to be O.S.S. and he knew me to be their boss. Who am I trying to fool? If we hadn't been friends. . . . I think the O.S.S. and I would both have been invited out of China—guilty of the same high-handed faults, and punctured by the same treatment—that the British had received a few months previously."[16]

These beginning episodes had a profound impact on future American intelligence operations in China. From this early scare, Miles became keenly aware of several key factors for a success in cooperating with the Chinese.

First, the Americans must completely appreciate the Chinese dislike of the British; second, and closely related to the first, the Americans must completely be void of any display of the odious treaty port mentality, as supposedly carried by these hated Old China Hands now working for their Western governments as military and intelligence officials; and third, civilian intelligence agents were to be strictly controlled by military authorities lest political and ideological penchants dominate the agenda and undermine major military objectives.

Miles's actions were swift and even ruthless to some. As the boss of all the OSS activities in China, he sent Hayden away from China and to General Douglas MacArthur's theater for an eventual recapture of the Philippines, where Hayden had once been a vice governor. Miles also suspended the entire Duff mission for collecting secret intelligence in China in collaboration with the British and without approval from the Chinese authorities. The Tolstoy and Dolan team was ordered to leave Tibet immediately and to report to Miles in Chungking for new assignment.

But far more significant was Miles's new policy he boldly announced to Donovan in Washington as to what kind of OSS men Miles would like to recruit in the future. "Almost my first words back to Colonel Donovan," Miles explained, "concerned the men to select for duty. The Chinese objected to ones we call 'Old China Hands'—foreigners who had worked, usually as bosses, in China before the war. They suddenly belonged to a past era because the Chinese weren't buying any more white supremacy."[17] He sent personnel recruitment requirements back to the Navy Department, asking for "good men, better than average, sturdy but slightly crazy, know more than one job, no high hat, rank conscious, red tape clerks or Old China Hands."[18] On another occasion, Miles reiterated his recruitment standards to Captain Metzel at the Navy Department, "[The new recruit] should not be an 'Old China Hand,' a title highly disapproved by Chinese as indicating a special privileged group with contempt for Chinese inferior methods and shortcomings. The less our recruits know about China, the less they have to unlearn."[19]

Roy Stratton, one of Miles's subordinates in wartime China, sums up the complex new Chinese psychology behind Miles's bold action. "Chiang and Tai Li resented [the Old China Hands] as they did the British and some other white people. They felt that white men had, from the earliest days of the Opium War, misused the Chinese and had been in the Far East for one purpose only: to exploit China's uneducated masses of cheap labor, export its wealth of products at cheap prices, and, in turn, import their own products and philosophies under the guise of uplifting 'the Heathen Chinese.' In so doing

... they had become arrogant, insisted that their household servants call them 'Master' and, in general, lived as if they were China's rulers."[20]

Miles further believed that "Opinions in China as to the merits of outsiders historically swung like a giant pendulum. Just now it had reached the same back stroke as in the days of the tea trade, when the Chinese court was sure the Chinese were the only cultured race on earth and all others were barbarians. The "Taipans' (foreign big shots) of the palmy days before the war were left out of touch."[21] To make sure that his Chinese partner understood his position on this issue, on 19 December 1942 Miles sent a long and carefully crafted letter to Tai Li, the essential part of which reads as follows:

> There are too many people who have lived a long time on the China Coast that now have no jobs in America and who think that they are real "experts" on China. Many of these people think that they will be very valuable to the United States if they can only get to China and they don't intend to do China any harm but are patriotically trying to help the United States. They do not think of China as a full fledged nation just the same as the United States. They think that spying is necessary to get information from the Chinese for the United States. It is one of my main purposes in this job to guard the China that I am very fond of from being "infected" with this type of foreigner. I am very critical of persons that have this attitude. If any such attitude exists in any of my men I wish to send them home immediately. Colonel Donovan promised me that if any person that he sent out was not up to my standard I could return him. I am particularly on the lookout against "Old China Hands" for whom I have a well founded dislike.[22]

But Miles's concern about overbearing foreigners was not just a cultural observation and moral concern. It had strong military use as well, because without trust and respect for the Chinese allies, a white man fighting against the Japanese could never get close enough to finish the military objective. "I emphasized," Miles later recalled, "that our people must be prepared to work without friction under anyone, perhaps Chinese if the situation required. The nearer we went to the enemy the more vulnerable we were."[23] As the Friendship Project grew and more and more U.S. personnel reached Chungking, Miles developed a standard orientation lecture for the newcomers, "You must implicitly trust your ally, and he you," he told his new recruits. "He is a native of the province in which you will be stationed. He knows it like the back of his hand, its villages, its roads and paths. He must like you and admire you as well as trust you. He must want you to live as much as he wants to. If not, he can leave you to be captured, change his clothes and become just another of the millions of Chinese who look exactly like him."[24]

From that moment on and throughout the entire enterprise, Miles was the most vigilant enforcer of utmost respect for America's Chinese colleagues. Lieutenant Commander Joseph E. Champe, one of Miles's subordinates during the China years, recalls, "I can't imagine Mary Miles calling a Chinese a 'gook' or anything like that."[25] To integrate with the Chinese personnel, Miles ordered that all Americans in the project eat Chinese food for most meals and that the Americans "treat the Chinese around the camps and station with the respect due to a soldier fighting for his country, [for] they are not paid servants, but are dedicated volunteers . . . To kick such a man or swear at him about clean floors or dirty laundry is unthinkable."[26] To prevent any verbal abuse or racial slur against the Chinese coworkers, Miles compiled a list of "do's" and "don'ts." Among the "don'ts" were "don't use the insulting word 'Chinaman,' don't use the word 'coolie,' don't call American food 'civilized,' don't talk Pidgin English such as 'go askee one master what for he do this.'"[27]

In fact, in Miles's way of thinking, the Chinese had fought the war for many years in their own country, and they had much to share with the Americans in the common pursuit of defeating the Japanese. The Chinese intelligence agents were just as good as the Americans when it came to operating in China. In this war, the Chinese and the Americans were in it together. With mutual trust and cooperation, they could be integrated into one unified military unit, and in some cases, the Chinese could even be Americans' commanding officers.

Miles's was a most revolutionary thinking at the time in foreign military and intelligence operations. By suggesting as such, he became the target of a vicious campaign through the entire war by forces motivated by a variety of reasons ranging from blatant racism to zealotry for turf and command control. "My suggestion raised a storm in Washington," Miles bemoaned, "since by now the foreigners who were caught in the Chinese coastal cities had escaped one way or another and were volunteering in Washington to help with the War in the place they knew best—China. Except that since Pearl Harbor it wasn't the place they knew at all. The Old China Hands went gunning for me—as a renegade white man 'gone native!'"[28]

In fact, Miles's willingness to cooperate with Tai Li in a mutually respectful way, especially the ease with which he integrated American forces with the Chinese, to have Chinese commanding officers over the Americans was the most important source of the inordinate difficulty and vicious attacks he and

SACO would endure during the rest of the war. "It pitted the Joint Chiefs of Staff against one another, caused the American Ambassador to China to request relief, fomented open warfare between O.S.S. and the Navy, and violated the Army's most sacred precept—nonintegration of American troops with those of any other nation."[29]

But there were numerous nuances in Miles's approach to cooperation with the Chinese. He was not uniformly against Old China Hands. In fact, an overwhelming majority of the Old China Hands truly loved and respected China and its people. But because some of them, especially the British, had behaved lordly over the Chinese, most Chinese people reacted with scorn and discomfort against Westerners.[30] There was no doubt to Miles that the Old China Hands' knowledge about China and their experience with the remote Asian giant would greatly help win the war over Japan. What Miles objected to was the attitude of some Old China Hands toward the Chinese.

In fact, throughout most of the SACO years, Miles's second in command was a prominent Old China Hand, David Wight, who joined Miles in January 1943 after he was treated badly by the Japanese in Singapore and had to swim to Java for survival and came to China to be rescued by the Chinese. Wight spent months "unlearning" his attitude as a white man with many years of Asia experience and getting rid of "any feelings he might have had for white supremacy in all things."[31] Gradually, Wight came to understand and admire Tai Li for his outstanding military and intelligence performance. "Tai Li was a very able person of the highest ability," Wight wrote. "He was probably very relentless in pursuing his aims, but they were entirely patriotic. . . . I have no way of knowing whether some of the stories about him are true, I have yet to meet any general officer of his caliber who was not somewhat merciless in gaining his objective."[32]

Equally nuanced was Miles's approach toward OSS projects. While he objected to many civilian-run projects, some of the military-oriented projects met with Miles's approval. A case in point was the Eifler mission, which OSS originally designed to have operated inside China. But General Stilwell did not believe in any commando-type special operations and could not see any value in what Eifler was supposed to do. As a result, he strenuously objected to sending Eifler to China, which would be objected to by Tai Li anyway. Miles and Stilwell agreed completely on the futility of Eifler's operation in China. When asked by Stilwell what to do with the Eifler bunch, Miles suggested they be sent to Burma to conduct jungle warfare to harass the Japanese there. If they could create some "bangs" in the Japanese-occupied jungle nation, that would be fine. But if they should not accomplish anything there, at least they would not make any trouble to Miles's setup in China, which would also be a great idea.

For Tai Li, these initial months of trying to figure Miles out proved equally significant. Weeks after his arrival in China and mindful of Admiral King's instruction to prepare for a future landing along the Southeast Chinese coast, Miles requested to go to inspect the Japanese-occupied region of that coast. With rare alacrity afforded to a foreigner, Tai Li agreed to go along to make this thousand-mile long trip to the Japanese-occupied area of the Fujian coast, just across from the Japanese colony of Taiwan. This would be the area most likely to be chosen for a U.S. amphibious landing if Admiral King's Pacific strategy should go as planned. By the time the party reached its destination, a small city called Pucheng, near the Fujian coast, both Tai Li and Miles had gained substantial respect for each other as military men. Tai Li was impressed by Miles's unusual aplomb under Japanese fire in Amoy during a frontline inspection of the Japanese naval installations; Miles was in complete awe of the vastness of Tai Li's espionage network as dozens of agents from the entire East Asia came to report to the "boss" in that little city.

Miles later wrote how he felt as the agents reported to Tai Li. "As I listened, my admiration for General Tai's organization and personal ability increased. In fact, by the time we began to make our plans to move on, my belief in Tai Li, as well as in his Secret Service and his guerrillas, had so increased my confidence in the organization I hoped to be able to create that wider plans began to evolve than any that had previously entered my head."[33]

It was this mutual admiration for each other that caused a turning point to be made in the history of Sino-U.S. military and intelligence cooperation. While in Pucheng, Japanese intelligence heard that Tai Li and some Americans were in the coastal area. Soon, eleven Japanese planes flew over Pucheng and ferociously bombed the small city, forcing Tai Li, Miles, and their entourage to hide in the rice paddies outside. If Miles had not by this time formed a clear idea as to what those aforementioned "wider plans" might be, Tai Li certainly had. In the rice paddy, a great decision was made between the Chinese secret police and the United States Navy, as Miles vividly described:[34]

> General Tai showed no useless anger. He, too, was watching the circling bombers but he had other thoughts in mind. He turned presently toward Eddie Liu [the interpreter] and spoke to him in Chinese.
>
> He referred to me, and used my honorable new Chinese name which in this case, took the form of "Winter Plum Blossom Mister."

"Tell Mei Shen-tung, " he said, "that I would like to have him arm fifty thousand of my guerrillas and train them to fight the Japanese. Can he do it?"

I thought I had heard that straight but I listened carefully while Eddie translated. This business of conversing in two languages gives convenient intervals for thinking.

"The United States wants many things in China," he went on,"— weather reports from the north and west to guide your planes and ships at sea—information about Japanese intentions and operations—mines in our channels and harbors—ship watchers on our coast—and radio stations to send this information."

He paused while Eddie Liu translated.

"I have fifty thousand good men. . . . They have been chosen from among those who have most reason to hate the Japanese invader. But they are armed only with what they have been able to make or capture and most of them are almost untrained. But if we are able to give you all you ask for, your operations will need to be protected and you cannot bring in enough men for that. So, if my men could be armed and trained, they could not only protect your operations but could work for China, too."

My mind was filled with a jumble of thoughts as Eddie Liu made his meticulous translation. . . . Here, surely, was a proposition that demanded careful consideration. . . . What a situation, I thought, for a land-locked naval officer! I had reached China—alone—only a month before. Yet here was I, sitting out a bombing attack in a rice paddy with the country's most inaccessible general—one who rarely permitted himself even to meet a foreigner. And more remarkable still, he was actually offering a most unexpected kind of partnership in a fifty-thousand-man army!

"Would your country allow you," he asked, "to accept a commission as general in the Chinese Army, so that we could operate these men together?"

Could the U.S. Navy use a part interest in fifty thousand guerrillas? From the way the general had phrased his idea it was plain that I would be given some sort of inside track in their control. Training and equipping them would be a big job, of course, but what if we could manage to make it possible for them to gather and report the kind of intelligence we needed for the Fleet?"

"O.K.," I replied.

It is an expression that means the same both in China and in America and no translation of it was necessary.

Out came the general's hand and I took it. This, I knew, was a rare foreign gesture for him to make.[35]

This of course was a decision of enormous scale and consequence for China's entire war efforts. Miles was keenly aware of the uniqueness of the situation and believed that "too often there are no second chances. And in this situation, if I was not, perhaps, the best man for the job, at least I was here. The general had never made any such offer before. He might not again."[36]

But Tai Li wanted more. Extraordinary as it was, a handshake in a rice paddy alone could not make the deal on such a scale a reality. Key factors such as the bitter lessons Tai Li learned from the British China Commando Group, Donovan's unauthorized dispatch of intelligence missions of various kinds to China and the suspicion of Donovan's symbiotic ties with the British, General Stilwell's monopoly of the entire Lend-Lease material distribution, the U.S. Joint Chiefs of Staff's guaranteed protest over Miles's joining the Chinese army—as it did to Chennault's appointment in the Chinese army—to train tens of thousands of guerrillas commanded by Chinese officers, and China's need for modern intelligence devices such as radar and technologies such as cryptology and counterespionage skills, all convinced Tai Li that a comprehensive legal document should be drafted to seal the agreement reached in the rice paddy with Miles and to set a wider perimeter of Sino-American intelligence cooperation.

Tai Li went straight up to Chiang Kai-shek, who summoned Miles and Tai Li in September 1942 to his residence. Chiang told Miles "with a smile that the competition for the services of his trusted General Tai was becoming too involved. We should work out a written agreement acceptable to both of us and have it signed, preferably by the Presidents [of both the United States and China], or at any rate by the highest possible authorities from both our countries."[37]

Tai Li's explanation to Miles for such a comprehensive document was that he would like to prevent a similar mistake or misunderstanding to those he had encountered with the British in the China Commando Group fiasco.[38] Miles personally would not have any problem with such a document, but he was afraid of a prolonged bureaucratic debate in Washington, D.C., for its approval.[39] However, Tai Li would not relent, and Miles finally decided to prepare a short draft, which Tai Li vetoed. The Chinese general believed Miles's first draft was too vague. Grudgingly, Miles was drawn into a long process of drafting a legal document in which he had no expertise. There were four key issues in the document. They were the command of Sino-U.S. joint intelligence operations, that is, who would be in command of such a huge organization, the Chinese or the Americans; the training and supply of the guerrillas; cooperation in signal intelligence; and an FBI-style school specializing in counterespionage and internal security. For several weeks, as Roy Stratton describes, "Miles and Tai Li met daily. Each paragraph took hours of discussion and compromise. Each section had to be translated into Chinese and English so there would be no misunderstanding of its meaning. Both of them, however, were determined to reach a mutually satisfactory agreement, and their work bound them closer together."[40]

Toward the end of 1942, a final draft finally came out to both Miles's and Tai Li's satisfaction. It was called the SACO Treaty and was immediately sent to Chiang Kai-shek and his chief of staff, General Stilwell, for approval. On the last day of 1942, T. V. Soong, Chiang's brother-in-law and China's foreign minister, met with Tai Li and Miles. Soong announced that Chiang and Stilwell had both approved the draft, but that Stilwell had stated that he would devote his entire energy in 1943 to the campaign to recapture Burma and would have no extra war materiel and hump tonnage spared for the proposed new organization. Because of this, T. V. Soong demanded that both President Franklin Roosevelt and President Chiang Kai-shek had to sign the document to make it more binding.[41]

Without any delay, the final SACO draft was carried by Al Lusey, who left for Washington on the New Year's Day, 1943. Attached to the SACO draft was also a letter from T. V. Soong for Admiral King for the establishment of an independent Navy-run air supply route to sustain the SACO enterprise. Upon Lusey's arrival in Washington, Admiral Purnell, the commanding officer of the Miles-Tai Li set-up in Chungking at the Navy Yard, and Captain Metzel, his executive assistant on the SACO matter, called up Colonel Xiao Bo for consultation. It was immediately clear to everyone that the key to the overall approval in Washington's bureaucratic maze was to gain consent from the U.S. Army, especially General George C. Marshall. And the prospect of General Marshall's approving of such a Navy-centered plan was grim. Undaunted, Captain Metzel came up with a brilliant strategy to crack the Army defense. As he cabled Miles, the key, it seemed to him, was General Stilwell, "[Although] you can be sure that complete effort will be forth coming . . . you have got to work on General Stilwell, because everybody from General Marshall down insists that they are giving him everything that can possibly be given and that only he can decide whether your stuff is sufficiently important compared to other things in his area, and his effort, to justify lugging any or all of your freight . . . so don't relax your work on Uncle Joe."[42]

While Purnell, Metzel, and Xiao Bo were waiting in Washington for President Roosevelt and General Marshall to return from meeting the British high command at Casablanca in North Africa, Tai Li, in Chungking, grew impatient and anxious because he would not tolerate any undue British meddling in this. His station chief in Washington, Colonel Xiao Bo, wired back to Chungking, suggesting there might be some revision of the draft by the U.S. government. This prompted Tai Li to send a long cable to Admiral Purnell that stressed three major points: (1) No essential revision of the SACO draft by the U.S. side was desired; (2) The British should in no way be involved in SACO; and (3) SACO's command control over OSS's secret intelligence (SI) activities in China was to be absolute.

Purnell was taken aback by Tai Li's hardball tone and quickly replied (A) "Please be assured of our fullest cooperation and enduring good faith. Any changes made in the SACO agreement are made to assure full understanding now and to prevent future doubt of our frankness; such changes are considered minor so far as the complete plan is concerned"; (B) "The British are in no way mixed up in our affairs"; (C) Regarding OSS's SI [Secret Intelligence] plan, "our only principle in which Donovan heartily concurs is to send in SI and all other fields only people you request or approve with every individual for any and all duty wholly under SACO command. Our trust in SACO is complete."[43]

Back from the 14–24 January 1943 Casablanca Conference, the Joint Chiefs of Staff began discussing the SACO draft. Admiral King gave his enthusiastic approval immediately. President Roosevelt also agreed to it in principle, although he believed that since it was a secret intelligence initiative, even though the draft was written as a treaty, it was therefore a good idea to change it to an "agreement" rather than a treaty so that it would not have to go through the open Senate confirmation process, thus endangering the required secrecy.

In spite of all these blessings from the president as well as from Admiral King, General Marshall, as expected, strenuously objected to the entire draft. What particularly upset Marshall was Article 5, which dealt with the command structure of the proposed SACO, that is, under the new establishment, the director of SACO would be Chinese and the deputy director would be American. This went directly against Marshall's military philosophy of "unity of command," preventing at any cost American uniformed personnel from serving under foreign command. But the worst thing this command structure might inflict on the U.S. Army and General Marshall would be the reduction of the Army's authority in the China theater, because under the new scheme as stipulated in the SACO draft, Miles would undoubtedly be under Tai Li. Since Tai Li directly reported to Chiang Kai-shek, Miles would directly report to the Chinese military authority, not to Stilwell, to whom Marshall would like to give total control over all American personnel, Army and Navy.

Article 10, which called for a joint Sino-American air survey along the Chinese coast also met Marshall's objection. The reason was quite simple—the Army had great problems with Admiral King's strategy of landing on the China coast, and General Marshall was particularly loath to the idea of the U.S. Navy teamed up with the renegade Claire Lee Chennault to create "bangs" in China to dwarf General Stilwell's profile in a theater that cried out for an overall commander, who in the opinion of many happened to be an old-fashioned infantry commander without much modern concept of warfare. In addition, Article 18, which would require the United States to provide hundreds more radio intelligence (RI) specialists to Tai Li's cryptographical team in Chungking, was also objectionable to General Marshall, whose chief concern was the maintenance of MAGIC intercepts security.

Thus, a stalemate was reached whereby the White House and the Navy approved the SACO draft, but the Army vigorously objected to it. In the end, the two sides reached a compromise. The Army proposed and the other side agreed to a plan to ask the theater commander, General Stilwell, in Chungking, to comment on the SACO draft, and Stilwell's comments would be the final decision on the fate of the SACO enterprise. On 16 February 1943, Marshall drafted a cable, signed by Admiral King, to Stilwell, in which Marshall stated, "Joint Chiefs have made theater commander responsible for psychological warfare in the theater. . . accordingly we contemplate charging you with responsibility for Captain Miles's project and placing him together with his O.S.S. and Navy personnel under your command." Marshall then listed his requests for revisions of Articles 5, 10, and 18 as a condition for sending the draft from the JCS to Roosevelt for final approval.[44]

Knowing Stilwell's penchant for command control in the China theater, Marshall was confident that his protégé in China would concur with him on his demands for revising the SACO draft. Admiral King was pessimistic that the SACO draft would survive without the significant changes demanded by the Army—so much so that Admiral King simultaneously sent a warning message to Miles in Chungking stating that all changes demanded by General Marshall were unavoidable and asking for Tai Li's understanding that all the changes were "necessary for effective support of our cooperative project and will be the foundation for its greater success."[45] Tai Li reacted violently to this and threatened to pull out of any involvement with the Americans entirely.[46] Miles panicked and warned Washington that "such action [Tai Li's threat to withdraw] would mean SACO breakdown and grave danger to present military cooperation and future Sino-American friendly relations."[47]

Whatever transpired at this juncture in Chungking, especially at Stilwell's headquarters, is not entirely known. But at the end of the day, the news was a surprise to everyone. After receiving Marshall's cable for comments, Stilwell quickly drafted a letter completely concurring with Marshall's proposed changes. But before Stilwell sent the cable to Washington, Miles rushed to see the general and had a long talk with the otherwise curmudgeony Vinegar Joe. It should be noted that, both men of action, Miles and Stilwell had formed a friendly and cordial relationship and respected each other as professional soldiers. They shared a similar disdain for red tape and amateur warriors, especially the style and attitude of the British-leaning OSS, and both desired to rein in Donovan's far-flung missions in China that were going in all directions. After listening to Miles's plea and explanation, Stilwell tore up the original reply and redrafted and sent to Washington the following remarkable message on 21 February 1943: "After investigation I believe that the Chinese will not accept the SACO agreement if any agency comes between them and Miles. Tai Li's organization is super-secret and super-suspicious. Miles work would be hampered if they knew he was under my command. I have enough confidence in him to recommend that in view of the peculiar and unusual circumstances connected with this matter he be allowed to operate as heretofore, and I believe that any conflict that arises can be adjusted between us."[48]

When Stilwell's reply reached General Marshall in Washington, the latter was completely surprised by the development. Now Marshall had no choice but to approve the entire SACO draft as originally proposed by Tai Li without any changes. Tai Li was ecstatic over the passage of the SACO Agreement. He sent Miles back to Washington to make it an air-tight case.

On 15 April 1943, in Washington, Secretary of the Navy Frank Knox, OSS Director William Donovan, and Milton Miles, representing the United States, and Foreign Minister T. V. Soong and Lt. Colonel Sin Ju Pu Hsiao (Xiao Bo), representing China, signed the official Sino-American Special Technical Cooperative Agreement Agreement, without any changes.

Tai Li's signature would be added later when Miles took the documents back to Chungking.

To the Navy, Tai Li, and Miles, this turn of events was too good to be true. Mindful of possible change of minds from Stilwell and the Army, Admiral William Leahy, the chairman of the Joint Chiefs of Staff, gave Miles a secret memo summing up what had just been achieved:

You are advised that the Joint U.S. Chiefs of Staff take note of the proposed Sino-American Technical Cooperation Agreement for the conduct and support of special measure in the war effort against JAPAN, and, further, of the exchange of despatches between General Stilwell and the Chiefs of Staff in which General Stilwell expresses approval of the conduct of American participation in these measures by you directly under Chinese command. The Joint Chiefs of Staff approve this arrangement and desire that you cooperate with the responsible designated Chinese authorities in every way practicable for the prosecution of war measures against the Japanese.

The President has been informed and has given approval of the plan to place you in direct charge of the American participation, as set forth in the proposed agreement.[49]

With this development, the casual coffee klatches at the Navy Yard had grown into a gigantic Sino-American military and intelligence enterprise involving the highest authorities of both countries in a time of global war. As for Tai Li, the importance of SACO was supreme in his mind, "Every time we meet," Miles wrote to his superior in Washington, "he produces a toast to SOCKO! It seems to catch, and is the only American word that I have ever heard him say. He is a grand guy, with one hundred percent loyalty both up and down the line."[50]

Chapter 6

UNCLE SAM'S CARBINE
Military and Financial Aid from the United States in Wartime China

DESPITE THE GREAT PROMISE and potential of wartime cooperative military and intelligence operations such as the Sino-American Special Technical Cooperative Organization (SACO) between the United States and China, the overall picture of America's wartime aid program to China was riddled with institutional and man-made obstacles.

Without doubt, the most significant foreign military aid and assistance to China during the entire eight years of the war came from the United States. Though the Soviet Union had provided the most substantial military and financial aid to China in the first two or three years of the war, the United States was the only other foreign nation whose top leader made it a national policy to provide military and other help to China. Indeed, China could not have found a better friend than President Franklin D. Roosevelt, especially after the Japanese attack on Pearl Harbor.

Before the Soviet divestment from China in the spring of 1941, the United States remained vigilantly isolationist. Between July 1937, when the war started in China, and April 1941, when the Soviet Union signed the Soviet-Japanese Neutrality Pact and withdrew all military aid to China, the United States provided China four loans totaling $120 million, compared with the $250 million in loans the USSR gave China during the same period. They were the February 1939 loan of $25 million, the April 1940 loan of $20 million, the October 1940 loan of $25 million, and the February 1941 loan of $50 million. The terms of these loans were harsh, strictly banning their use for the purchase of arms, while the Soviet loans were solely for the purpose of buying weapons. The interests for these U.S. loans were also relatively high, ranging from 4 to 4.5 percent, compared with the Soviet interest of a flat 3 percent.[1]

But things began to shift in China's favor very soon. Determined to become the "arsenal of democracy," the United States gradually changed its policy of nonengagement in war-torn Europe and Asia. In November 1939, the "Cash and Carry" regulation went into effect. But China did not have enough cash, and the American loans granted to China were specifically excluded from arms purchases. However, on the eve of the Soviet-Japanese Neutrality Pact, on 11 March 1941, the United States passed into law the historic Lend-Lease Act, promising to provide massive military hardware and other war materiel to countries fighting fascism on a "lend and lease" basis without any cash down payment. Four days later, President Roosevelt announced that "China . . . expresses the magnificent will of millions of plain people to resist the dismemberment of their Nation. China, through the Generalissimo, Chiang Kai-shek, asks our help. America has said that China shall have our help."[2]

On 6 May China was officially categorized as a qualified nation to receive the American Lend-Lease materials, and President Roosevelt solemnly declared that helping China to defend itself against Japan was "vital to the defense of the United States."[3] Thus began an epic China aid program, originated in Washington, to replace the previously robust China aid program originated in Moscow.

As we briefly mentioned before, Chiang Kai-shek designated his brother-in-law, T. V. Soong, the unmatchable expert lobbyist with a Harvard PhD in economics, to be the anchorman in Washington handling the ambitious military aid program. Soong immediately established in Washington a company called China Defense Supply (CDS) to solely handle the China-bound Lend-Lease materiel.[4] For his part, President Roosevelt designated his Canadian-born White House aide, Lauchlin Currie, to be in charge of the China aid program under the Lend Lease Act. On 31 March 1941, T. V. Soong sent the first list of items China immediately wanted from the United States: 700 pursuit fighter planes, 300 bombers, weapons and materiel to equip 30 divisions of infantry, and materiel for improvements to the Burma Railway from Rangoon to Lashio. The proportionally large number of pursuit fighters on Soong's list is of particular interest, coming at the time when the dominant air force emphasis was on bombers. The leading proponent for pursuit fighters in the entire U.S. Army was Claire Lee Chennault, who had one year earlier acquired 100 fighter planes from the United States on his own initiative. Undoubtedly, the request of 700 pursuit fighters on Soong's list was influenced by Chennault.

The Army, however, felt Soong's list of requested items was too vague and grandiose. From this early moment on, the Army adopted a generally pessimistic and suspicious attitude toward China's wartime aid programs. To make matters more complicated, the Army decided to send a military mission to China to directly report on and handle Lend-Lease matters. Code named AMMISCA, the military delegation was announced on 26 August 1941, to be led by the reticent Brigadier General John Magruder. The official mission of the Magruder delegation was "to aid China in procurement of Lend-Lease goods, to train Chinese personnel in their use and maintenance, to aid in obtaining their orderly flow to the Chinese forces, and to aid in creating an adequate line of communications."[5]

Official U.S. Department of Treasury data indicates that in 1941 total military assistance from the United States to China was $25.821 million.[6] Though this is a small portion of the entire U.S. Lend-Lease programs world-wide, it did mark a promising start. The first cargo ships loaded with the Lend-Lease materiel bound for China set sail in May 1941, with a total 7,552 tons of weapons. By December 1941, in parallel with the Pearl Harbor attack, a whopping 66,675 tons of war materiel were on their way to China.[7] These China-bound items included military aircraft, cannons, grenade launchers, machine guns, ammunition, and military communications equipment.[8]

The attack on Pearl Harbor added great momentum to the U.S. aid to China's war efforts. The infamy at Pearl Harbor, Hong Kong, Malaya, the Philippines, and elsewhere in the Pacific threw open foreign support for China in most unambiguous terms. China, the United States, and Great Britain had finally become allies fighting the same enemy. Much more important was the enthusiastic, albeit belated, appreciation by the Americans and the British of China's four years of tenacious resistance against the Japanese without any steady international allies—Stanley Hornbeck, the preeminent State Department political adviser on East Asian affairs, characterized China's protracted war against Japan as "a miracle in war-making."[9] The Americans were in a grim mood, ready to grant China much-needed assistance.

China's needs at the time of Pearl Harbor did not just concern military hardware. Equally desperate was China's war-torn economy. As Chiang Kai-shek's chief foreign financial adviser, Arthur N. Young, curtly put it, "Financially China's difficulties were as grave as they were militarily. By the end of 1941, prices had risen about 20-fold from prewar. How to cope with acute and ever-faster inflation in an overstrained economy stood out as a major issue."[10] The war was extremely costly to the Chinese government. The government's budget for 1942 was C$15 billion, with only a gross annual revenue of C$5 billion. The monstrous C$10 billion deficit for 1942 alone would mean a cata-strophic inflation spiral, because the only way China could fight on would be to print more paper money without any solid financing backing.[11] Facing this dire financial woe, on 30 December, Chiang Kai-shek delivered a request to both American and British officials for loans totaling $1 billion—$500 million from the United States and £100 million, or close to $500 million, from Great Britain.

The British were stunned by this huge request and waited for Washington's consultation. But Washington was now in no mood to stall any further aid to China, financial as well as military. Ten days later, on 9 January 1942, President Roosevelt granted his approval for Chiang's request and instructed U.S. Secretary of Treasury Henry Morgenthau in a historic memo as follows: "Memo to the Secretary of the Treasury: In regard to the Chinese loan, I realize there is little security which China can give at the present time, yet I am anxious to help Chiang Kai-Shek and his currency. I hope you can invent some way of doing this. Possibly we could buy a certain amount of this currency, even if it means a partial loss later on. FDR"[12]

Following White House instructions, Henry Morgenthau dutifully went about "inventing" a way to satisfy China's request. The solution finally arrived at by Morgenthau was for the United States to directly pay for the salaries and maintenance cost of one million of China's soldiers, which would cost the United States $10 million per month. When presenting this idea to T. V. Soong, Morgenthau claimed his solution had been approved by both Roosevelt and Churchill. At first Soong seemed to accept this proposal of financial support, because, if it were to be carried out, China would receive a total of $20 million per month from the United States and Great Britain, thus greatly alleviating its wartime financial burden. But Chiang Kai-shek flatly refused Morgenthau's solution, fearing the political and command ambiguity it might create within the rank and file of Chinese troops whose loyalty to Chiang was essential in any military campaign.

Morgenthau became characteristically impatient with Chiang and Soong for China's strong reaction to his solution and decided to play hardball with T. V. Soong over the modality of the loan. A rare genius in persuasion, Soong appealed directly to President Roosevelt on 30 January 1942 in the White House. The president was completely convinced by Soong's reasoning against attaching any strings to the loan package. That same day, Roosevelt summoned Morgenthau, Secretary of State Cordell Hull, and Secretary of Commerce Jessie Jones to the White House, ordering immediate action be taken to grant China the $500 million loan with no strings attached. On 7 February, Congress passed Public Law Number 422, authorizing the treasury secretary, with the approval of the president, to provide China a loan or credit or other financial assistance not to exceed $500 million. Five days later, Roosevelt signed it into law.[13]

This was the most generous of all loans received by China from any foreign government during the entire eight years of war. In fact, it was a monumental gift to China rather than a loan, because the package did not specify the terms of repayment and had no interest rate enunciated, no collateral required, and no restriction on how the loan or credit should be used.[14]

Following the U.S. example of generosity, the British government felt pressured to show its friendliness to China. Almost simultaneously, Great Britain granted China a loan of £50 million, "at such times and upon such terms as may be agreed between the two Governments."[15]

Yet, after the Pearl Harbor attack, the most pressing aid China wanted from the United States was still military hardware. China was not disappointed by the American resolve to help on this ground either. The large Lend-Lease shipments to China continued after the United States officially became China's ally in the Pacific war. The ongoing and expected volume of shipments to China was so large that both China and the United States decided to strengthen and expand the coordination and delivery lines of the Lend-Lease inflow to China. In early 1942, Lieutenant General Joseph Stilwell was sent to China as the overall American coordinator over Lend-Lease materiel, among other military duties. The American military aid program for China immediately gained great momentum. For the year 1942 alone, the entire supply of American military hardware shipped to China amounted to $100 million, almost four times the $25.8 million for 1941. By 1945 the total supply of U.S. Lend-Lease military materiel for China would become $1.31 billion, by far the largest and most generous defense aid package China ever received in the entire eight years of war.[16]

Yet, China was soon to find out that much of the heightened enthusiasm for wartime aid to China in the immediate aftermath of the Pearl Harbor attack was based on wistful illusions, because a multitude of factors would unleash their destructive forces to make the wartime aid to China one of the most remarkable fiascoes of World War II.

One of the greatest myths of World War II has been that the China theater formed a strategic core in the mind of Washington war planners. Indeed, the rhetoric was all there and everyone was announcing how important the war in East Asia was to the overall struggle against fascism. Yet, in reality, China's chances of getting substantial Lend-Lease materiel, proportional to the rhetorical importance of the Chinese war efforts, were remarkably reduced at the Arcadia Conference in early 1942. There the United States and Great Britain bilaterally decided that the overall Allied grand strategy for the war would be "Europe First, Asia Second." Furthermore, in the Asian theater, it would be the Pacific theater first and the China-India-Burma (CBI) theater second. Thus, the war effort in China was treated as the least important among the three major areas of fighting. This overwhelming tilt toward the European theater was accompanied by an overwhelming neglect of Lend-Lease aid to China. Throughout the entire Lend-Lease program from March 1941 to the end of the war, with the exception of a very brief period toward the end of the war, China never received more than 2 percent of the available Lend-Lease materiel at any given moment. In fact, the percentage of the overall Lend-Lease materiel granted to China actually decreased after the Pearl Harbor attack. In other words, the percentage of the U.S. Lend-Lease materiel for China before the Pearl Harbor attack was larger than the percentage for China during the entire Pacific War except the several months immediately preceding the Japanese surrender in August 1945. The following table illustrates how little military aid China actually received during the war compared to the overall Lend-Lease program:

Year	Amount for all countries	Amount for China	Percentage of total for China
1941	$1.54 billion	$26 million	1.7%
1942	$6.893 billion	$100 million	1.5%
1943	$12.011 billion	$49 million	0.4%
1944	$14.94 billion	$53 million	0.4%
1945	$13.713 billion	$1.107 billion	8%
TOTAL:	$49.096 billion	$1.336 billion	2.7%

[Source: Letters from State Department, 10 January and 26 March 1958, cited in Arthur N. Young, *China and the Helping Hand, 1937–1945*, 350]

The remarkably inadequate distribution of the Lend-Lease materiel to China during World War II becomes even more mind-boggling when we compare China to other Allied countries, as shown in the following table, including the added year of 1946, which was not reflected in the previous table:

Countries receiving Lend-Lease materiel	Amount in U.S. dollars	Percentage
The British Empire, ncluding Australia, New Zealand, India, and South Africa	$31,267,240,530	64.65%
The Soviet Union	$11,260,343,603	23.2%
France and its territories	$3,207,608,188	6.6%
China	$1,548,794,966	3.2%

[Source: *New York Times*, 19 October 1946, as cited in Ren Donglai, *Forever Querulous Partners—The American Aid and Sino-U.S. Anti-Japanese Alliance* (Guangxi Normal University Press, 1995), 254]

This severe shortage of Lend-Lease materiel for China took place despite tireless and arduous efforts of the Chinese high command to solicit American help. The wartime foreign financial adviser, Arthur Young, bitterly complained after the war that "The United States failed to meet promises of aid [to China] and for some time did not send even the relatively small volume of items that could have been used. Again and again China's representatives, and those in the American government who agreed with them, pointed out that even granting the priority of the fronts in Europe, China was not getting a reasonable proportion of Lend-Lease items, as compared with Britain and Russia."[17] A look through the wartime correspondence between Chiang Kai-shek and Franklin Roosevelt cannot help but reflect the tremendous urgency and frustration from Chiang over the repeated incidents that impeded the American military aid to China in various bizarre ways, despite Roosevelt's constant instructions and promises to get the much-needed Lend-Lease materiel to China at any cost in the most effective way.

Almost every Allied leader realized the importance of keeping China in the war, which of course required massive military support for China. To their credit, leaders of the Western Allies such as Roosevelt and Churchill had provided China with great support by facilitating various ambitious military and financial aid programs for China. The $500 million loan and credit to China in 1942 by the U.S. government, the decision to ship $200 million worth of gold to China to stabilize China's currency and to slow the out-of-control inflation, the remarkable British approval of a £50 million loan to China in 1942, and many military items requested by China to fight the war, all provided sinews of great hope and friendship to China's cause and to the cause of the global antifascist crusade.

However, the leaders of the U.S. and British governments failed to provide adequate leadership to guarantee the delivery of what had been promised to China. Instead, their own fickleness in China-related policies, and their focus on the European theater tremendously damaged their reputation and credibility in China when it came to military aid. To make matters worse, their inattention to the China theater created a most unfortunate vacuum for low-ranking bureaucrats, self-important lieutenants, disgruntled misfits, and agents of unfriendly forces to manipulate the China aid programs, resulting in military paralysis and diplomatic frictions between China and its Western Allies, especially the United States. Without solid leadership and a clear chain of command, the near-chaotic wartime bureaucratic mechanisms and extraordinary interservice and interagency rivalry for turf and command and control were allowed to greatly undermine China's war efforts and its allies' commitment to China aid programs.

It is therefore quite unsettling for us to realize that most cables or telegrams President Roosevelt sent to Chiang Kai-shek during the war were first drafted by someone else with a partisan disposition one way or another. With very few exceptions, the president willingly appended his signature to whatever he was presented without any revision. Unless these harshly worded and ill-guided cables created diplomatic crises and strategic blunders, the president rarely gave his full attention to issues concerning China.

In the black comedy *MASH,* set in a U.S. mobile army surgical hospital during the Korean War, the unit commander, Army Colonel Henry Blake, lacks committed attention to daily routines in his unit and signs every form or letter his company clerk asks him to sign without any substantial review. In handling his China aid programs, and China policy in general, during World War II, President Roosevelt was the reincarnation of Colonel Henry Blake—a jolly good fellow big on abstract ideas but with little stomach for concrete measures to supervise and implement these ideas. Consequently, virtually all the major aid programs to China remained unfulfilled dreams or half-baked measures that made little positive impact on China's wartime morale and warfighting capability.

Caused largely by extraordinary specific restrictions imposed on China by Roosevelt's subordinates in the Treasury Department, only half of the momentous $500 million U.S. loan to China in 1942 was used by the end of the war. The big idea of a big loan was indeed encouraging to the Chinese. But China was greatly baffled by the trivial yet deadly bureaucratic regulations on Sino-U.S. interactions, the biggest of which was related to whom should bear the cost of maintaining American military personnel and American military operations in China. In fact, while receiving the U.S. financial aid meant to stabilize China's precarious wartime economy, the Chinese government was forced to pay a large portion of the bill, which further aggravated the inflation and canceled out much of the efficacy the U.S. financial loan was supposed to create.

On the crucial issue of the Burma campaign, President Roosevelt and Chiang Kai-shek had reached an agreement to press the reluctant Winston Churchill for a commitment on joint Allied operations in Burma to retake the vital supply route to China. This big idea led Roosevelt to invite Chiang to attend the historic Cairo Conference at the end of 1943 and to secure the trilateral commitment for the Burma campaign. Yet Roosevelt and Churchill unceremoniously changed their mind while Chiang was still on his way home. This snubbing was undoubtedly the crucial event that greatly soured the relationship between China on one side and the United States and Great Britain on the other. Ultimately, this led Chiang to stonewall on sending troops to Burma to fight alone, which in turn resulted in Stilwell's hardball handling of Chiang's stonewalling, and ultimately, to Washington and Chungking's mutual agony, which culminated in the bitter recall of General Stilwell from China.

To ameliorate China's abyssal crisis of finance, the U.S. government agreed to provide gold for China to sell to stabilize its currency. In 1943 President Roosevelt approved a $200 million gold loan to China. In July 1943, Treasury Secretary Henry Morgenthau also agreed to this gold loan. Yet, the shipment program of gold to China was sabotaged by lower-ranking officials at the Treasury Department. Nearly two years later, by May 1945, when Treasury Secretary Morgenthau finally found out about the "inexcusable" and "dishonorable" act of his Treasury employees, of the $200 million gold loan approved by the president and the treasury secretary, only $8 million was delivered to the Chinese, causing tremendous damage to China's wartime economy.[18] China never fully recovered until after the Nationalists lost the civil war to the Communists in 1949.

The most inexplicable loan ever granted to China came from Great Britain in 1942. Following in the footsteps of the Americans, the British felt it necessary to support China's war efforts by providing a historic £50 million loan, equal to about $250 million. This was the second-largest single loan granted to China during the entire war. But the British governing style had a reverse problem compared to the American one, although both reached the same destination of inefficiency and failure. In the American case, it was the top leader, that is, the president himself, who was most enthusiastic about helping

China, but who failed to provide a strong supervisory role over details and implementation, and whose big ideas and major policies concerning China were subverted by forces below, either in Washington or in Chungking. In the British case, the top leader, Winston Churchill, never believed China should be vigorously aided and repeatedly chastised the American attempts to help China and its war efforts. However, virtually all the British officials in the field who were intimately familiar with China's wartime situation became the most vigorous supporters for China aid. Most notable were the two British ambassadors to China, Clark Kerr and Horace Seymour, and General Sir Adrian Carton De Wiart, Churchill's special military representative to Chiang Kai-shek in Chungking, whose plans for aiding China were repeatedly vetoed by Churchill.[19]

Many have suspected that the £50 million loan to China was designed to please President Roosevelt and gain American support for British war efforts rather than to actually help China. Eventually, this British loan became something of a farce. After the grandiose ceremony of granting this loan to China, the British informed the Chinese that there must be a series of restrictions on how the Chinese government should use this loan. Because the simultaneously announced much larger American loan of $500 million had no restrictions, the Chinese pleaded with the British to do the same so China might use this loan to support its currency, not just purchase weapons from the British Commonwealth. As Chiang Kai-shek poignantly told Roosevelt on 9 December 1943, "China's economic situation is more critical than the military."[20] But the British insisted on imposing various restrictions on the use of the loan. The negotiations lasted for two agonizing years, between April 1942 and May 1944, without any substantial resolution on the key points of contention. Clearly, to most Chinese, the British never meant to actually provide the loan to China, only wanting to display the loan as a morale boosting symbol, like a painting hanging on the wall.[21]

Military aid to China for most of the war, especially since the active participation in the Pacific war in December 1941 by the United States and Great Britain, was highly inadequate, constituting less than 2 percent of all U.S. military aid worldwide. Of the extremely limited military aid that did arrive in China, mostly through the hazardous Hump flights, the overwhelming majority of the items was allotted to the American 14th Air Force under Major General Chennault, and to the "X" and "Y" forces specifically designated for General Stilwell's obsessed campaign to retake Burma. Overall, the Chinese military forces that confronted the Japanese forces in the vast expanse of China received extremely little from the United States for most of the

Pacific war, excluding the last few months of the war after Stilwell's recall. The grand strategy of "Europe First, Asia Second" played a decisive role in creating this anemic aid program to China. Yet, the commonly held myth has been that China did indeed receive an enormous amount of military aid from the United States during the war but refused to fight the Japanese nonetheless. This myth further enraged many Chinese officials and commoners, greatly undermining the credibility of the leaders of China's wartime allies.

On 28 September 1944, Winston Churchill gave a speech in London on the war and the international situation, in which he stated that China had received an "excessive amount" of U.S. military aid yet still managed to lose many air bases to the Japanese in East China.[22] Chinese public opinion erupted into resentment and public protest against Churchill's claim that China had received an "excessive amount" of the U.S. military aid. Various newspapers and government officials angrily pointed out that what the Chinese army facing the ten mechanized Japanese divisions in East China had received up to that point was not even enough to equip one American or British division for a week; that while the British received more than 60 percent of the entire U.S. Lend-Lease aid, China had received less than 2 percent—an excessively inadequate amount for a China theater, which all Allied leaders believed to be of great value to the worldwide fight against fascism.[23]

But this was not because of a lack of good intentions on part of President Roosevelt to help China get adequate military aid. On the contrary, President Roosevelt had been greatly supportive of military aid to China. It was Roosevelt who approved with alacrity the largest financial loan to China and who allocated extensive Lend-Lease materiel for the China theater. But the president's big ideas for unconditional support for China were sidetracked by many forces and various motivations—bureaucratic and command disputes, strategy disagreements, delivery quagmires, a chaotic system of communications between Chungking and Washington, and Communist espionage.

How did the Communists fare with regard to foreign military aid to China during World War II? First of all, it must be pointed out that while the overall amount of the U.S. military aid to China was miniscule compared to what China needed and requested, of the limited amount that did flow to China, all of it went to the Nationalist troops. Yet, the Chinese Communist Party's armed forces grew dramatically during the war, from under 50,000 in 1937 to more than a million at the time of the Japanese surrender in August 1945. Where did the Communist armed forces receive their weapons, considering Yenan did not have any meaningful arms manufacturing capability?

The first source of the Chinese Communist arms acquisition came from the CCP's massive cooperation with the Japanese-supported puppet troops in North China. Although officially at war with each other, both the Chinese Communist armed forces and the Japanese claimed to be the simultaneous occupiers of North China. Only one reality could come out of this irony: the Communist forces and the Japanese troops in North China for the most part coexisted without much serious fighting against each other, despite the unbelievable claims by the CCP official historians of the gallantry and valor with which the Communist forces fought the Japanese during the war.

An official history of the war published by the People's Liberation Army historians claimed that the CCP troops launched more than forty thousand battles against the Japanese in 1942 and 1943 alone, which is supposed to represent the ebb of CCP's efforts against the Japanese. If this were to be believed, it would mean that every twenty-six minutes the CCP launched a battle against the Japanese in China, which is nothing short of being impossible.[24] The often cozy coexistence in North China between the Japanese and the CCP troops was greatly enhanced by the large number of Chinese puppet troops, who were well equipped by the Japanese. Thereafter, Yenan developed a lucrative "cash-for-weapons" business with the puppets, buying weapons from the puppet troops to arm the CCP troops. In late 1944, Mao Zedong directly asked the U.S. intelligence apparatus for cash to carry on this business. General Zhu De, the CCP military commanding officer, gave the deep-pocketed American intelligence official a bill for $20 million to buy Japanese weapons from the puppets, in exchange for the CCP's intelligence cooperation with the covert U.S. intelligence activities in China.[25]

The CCP therefore had a dire need for cash throughout the war. But how did the Communists meet the huge demand for cash to buy weapons? The answer lies in the CCP's vast international network. Contrary to the much-propagated notion that the Chinese Communists were proverbial agrarian reformers with indigenous roots in the isolated plains of North China. On the contrary, during the war, the Chinese Communists had a highly efficient international network stretching from Moscow to London to New York to Washington, D.C., to Hong Kong to Chungking and ultimately to Yenan. To generate cash for Yenan to buy weapons from the puppet troops, the Communist underground organized a front group called the Industrial Cooperative, or "gung ho" in Chinese, meaning "fanatical spirit" in today's English vocabulary. Initially formed to provide a façade of nonpartisanship, many Kuomintang (KMT) and international luminaries were invited to join. When the issue of how to distribute the funds became a problem, the Communist underground set up an "International Committee" of the Industrial Cooperative based in Hong Kong to handle the huge amount of donations by international charities and overseas sources and directly channel them to the Chinese Communist headquarters in Yenan. In just two and a half years in Hong Kong before the Japanese takeover, this Gung Ho setup was able to send Yenan an astonishing total of $20 million.[26] This enormous sum alone would make the Eight Route Army and the New Fourth Army under the Chinese Communist command financially better off per capita than any KMT army groups.

The Communists also received willing aid from partisan forces within the U.S. government. In late 1944, with the help of John Paton Davies, Joseph Stilwell's former political adviser, and his selected assistants, the American intelligence agency, the Office of Strategic Services (OSS), eager to enter the crowded China theater, offered the Chinese Communists generous weapons supplies, deliberately bypassing the authority of the Nationalist central government that was officially supported by the U.S. government. Among other things, OSS secretly promised to bring to the CCP troops arms enough to equip 25,000 soldiers, a massive radio intelligence network covering most parts of China, and 100,000 single-shot assassination pistols.[27] This deal was promptly halted by Patrick Hurley, who was trying to broker a peace deal between Yenan and Chungking and was unwilling to allow unauthorized American bureaucratic elements to tip the delicate balance of power between the feuding parties.

Communist espionage also had a hand in the affairs of military aid to China during World War II. Leading the shadow warriors fighting against the Chinese Nationalist government was the NKVD (KGB; People's Commissariat Internal Affairs)-operated Silvermaster Group, which had sources deep inside the U.S. government agencies that dealt directly with wartime aid to China.[28] Thanks to the efforts of these covert forces, China suffered greatly during the war. Recent declassification of the KGB wartime traffic between the United States and the USSR has pinpointed the key figures that greatly undermined Chinese efforts to stabilize China's wartime economy. The top Soviet source in the U.S. government during World War II was Assistant Secretary of Treasury Harry Dexter White, who, with Alger Hiss, ranked as the second-most-important source to the Soviets, and Lauchlin Currie the third.[29]

Harry Dexter White was the most influential financial brain in the wartime Treasury Department and had spied for the Soviet Union until 1938. After two years of inaction, White resumed his activities as a Soviet source. To aid his efforts, in 1940 White hired eleven active Soviet sources into the

Treasury as a network. They included the Treasury's wartime chief representative in China, Solomon Adler, and Treasury's top person in charge of gold reserve, Frank Coe.[30]

Led by Harry Dexter White, the Silvermaster Group's Treasury Department ring accomplished several deeds detrimental to the military aid programs to China. First of all, they were able to influence the decision makers at the top through their control of bureaucratic processes at the operational level. Particularly crucial was White's overwhelming influence on Treasury Secretary Henry Morgenthau, a key figure in the China aid program. Historians John Haynes and Harvey Klehr write, "No individual had greater influence on Morgenthau's own thinking in the late 1930's and during World War II than White."[31]

During the time when the Soviet Union was actively supporting China's war efforts before 1940, Morgenthau was known to be the strongest supporter of aid to China in the entire Roosevelt cabinet. When the Soviets divested from China, Morgenthau became one of the primary doubters of the China aid programs, mostly thanks to White's influence. Secondly, the White clique inside Treasury was able to generate enormous amounts of ideologically tainted field reports from China, ruthlessly manipulating facts and statistics to influence the internal bureaucratic opinions of the key policymakers on wartime China and its leadership. Thirdly, the White ring was able to coordinate with international Communists in discrediting the Nationalist government led by Chiang Kai-shek and in aiding the Chinese Communists in Yenan led by Mao Zedong. A good example is the case of Chi Ch'ao-ting (Ji Chaoding), a Chinese-American member of the Communist Party of the USA (CPUSA).

Chi was the chief of the CPUSA's China Bureau and was in charge of maintaining a transportation channel of funds and materiel from the United States to Hong Kong and finally to Yenan. With the help of the International Longshoremen's Union, Chi had become a legendary figure in helping wartime Communists in China with materiel as well as financial shipments. When the time came for Chi to penetrate the KMT financial nerve center, it was Harry Dexter White who coordinated with Comintern chief Georgi Dimitrov and the CCP chief Mao Zedong. It was White who used his high position in the U.S. government to plant Chi Ch'ao-ting deep inside the Nationalist Ministry of Finance to do further damage.[32]

Yet, the most damaging operation conducted by the White ring against China during World War II was the gold shipment incident. As we have briefly discussed earlier, the tenacious efforts conducted by the U.S. Treasury in stopping the shipment of gold to China as approved by President Roosevelt and

Treasury Secretary Morgenthau at the most crucial period in China's wartime economy did significant damage to China's financial stability. Of the $200 million gold loan approved by the president and treasury secretary in writing, only $8 million was delivered to China in the crucial two years of the war, thanks to the Silvermaster Group's adroit efforts to manipulate the bureaucratic process and sabotage the essential shipments of gold to China. Not until May 1945 did Treasury Secretary Morgenthau discover the shameful acts of his subordinates on this matter and exploded, charging the incident as "inexcusable" and "absolutely dishonorable."[33] The perpetrators involved were a "Magnificent Three": Harry Dexter White, the ringmaster of the operation and at the time the number two man in the Treasury Department, and two of his aides, Frank Coe, the wartime director of monetary research in the Treasury Department, and Solomon Adler, an active member of the CPUSA hired by White as the chief agent in China for the Treasury Department.[34]

Arthur Young provides a salient evaluation of the impact of this U.S. about-face:

> Sale in China of gold provided under the [$200 million loan] credit could have helped much more than it did to check inflation [in China]. Gold sales were a recognized wartime expedient in several countries for raising money by noninflationary means. The Treasury was selling gold to raise local currencies in the Middle East and India at the very time it was denying gold to China, despite China's urgent pleas. The Treasury had a clear commitment to supply China with gold. China was handling gold sales well, on a cash basis, so long as the Treasury loyally sent gold. Official selling prices were kept closely in line with prices in the free market. When the Central Bank [of China] no longer had gold, it did not dare to stop sales, lest the price skyrocket with a serious effect on general prices. Trusting in the Treasury's commitment, the Bank began to sell gold for future delivery, which did not soon materialize.... [Harry Dexter] White and his associates held back for reasons which they admitted were largely specious.... The Treasury's foot-dragging came at a time when inflation was growing dangerously in China, and when Japanese troops were seizing the East China air bases and even threatening Chungking.... On the gold issue, I felt at the time and still feel that the American position was wrong and hurtful to China. Even then those of us on the Chinese side suspected skullduggery.[35]

To reward Adler and Coe's stupendous service to the Chinese Communist cause during World War II, Beijing granted life-long protection and safe haven for this duo after they fled to Communist China in the late 1950s. Both worked for their "socialist motherland" for several decades in Beijing in the CCP's propaganda and intelligence agencies. Frank Coe died in Beijing in 1980; Solomon Adler died there in 1994.[36]

The inadequacy of the Allies' military aid greatly demoralized China. It also created constant bitterness between the Chinese and the U.S. military and civilian leaders. But more important, it caused the deterioration of China's wartime economic and military conditions, making the China theater inconsequential to the final victory over Japan. Yet, most damaging of all, was the growth of a profound distrust of the KMT government by many high-ranked U.S. officials, including the new president, Harry S Truman.

In the immediate aftermath of the war, Admiral William Leahy, the wartime chairman of the Joint Chiefs of Staff, poignantly stated, "I could never understand what happened in China. I know at Cairo President Roosevelt assured Chiang Kai-shek of his and America's support in every way. He meant it, too! Over and over he told me we were going to get behind China. But something or somebody got between him and his plans. We were all too busy to push them or to find where the hold-up was. The President mentioned it to me frequently until the time he died. He intended to find out what was happening—why we were not supporting Chiang. But after he died, the matter dropped."[37]

Hopefully, this narrative has partially answered the good admiral's question.

THE CURSE THAT WAS SACO

WITH THE PROMISED MORE THAN fifty thousand guerrillas at Tai Li's and Milton Miles's disposal, the Sino-American Special Technical Cooperative Organization (SACO) started with renewed energy and expanded ambitions. Nine camps were set up throughout China, with the majority of them located along the coastal area of China to prepare for the eventual landing of the U.S. forces there as planned by Admiral Ernest J. King. To fulfill the need for weather intelligence for the fleet in the Pacific, SACO also had units deep inside China's Northwest near the Gobi desert to observe and report the origins of many important weather patterns. While the majority of the camps were U.S. Navy-related, there was Camp Three in Linru, Henan Province, which was run by an OSS (Office of Strategic Services) team led by Major Arden Dow and Lieutenant Frank A. Gleason, both industrial espionage and demolition experts. Tai Li also got a trade-off from Miles by establishing a school of intelligence and counterespionage inside SACO headquarters in Chungking. Known as Camp Nine, this was the most controversial of all SACO units, because it was, in Miles's words, "General Tai Li's baby."[1] Essentially, it was a modern police training school run by Charlie Johnston who arrived in SACO in May 1943. Yet because of heavy political pressure from all sides, Camp Nine did not really start until January 1945 and only trained about a hundred graduates at a remote site in Xifeng, Guizhou Province.[2]

However, SACO was born with a debilitating birth defect. The inclusion of OSS in SACO was a fundamental mistake and would prove devastating to Miles's enterprise. The differences and disagreements between Miles's Navy contingent and Donovan's OSS gang inside SACO could not be more startling and would render the whole Sino-American wartime cooperation in intelligence a legend in chaos and internecine infighting.

The most obvious problem was that Miles and Donovan belonged to completely different types of human professions. It was a classical clash between career military men, who prized straightforwardness and bluntness in communications and placed utmost importance in seeing actions and results, and lawyers, who thrived on legal and conceptual ambiguity and linguistic manipulations to get ahead of things. In other words, it was a battle between men of action and men of words. It was this difference in profession that had bound Joseph Stilwell and Miles together as two professional military men and forged a friendship and mutual respect for each other in the culturally intriguing and politically complex scene of wartime China. However, to a large extent, it was this very difference that made Miles and Donovan, and the organizations they each represented, acrimonious toward each other throughout their cooperation.

In case after case, Miles's military mind and Donovan's legal mind collided. In November 1943, during his first visit to Chungking, Donovan got into a heated argument with Miles in Tai Li's headquarters over command issues of SACO. Miles's vivid description of the travesty reflects the essence of the stormy SACO-OSS relation. Miles recorded:

> We did a tremendous job of arguing, and, although I understood most of what they were talking about, I am afraid I enjoyed the situation too much to let it pass as simply as that. To an outsider it would have been amazing to see one poor little Naval officer being harangued on three sides by expert professional lawyers with a very innocent look on the Naval Officer's face and a continued insistence that he did not understand all those big terms, such as assessments, procurare, assizes, testaments, instruments, pax vobiscums, etc. Finally it was necessary for the simple little Naval Officer to tell them that he had had absolutely no law training and could they tell it to me in common American slang. This they did in about three sentences and it seemed to work, much to the lawyers' relief.[3]

This lawyerly approach to intelligence operations in wartime China formed a unique feature of OSS. Donovan himself was a lawyer, who hired almost his entire law firm into OSS to be in charge of various branches of the spy organization. The leadership core of his China team, including the second and longest-serving chief of OSS/China, Richard Heppner; Donovan's executive assistant, Edwin Putzell; his special intelligence chief, Duncan Lee, who in reality was a KGB mole inside the OSS; and the superlawyer James Donovan (no relation to William Donovan), who would play a key legal role in the Nuremberg Trials after the war, were all lawyers by profession.[4] As such, they were used to treating signed documents with legalistic creativity, not necessarily compliance with the obvious intent of those documents.

To Tai Li, Miles, and the Navy, the SACO Agreement was a strict guidance in their planning and enforcement of actions. To Donovan and his OSS lawyer/agents, it was just another document subject to various linguistic deconstruction and not necessarily binding 100 percent. And they often did try to interpret it differently from what was commonly understood.[5] This situation often brewed suspicion and distrust between the Navy and OSS. Quite often, when there was a working dispute between the two organizations, Donovan's first instinct was to send his lawyers to form a committee with the Navy and flood that service with legal documents and long memos to make simple matters unnecessarily complicated. Or even worse, it frequently resulted in creating an atmosphere in which the Navy suspected the OSS was trying to cover things up or to usurp the Navy's predominant role in the SACO enterprise.

In early 1944 Captain Jeff Metzel sensed a plot by OSS to oust Miles out of China and reported to his superior, Rear Admiral W. R. Purnell, "It may be that I am drawing wrong conclusions from natural behavior of professional lawyers, but we are beset with demands for documentation and with documents which we are requested to verify as we would testimony and make matters of record. If we are to hold our own in this sort of thing as a regular diet, it will be necessary to take a number of good lawyers full time on our SACO staff both in Washington and Chungking."[6]

More exasperating was the legal manipulation of simple organizational matters with regard to major SACO initiatives. For example, a dispute arose between the Navy and the OSS over the minutes of a meeting jointly held in Washington on the SACO. Metzel wrote in agony, "We do not have a court stenographer and have not considered it necessary to make word for word transcriptions of our meetings. The O.S.S. version covers a great deal of detail, much of which is correct, but the emphasis and tone throughout looks like an attempt to pile up evidence for future charges that Captain Miles made conflicting and incorrect statements malignant to O.S.S. and designed whatever he found convenient to remember. . . . Given a week of concentrated effort, I could refute something in almost every sentence on the paper. I have told Commander Halliwell [of the OSS] that we simply do not have time to argue these records to an agreement and that they would have to stand purely on the O.S.S. version."[7] Metzel's summary of this episode with the OSS lawyers was classically poignant. "My conclusion from the whole thing is that the reserve officers in O.S.S., particularly their lawyers, are by their experience in the cold, hard world unable to realize that regular officers can think and work and form opinions objectively and act as they see their duty requires without personal or ulterior motives, but I do not believe that anyone could have handled Captain Miles's very complex and difficult duties more ably, honestly and thoroughly than he has."[8]

Yet, SACO's record of constant frustration in carrying out its intended missions did not stop at this clash of professional differences in styles and work ethics, it was also riddled with international intrigues and manipulations. The most telling episode in this regard is SACO's involvement in organizing intelligence and sabotage groups in Thailand and Indochina.

From the beginning of China's open alliance with Western democracies in a common war against Japan, Chiang Kai-shek had been designated by the Allies as the overall supreme commander for a large area that extended far beyond the Chinese borders. In fact, Chiang was given an area to operate military activities that included China, Burma, Korea, Thailand, Taiwan, and the Indochina peninsula. It was a commonly understood designation for Chiang. Therefore, Article 8 of the SACO agreement specifically mandated that special intelligence operations be launched in "Burma, Thailand, Korea, Taiwan and Annan [French Indochina]."

Yet, those regions were rife with ambiguities and international intrigues, which made SACO's intelligence efforts difficult, confusing, and at times demoralizingly frustrating. Before the war, Siam, which was renamed Thailand soon after the war started, was the only independent kingdom free from Western colonization in Southeast Asia. When Japan waged a widespread war in December 1941 on all major Western powers that had colonies in East and Southeast Asia on the pretense that it was fighting Western colonialism and chasing the Westerners out of Asia, Thailand became an important diplomatic stunt for Japan to illustrate its ostentatious virtue of anti-Western colonialism. Accordingly, although Japan needed to control Thailand in its swift and brutal drive southward that had occupied Burma, Malaya, French Indochina, and Hong Kong, this could not be done overtly, lest the nominally independent Thailand be seen as a Japanese-occupied nation, thus revealing Japan's hypocrisy. Accordingly, enormous pressure was exerted on Thailand. To preserve their country's independence, the Thai played along unwillingly. On the one hand, Thailand officially joined the Japanese in its war against China, the United States, Great Britain, and the Netherlands, and was on paper a member of the Axis alliance. On the other hand, Bangkok also kept secret contact with the Western powers at war with Japan. The United States State Department, for example, was extraordinarily careful not to classify Thailand as in the same category of such enemy countries as Japan and Germany. As Miles put it, "Siam declared war on us, but we didn't on them. It put the diplomatic proceedings in some doubt."[9]

But this diplomatic subtlety was never to be openly discussed or contemplated. Only a handful of top officials in Western capitals were aware of it. When it came to carry out military and intelligence operations in Thailand, it was difficult to be implemented into actual military policies in the field. As a result, any overt or covert military and intelligence operations would encounter complexity and internal rankling among the Allies.

SACO had strong interests in running an intelligence and special operation team in Thailand. For Miles, it was important that he could gather weather intelligence from a wider scope that would include Thailand. Tai Li had long harbored interest in penetrating into Thai territory to consolidate his intelligence-gathering capabilities in Southeast Asia. But overall, the most enthusiastic about operating in Thailand was Donovan's OSS, now officially inside SACO, whose Asia projects were under the overall command of Miles. For preparing operations in Thailand, OSS had already recruited twenty-three college students of Thai origin from American universities. They were trained in the United States in various espionage schools on skills ranging from radio and cryptography to demolition and assassination. At one point, they were on a school assignment to practice their espionage skills and managed to get arrested in Idaho, where the all-white locals were not used to seeing Asians roaming around carrying secret devices. "During a war with Japanese," Miles mused, "Asiatic foreigners loose in the West attracted attention—especially with little spy radios."[10]

Immediately after SACO came into being, Miles assumed command of the Thai project. Miles ordered them to report to SACO headquarters in Chungking. Quite unexpectedly to Miles, managing these Thai agents turned out to be a tough task. First of all, these agents were trained in the United States and learned skills not useful to Asian conditions. "We gave them another dose of school," Miles records, "to unlearn some of the things they had been taught and to bring them up to date on the conditions they would meet."[11] Moreover, this was a colorful bunch of Thai, with great difficulty adjusting to the military lifestyle and discipline. Miles vividly describes one of his Thai subordinates:

Some of the lot were prima donnas. One was a pretty important prince of the royal blood. He was a nice boy, but being brought up as an oriental prince gave him no experience in obeying orders. As a matter of fact, he was downright insubordinate over some subject or other. . . . With no special experience in how to discipline a prince, I put the young prince 'under hack,' restricting him to a special room. . . . As a result of my investigation I preferred charges against him, signed "M.E. Miles, Captain, U.S. Navy, by order of the King of Siam. . . ." I don't know about my authority, but I signed it. After a little bit of talking the young prince agreed I did have a legal right to court-martial him, but that wouldn't look very well, so he would do better to conform. He never caused us any trouble after that.[12]

But Miles was fortunate in that the Thai group did have an effective leader in Colonel Kharb Kunjara, who was a grandson of a Siamese king. A graduate of Britain's Royal Military Academy, Kunjara was "effervescent, volatile, easy-come and easy-go," Miles observed, and "it took [Kunjara's] inexhaustible physical bounce to stay on top of his crew."[13]

Both Tai Li and Miles had great hopes for the Thai operations. The plan was to slip these agents into Thailand to instigate an uprising to overthrow the Thai government, and then Tai Li would send in ten thousand Chinese guerrilla troops disguised as Thai from the border region of Puer (Puerh) to invade Thailand. Preparations began in earnest, with SACO spent a fortune buying horses from the nearby Tibetan regions to equip this group. The irony of a U.S. naval officer stuck in the thicket of China during wartime training a Thai guerrilla contingent that had the penchant for horses as the preferred way of operation did not go unnoticed. Miles confessed:

Now for the horses—an odd sort of business for a Naval officer. Colonel Kunjara's professional Army officers were all anxious to organize a liberation army. . . . General Tai Li was in touch with a group of 10,000 well-trained Chinese . . . at the point nearest Thailand. We flew down to look them over and were amazed and delighted that the troops looked Siamese even to the Siamese. The boys thought that with those troops they could shove out the Japs practically single-handed. At the least, I thought, we could cause a diversion of the strength facing Stilwell in Burma. It was horse country and they were to be the first SACO Navy cavalry raiders.[14]

But the Thai group organized by SACO met an unexpected opposition—the British, who suddenly and strenuously objected to the SACO-run guerrilla and intelligence operation in "their territory" that included Thailand. Miles and Tai Li were caught completely by surprise by this British intransigence. As Miles observed, "We were going along dumb and happy under an agreement of the A.B.C.D. [American-British-Chinese-Dutch] combined Chiefs of Staff, giving Generalissimo Chiang Kai-shek control over all operations on the China mainland including Siam, Indo-China and the Malay Peninsula."[15] Not only did the British object to SACO's operation in Thailand, but London was also poised to oppose any U.S. military intelligence operations in Burma, a territory dear to Stilwell, whose entire energy and efforts were focused on launching a military campaign to retake Burma from the Japanese.

In August 1943, as SACO's Thai operation was proceeding in full gear, high politics befell Chungking, because the Quebec Conference arbitrarily created a new Southeast Asia Command, with total British control under Admiral Louis Mountbatten. Miles reported on the grave situation at the time, "In late August the South-East Asia Command was set up under Admiral Mountbatten. There was a real snafu. Stilwell was already operating in Burma—Generalissimo thought Eastern Asia was his theater—and Mountbatten was cutting across all those lines through an agreement made at a meeting in Quebec that wasn't even attended by the Chinese."[16]

Stilwell was horrified by the prospect that Washington and London might pull him out of Burma entirely. In fact, he had long suspected the British might do something like this. To prevent such an eventuality, Stilwell had already decided to stop SACO's Thai operation to save his Burma campaign. Essentially, he wanted Miles and Tai Li to stop sending any Thai agents and Chinese troops into Thailand. Stilwell told Miles face to face, "The British are hostile to the whole idea and we would have to screw the British to get them in." Miles was surprised by Stilwell's determination to end the Thai project and evoked the OSS shield to try to save it, as he pointedly asked Stilwell whether Donovan was on board to scrap the Thai operation. Never mincing his words, Stilwell exploded in front of Miles, "Donovan is out to screw us. [I] do not like the whole idea. Because I am supposed to be playing an open hand with the British, due to the operations coming up. I think it's just asking for trouble bringing these [people] in."[17] With Stilwell's strong demand to pull the plug on the Thai group, SACO had no choice but to put the Kunjara group in abeyance, which caused great bitterness on all sides.

Most angry were the Thai, who were now stuck at the SACO headquarters in Chungking without a sense of direction and purpose. Months of idle waiting prompted Colonel Kunjara to take things into his own hands, and he proceeded to enter Thailand anyway in early 1944. When Kunjara's people arrived at the Chinese-Thai border, however, they were promptly intercepted by SACO and Stilwell's people at the border crossing. "Until the political situation is cleared up," Major Hoffman, Donovan's representative inside SACO reported to Stilwell on 25 February 1944, "General Donovan concurs that Kunjara personally would not proceed into Thailand proper."[18] A couple of weeks later, an official order was issued to seal the fate of the Thai project. "Until we have had further talks with the British on the subject, Kunjara will not be put into Thailand. Thailand will not be infiltrated from the North [from China] until we have informed the British."[19] Of course, the British would never allow any Chinese-run or American-run military and intelligence operations inside "their territory," Thailand, throughout the whole war.

The Thai project was yet another frustration SACO suffered. Miles bit-terly complained, "Everything SACO had been doing for them [the Thai group] was either cancelled or side-tracked. Even though it had been thoroughly discussed and OK'd and Stilwell was counting on it for southern diversion, the whole Puerh invasion plan was cancelled. I was left to take care of a heap of broken promises, the Chinese troops all trained and no place to go."[20]

Yet, a more colorful group unfolded a more dramatic play of wartime politics and intrigues in China. This was SACO's attempt to operate intelligence and sabotage activities in Indochina, administered on paper by the Vichy French authorities, but in reality controlled by the Japanese since late 1940. "It was a good spy story," Miles wrote, "including a pretty princess, a gay and witty French officer, [and] a dedicated priest who carried guns under his robes."[21] If Miles was relishing the delightful characters involved in this mission, he was certainly understating the complexity of its politics. It involved the French, Chinese, British, and several Indochinese indigenous groups, none of whom shared any substantial political ambition or military objectives with each other.

"All the native people," observed Miles, "were afraid of the Chinese who might invade from the North and heartily disliked the French for not giving Indo-Chinese enough liberty and responsibility."[22] The French had lost their country to the Nazis early in the war in Europe. The British saw the opportunity and started to support and finance a French political entity in exile in London led by Charles De Gaulle, who had dispatched his own diplomatic mission to Chungking as representative of the legitimate French government. The De Gaullist French mission in Chungking was led by General Zenovi

Pechkoff, the adopted son of Joseph Stalin's proletarian model writer, Maxim Gorky. Pechkoff's chief of staff in Chungking, a Colonel Emblanc, was an abrasive officer in the old French army, who was regarded by many as "volatile and combative" in Chungking.[23]

Yet, because the British were openly financing and supporting the De Gaullist French mission in China, the deeply Anglo-phobic Tai Li would have nothing to do with Pechkoff's establishment. Not only that, the entire French underground in Indochina and inside China deeply resented De Gaulle's French mission to China and refused to cooperate with it. The loyalty of those stateless French men belonged to their hero, the legendary French general, Henri Giraud, who had been a chief rival of De Gaulle and had been running his resistance warfare out of North Africa.

When Miles was ordered to organize an Indochina operation, he was asked to approach the then most-recognized fighting French man, General Giraud, who saw the importance of SACO's efforts and readily recommended his staff officer, Commander Robert Meynier, to head the China project for Miles.

The only French submarine officer who refused to surrender to the Germans, Meynier drove his sub away, escaping from Toulon in 1942 and joining General Giraud in North Africa. Miles and Meynier immediately hit it off. "Altogether, the commander was a colorful guy," Miles excitedly observed, "I liked the cut of his jib. We knew at first meeting we could work together."[24] And a major reason why Miles thought this project might work well was because Meynier's wife was a Vietnamese (Annamite) princess, whose father and uncle were influential Indochinese politicians of considerable clout. But the problem was that she was captured by the Germans at the fall of France and was now incarcerated in a German concentration camp in occupied Europe. Miles requested that OSS approach the British SOE (Special Operations Executive) to organize a jail break and rescue Madame Meynier from the German camp.

In the end, a dramatic rescue mission was indeed carried out, with success, costing the lives of several British agents and French resistance fighters.[25] "Half-pint size, cute, curvaceous," and once a winner at a beauty contest, Madame Meynier, whose escape from the German concentration camp and trip from London to Asia were a legendary part of the World War II lore, arrived in Chungking in late 1943.

The Meynier group, as it was commonly known at the time, had some grand plans for their operations, which include the establishment of "a network of informers, propagandizing natives to resistance, preparing ground for favorable reception of [Allied] forces when they should come in, organizing contraband such as rubber and tin for smuggling into China, and in various ways annoying Jap shipping."[26]

Madame Meynier proved a crucial asset to SACO. Her connections among the indigenous Indochinese were immense. Somewhat doubtful of her usefulness as an intelligence handler at first, Miles was soon impressed with her ability to extend influence and incite disenchantment among her native people under Japanese and Vichy French dual occupation. "The Madame was a natural for reaching the native residents," Miles admitted.[27] Commander Meynier was also enthusiastic in organizing his SACO agents. One of Meynier's faithful agents was a Catholic priest, Father Bec, who had been in Indochina since before the war. Father Bec was able to use his network of congregations to set up communications with other priests in the region and provided a great deal of intelligence about the Japanese and downed Allied flyers throughout the region. As Meynier's boss in SACO, Miles was happy to record that "[Robert] Meynier had already signed up a great many French agents . . . during the whole rest of the war, I received continuous information—weather, prisoners, status of wounded, intelligence on shipping and Jap planes, and an amazing amount of maritime and port information. I turned it over to our Fleet, and of course the O.S.S."[28]

But politics was never far away from SACO. The Meynier project met fierce opposition from the British-dominated De Gaullist establishment in Chungking. The French mission under General Pechkoff insisted that the Meynier group should stop reporting to SACO and General Henri Giraud in Africa—that, instead, the French mission should take over the command of the group, and that failing to do so would result in banning Meynier and his agents from going into Indochina at all. When Meynier's connection with General Giraud continued, De Gaulle ordered Pechkoff to send stern orders to Meynier to cease operating.

Lieutenant Commander Robert Larson, SACO's liaison officer and interpreter for Meynier and Miles, and the entire SACO staff wasted a great deal of time and money on making the squabbling French happy. The French twist was so immense that Miles angrily admitted that "the actual dollar value of the small amount we were allowed to accomplish in Indo-China turned out to be more than the whole cost of SACO to the U.S. in the war!"[29] "I can't begin to list the roadblocks put in the way of the Meynier group by the French Mission in Chungking," Miles continued, "General Tai grinned—'I told you so'—for according to him the main effort of the Mission was to see that nothing was done in Indo-China."[30]

Pechkoff's chief of staff, Colonel Emblanc, tried to deport Father Bec to North Africa; "Meynier was completely ham-strung by his own countrymen. He was forbidden to see any French officials—a ludicrous stipulation if he was to organize them to cooperate with the Allies. But for a while he got around that by sending Larson to talk for him. Mme. Meynier was forbidden to go into Indo-China at all, in spite of the important letters she carried written by Giraud and later by De Gaulle."[31] In utter frustration, and caught in this intense Giraud–De Gaulle fight for turf and command, Commander Meynier finally gave up and left China and SACO in disgust of his own countrymen in Chungking.[32] SACO's Robert Larson, befuddled by the French infighting and speaking on the general situation in China, poignantly commented, "It seems the war in China is more between the Allies than against the Japs."[33]

Who should be responsible for the French disconnection in Asia? Miles had a unique perspective—he blamed Washington for its failure to stand up to the British and French colonial ambitions in Asia. "Instead of leading, we played follow the leader in the Far East to Britain and France, whose interests and history had been in subjugating, not liberating people," Miles suggested, "a new deal and a firm united stand for our own principles at this time could have forced the old countries in the new pattern in time to change the course of conflicts after the war. At least in Indo-China the organization Meynier was engineering would have given powerful but moderate native leaders a stake in the success of the war and backing for more representation in their government. These were the men who could have stolen the thunder of the radicals."[34]

However, in addition to this policy paralysis in Washington, SACO faced another major challenge in China—the clash over how to respond to the rising Chinese nationalism was a far more explosive issue. And this had much to do with a historic dispute between the Navy and the OSS. Key to Miles's success in gaining Chinese trust and cooperation was his extraordinary appreciation of the rising Chinese nationalism and the Chinese demand for international respect. His empathic stress on not hiring Old China Hands was mostly based on such a realization. Not all Old China Hands had developed racist attitudes of white supremacy, which made Miles's tough policy at times unreasonable and over the top. In fact, his superiors in Washington, while sympathetic to his concern, did warn him not to get too strict on the Old China Hands. Captain Metzel wrote to Miles in August 1943, "You've got to make Wild Bill and Uncle Joe [Stilwell] feel you are on their side," which prompted Miles to grudgingly relax his Old China Hands policy a bit. "My stand on the Old China Hands situation," Miles wrote back to Metzel, "is naturally somewhat modified with the increasing demand for personnel."³⁵ But overall, Miles was particularly careful not to be disrespectful of his Chinese interlocutors.

In sharp contrast, the OSS took no effective measures to indoctrinate its agents and officers on respecting Chinese sensibility and often acted as if the Americans were the saviors of the Chinese nation from Japanese aggression, which created the feeling that Chinese resistance efforts and leadership, from Chiang Kai-shek on down, was not worth much. In fact, this was at the root of Donovan's difficulty with the SACO enterprise and his Chinese collaborators, and many of OSS's excellent opportunities in China were ruined by such insensitivity.

In mid-October 1944, a senior member of OSS's Washington Planning Board, Brigadier General Lyle Miller of the Marine Corps, was on Donovan's order to visit Tai Li for OSS's reorganization matters in light of the impending Stilwell recall from China. After otherwise amicable and cooperative consultations with Tai Li during the day, Miller revealed his unsavory sentiment toward the Chinese in the aftermath of some Chinese liquor. The OSS official carried on a racist tirade at the banquet hosted by Tai Li in his honor. Captain Ilia Tolstoy, an OSS officer from the Army attached to SACO, who was at the scene, felt ashamed "as a member of O.S.S. or the white race," because he had "just seen the most disgraceful thing that he had ever seen in the army."³⁶ An official OSS report to Donovan in Washington, D.C., from Chungking describes only the printable version of what had gone on:

Very grave diplomatic relations have arisen. A full report is herewith submitted. General L. H. Miller attended a conference and a dinner on the afternoon and evening of the 22nd of this month by TL [Tai Li]. During the dinner liquor was served and General Miller, both in speech and conversation, spoke most disparagingly of Madame Chiang Kai Shek, her husband, the Chinese people and the country itself. Listed bellow are the statements made by the General: (1) Again and again Miller demanded that TL afford us the opportunity of being entertained by Sing-song girls. He requested that TL produce such maidens. TL attempted to switch the conversation into other channels but Miller was adamant. (2) Miller asked TL about Chiang Kai Shek's new women and wanted know if this was the reason for his wife's long absence. (3) The General denied that China is a front rank power. He stated that the country could not even be a 5th or 6th rank power and that they were just about 12th. (4) He stated that China was guilty of "God damn obstructionism." (5) Miller asserted that China would now be under Japanese domination if it had not been for the United States of America guarantees that China is a front rank power and also guarantees China's territorial integrity. According to Miller, 40–50 years will be required for China to assume a leading position. (6) In order to protect China from U.S.S.R, it is necessary for China to have our support. (7) Throughout the evening Miller time and again called the Chinese "Chinamen." (8) The General said "you Chinamen must open your eyes and stop sleeping like that idiot over there." Miller designated one of the Chinese guests as an example of what he meant. (9) Miller said that in the Philippines he would get Japanese genitalia and ask the Chinese to a dinner at which they would be served. The General's tirade went on for more than 2 hours, punctuated with a good deal of table pounding and swearing. Both myself and Colonel Tolstoy attempted to break it up but were ordered to remain quiet by both TL and Miller.[37]

Of course, this kind of behavior did not go well with OSS's efforts to forge an alliance with the most powerful intelligence boss in China. Donovan's China plans were therefore constantly frustrated by his organization's insensitivity to the rising Chinese nationalism.

On orders from President Franklin Roosevelt in the White House, the U.S. Army conducted a thorough investigation of the Miller incident. It came out on 5 November 1944 and concluded that Brigadier General Miller, who represented the chief of OSS on an official business trip to China, had made "insulting, embarrassing, and profane remarks about the Chinese, China, Generalissimo Chiang Kai-shek and Madame Chiang Kai-shek" and behaved "in a thoroughly disrespectful and disgraceful manner . . . [which was] discrediting to a standard far below that of a general officer of the United States."[38] The report did not stop at denouncing Miller's behavior; it further pointed out the impact of this sort of racist attitude toward America's war efforts in a culturally sensitive Chinese environment, as it concluded: "Now it appears, due to General Miller's offending remarks as a representative of the Chief of the Office of Strategic Services, that the desire of the Chinese to have the O.S.S. in SACO is jeopardized and its future is in a delicate balance. We have always felt that the presence of O.S.S. in SACO is to our advantage and now we are in a position where to talk cooperation and sincerity of purpose with the Chinese seems futile. Instead of assistance from the Chief of Office of Strategic Services we have gained added hindrances and responsibilities."[39]

Facing such devastating charges by the U.S. Army's theater inspector general, Donovan fired Miller from OSS's employment the next day.[40] On 14 December 1944, almost two months after the Miller incident, a humiliated

Donovan sent Tai Li the following letter of apology trying to save his OSS from being kicked out of China entirely:

My dear General Tai Li:

May I offer, for myself personally and officially on behalf of the Office of Strategic Services, my heartfelt apologies to the Generalissimo, to you and to the Chinese people for the conduct of General Lyle Miller at the banquet at which he was your honored guest? As I stated in the apology I asked to have personally tendered to you at the time, the remarks were inexcusable even if due to the officer's inability to partake as a gentleman of your hospitality. I am grateful, indeed, for the characteristically generous and farsighted view you have taken in our relations and those of our government and for your refusal to magnify the act of an individual beyond its proper scope and significance.

I know I do not need to tell you of the high regard in which I hold you and the Chinese people. Although I have always been forthright and direct in my relations with you, stating my intentions and differences of opinions clearly and unequivocally, I have done so to you as a man for whom personally and as a representative of the Chinese people I have the greatest admiration, respect and devotion. And may I add that my deep conviction of the greatness of the Chinese people has never diminished.

In closing let me express my personal wish for your health and welfare and the hope that I may soon be privileged to meet with you.

Sincerely William J. Donovan, Director[41]

However, the disunity of goals and styles between the Navy and the OSS did not stop here. Another contentious issue was about the command over intelligence operations in wartime China. To the Navy, it was China's war, and the Chinese had been fighting it alone for more than four years before the Americans participated in the common objective of defeating Japan. It was abundantly obvious to the Navy that the Chinese were far better in organizing irregular warfare against the Japanese in their own country. As such, the Navy had no problem sharing command with capable Chinese officers such as Tai Li. Consequently, in all of Tai Li–Miles's initiatives, it was explicitly arranged that Tai Li would be the commanding officer of the SACO enterprise and Miles would be Tai Li's deputy, with both sharing veto power. But for a close and trusting partnership, such ranking order would not, and did not, matter much, for Tai Li and Miles worked perfectly well as a team with complete mutual respect. One OSS officer inside SACO remarked that "no one knew which was the 'shadow,' [because] Tai Li and Miles were always together in person or policy."[42]

At the outset of the enterprise, and before he went to China and met Tai Li for the first time, the very first request Miles made of the Chinese side was "one hundred percent cooperation between the Chinese and myself. I expect to keep no secrets and will return one hundred percent cooperation."[43] Yet, to Donovan and the OSS, the primary goal of operating in China was to establish an intelligence network entirely independent of the Chinese, the U.S. Navy, and the U.S. Army. The participation in the SACO enterprise was only Donovan's expedient cover to penetrate into the China theater. As Donovan made clear to the U.S. Navy official in charge of the SACO endeavor, "The American and Chinese intelligence services must each be free to act independently!"[44] Donovan's philosophy of wartime intelligence operations was a major contributor to the SACO/OSS infighting, because it collided head on with Miles's operating principle that the intelligence command had to be shared with the Chinese. As Donovan explained aptly to the Navy, "(Mile's) double allegiance and double command with resulting conflicting obligations will not work."[45]

With this understanding of command authority in China, and with SACO as a legal cover, Donovan went on to conduct a series of intelligence initiatives without the knowledge of the Chinese, the Navy, and General Stilwell's headquarters. The first such scheme was the setup of an OSS secret intelligence (SI) network in wartime China. In Donovan's mind, OSS could nominally cooperate with the Chinese and the Navy in special operations (SO) only for the purpose of gaining confidence and access to independent SI operations in wartime China. Putting Miles in charge of the OSS inside SACO had only utility value too, as Donovan instructed his China team, "although Miles will be in complete charge, his principal work will be on the SO side."[46] The person Donovan wanted to run secret SI project inside SACO was Alghan Lusey, who would, as Donovan ordered, "assist Miles generally, but will also carry on other duties independently. SI work will be under his [Lusey's] sole supervision and direction."[47]

Subsequently, Lusey dutifully proceeded with his secret work. The plan was to send as many OSS men into Tai Li's organization as possible for the ostensible task of SO, but after gaining trust and confidence from the Chinese to gradually turn them into SI men. "None of the [SO] men sent to China as instructors [for the Tai Li-Miles project]," Lusey explained, "should be told they will eventually be used as SI men, or that they will be used for anything except instructing the Chinese SO people; when the time comes for them to do SI work, we will work them in."[48] Of course, this plot had to be kept completely secret from the Chinese and the Navy, as Lusey poignantly explained. "This would have to be handled very carefully, as our whole show would blow up if the Chinese ever found out we were doing anything like this."[49] Lusey assured Donovan that "in my case, of course, the Chinese know that I am to act as your personal liaison with Tai Li. You may be sure that I will never give myself, or our plan away."[50]

Miles was seen as a renegade American military officer who unduly collaborated with the Chinese against the OSS rule that the Chinese and the Americans should not mingle. Even though for convenience's sake, Donovan designated him as the overall chief of all OSS activities inside SACO, as Lusey further elaborated, "Miles should not be told of our SI plan; not that I don't trust Miles completely, but he is not a permanent member of our organization; he will return to the Navy. For that matter, I am taking an awful lot for granted in saying 'we.'"[51]

Such duplicity on the part of OSS was foolhardy, to say the least, because the Chinese could find it out easily. In addition, Miles would feel completely cheated anyway. But most important, this kind of double-dealing with a wartime ally in a country geographically and culturally afar would not bode well with America's publicly stated policy of friendship and goodwill with the Chinese people and their internationally recognized government. Even Donovan's many China scholars resented such a scheme and openly challenged its validity and usefulness.

Ernest Price, Donovan's top China scholar in charge of SI planning in OSS's Washington headquarters, protested with a sound reasoning:

We cannot . . . carry on espionage or subversive operations in Chinese territory against the Japanese without the knowledge and cooperation of the corresponding Chinese agencies; they would soon discover it in any case, would resent our having attempted it, and would put our agents out of the country, as they did the British. We cannot hope to set up in China a completely independent system of radio or other communications of our own. I would go further and say that for intelligence or subversive operations in China, all plans should be worked out jointly, all operations of each should be known and approved by the other, and all information pooled. On such a partnership basis, I believe we can conduct effective intelligence and subversive operations directed against the common enemy. Without it, we shall be handicapped by Chinese distrust, and by our own inability to conduct such operations on our own.[52]

But Price's most stinging indictment of his own organization's China policy comes down to this: "It is all very well to say that 'we must fight this war with our own men and our own weapons,' but we make ourselves the aggressors if we attempt to do so within the territory of a friendly nation without the full knowledge and consent of its government."[53] Ernest Price was promptly fired by Donovan in late September 1942 for "opposing the policies of Colonel Donovan in China."

Understandably, Miles grew furious when within a few months he found out about Donovan's SI scheme behind his back. "No SI man is wanted here," Miles angrily declared to Washington, "The very fact that he is here would put the Chinese on their guard against not only him but our whole Organization out here. Tai Li has to be on guard against people that slip in unseen and unasked, and I am going to help him do it. The job of SI in China is one of Tai Li's worries, and we can not step in here and expect to do any SI work anymore than we would knowingly let the Mexicans send SI men to operate in the U.S.A. The only difference there is that Mexicans might get away with it, while Tai Li would have an SI man spotted the minute he left the U.S."[54]

Donovan certainly sensed such an obstacle as Miles, who had apparently "gone native" on the Chinese side with regard to command control of intelligence operations inside China. To circumvent the SACO straightjacket, Donovan attempted other ways of conducting secret intelligence sub rosa. A chief tactic was to set up dummy organizations attached to other sponsors in the China theater while slipping major OSS human and materiel resources into China to operate without Chinese consent. At the time, the most obvious out-of-SACO sponsor with whom to operate was the famous commander of the erstwhile Flying Tigers and now a major general of the U.S. Army Air Corps commanding the 14th Air Force in China, Claire Lee Chennault.

It is still a minor mystery as to why Donovan went over to Miles and Tai Li instead of Chennault in the first place, because, from the start, Chennault showed great hospitality to Donovan's China programs. OSS's earliest China enthusiast, Joseph Hayden, was the first top official Donovan sent to China to find sponsors in early 1942. While encountering difficulty everywhere in Chungking, Hayden found Chennault was the most welcoming to OSS's type of work in China. Chennault, Hayden reported to Donovan, had "fought the Japs more successfully and dealt with the Chinese far more successfully than any other American," and had indicated to Hayden "how extremely valuable quick information concerning enemy air and sea movements up and down the coast would be. For example, if he could know that ten enemy planes had landed on a field near Hanoi that afternoon he could pounce on them before they took off tomorrow morning." In the end, Hayden told Donovan in Washington that "Chennault may be our best entry into this game;" that "[he] should be supported to the limit," and that "with the equipment we have lined up we could give him much information of the highest military value."[55] However, by the end of 1943, Donovan was determined that the SACO hookup with Tai Li and Miles was a mistake from which he could not easily escape. Considering the enormous prestige Chennault had commanded from the Chinese and the far distance between Chennault's headquarters, located in another province of Yunnan, and the SACO headquarters in Chungking, Sichuan Province, Donovan began to contemplate an escape plan. In December 1943, he instructed his China operatives to start "using Chennault air raids as cover for our operations . . . we should regard Chennault's position, the area in which he is located, as a definite front and should aid him by whatever means we can."[56]

Within a couple of weeks, OSS's China chiefs, John Coughlin and Carl Hoffman, found themselves in Chennault's Kunming headquarters negotiating a deal to set up a dummy organization to conduct OSS operations independently without the knowledge of SACO. As Chennault was in dire need of intelligence analysts and propaganda materials, for which OSS had plenty of talent, to be dropped in the bombing target areas, his staff treated the OSS initiative with welcoming hospitality. "They would give us office space," Hoffman reported to Donovan, "facilities for communications equipment to be installed and wanted personnel and possibly cash with which to hire agents. They wanted an R&A [Research and Analysis] group and an MO [Moral Operation, or black propaganda] group."[57] Of course, Miles and Tai Li were not to know anything about this, so Hoffman, a talented lawyer, used his legal acumen and came up with a name for this group that would not conjure up any connection with OSS. This new secret OSS setup was going to be called "Air and Ground Forces Resources and Technical Staff," or AFGRTS. Hoffman gloated to Donovan, "It was the most confused title I could think of at the moment."[58]

But this secret plan, designed to bypass Miles and Tai Li, had a serious downside to Donovan, that is, because it was secret from everybody and it was openly a 14th Air Force outfit, OSS might not get any credit at all for doing essentially all the work. As dozens of OSS agents and propaganda experts sneaked into China as AGFRTS members in direct violation of the SACO Agreement, Donovan's China chief nervously pointed out this problem to Donovan. "I have been very careful to be sure that all the important army personnel out here know just who the personnel are that are going into this unit, and why. I am certain that our identity will not be lost out here, and I don't think that it will be lost in Washington. It will be a touchy point with the 14th, as they will be very anxious to claim all credit. However, I think it will work out to the mutual satisfaction of both. Time should tell, and it shouldn't take too long a time."[59] In the end, AGFRTS operated until the very end of the war. Although the OSS provided all the resources for its operations, much of the credit indeed went to the 14th Air Force, and this identity problem never was completely solved for Donovan.

If Donovan's secret dalliance with Chennault' s 14th Air Force in the affairs of AFGRTS was innocuous in purpose and nature, OSS's liaison with the Chinese Communists was far more consequential and dangerous. In addition to the desire to get out of the SACO straightjacket, OSS had strong reasons to cooperate with the Chinese Communists because of the fabled guerrilla warfare the Chinese Communists were able to conduct in North China. International experience also buttressed Donovan's desire to work with Mao Zedong. OSS, along with its British counterpart, the SOE, had made some successful arrangements in Yugoslavia with Tito's Communist guerrilla groups against the Germans. OSS's Yugoslavia experience was so important to Donovan that he went to Cairo to report to President Roosevelt and Prime Minister Winston Churchill in late 1943. Donovan was strongly inclined to duplicate his Yugoslavia experience in China with the Chinese Communists. To do this, he had to first completely bypass the Chinese government and the SACO restriction. In fact, OSS's top Yugoslavian handler, Walter Mansfield, was quickly transferred by Donovan to China to make preparation for such a rendezvous with the Communists.[60] But the contact with the Chinese Communists could not be attempted by OSS alone, because it would ignite an immediate fire of destruction because of Donovan's tie-up with SACO and Tai Li, who was among the most ardent anti-Communists within the Chinese government. As it turned out, the opportunity soon came to Donovan and it was from the U.S. Army. The specific venue was the Dixie Mission.

Led by the pro-Communist wing inside Stilwell's headquarters, especially John Paton Davies, Stilwell's political adviser on loan from the State Department, the Dixie Mission was a U.S. Army-led intelligence initiative in an effort to gain political and military leverage against the Nationalist government under Chiang Kai-shek. It was an essential part of the Chiang-Stilwell internecine fight over command and control of the China theater. But to the managing operator of the Dixie Mission, John Paton Davies, it had a strong anti-SACO motive. Among the initial eighteen Dixie Mission members, five were from the OSS via AFGRTS, and none of these were directly related to

SACO. Among them were Raymond Cromley, who, as the Tokyo bureau chief for many years for the *Wall Street Journal*, was an expert in Japanese order of battle; John Colling, who was a photographic unit man specialized in making film documentaries; Charles Stelle, an intelligence analyst with a penchant for daring guerrilla raids against the Japanese; and Brooke Dolan, Donovan's famed Tibetan explorer.

If in the beginning the role of OSS in the Dixie Mission was rather small, Stilwell and his political adviser team under John Paton Davies soon realized that the OSS had two enormous features that could be used abundantly: secret cover and an unvouchered slush fund. In late 1944, Davies led a major effort to arm the Chinese Communist troops by using the OSS as a conduit to channel arms and money to Mao's headquarters. The Chinese Communists needed arms because of the embargo against them imposed by the central government. They needed money from the Americans in order to bribe the well-equipped Chinese puppet troops working for the Japanese in North China. Eventually, the Chinese Communist army chief asked Donovan for an astonishing $20 million with which to buy weapons from the puppets.[61]

After Stilwell's recall in October 1944, Davies remained in the Army's theater headquarters in China as a State Department political adviser, and he sped up the effort of using the OSS to arm the Chinese Communists. On 14 December 1944, accompanied by Davies, now under a new Army commander, Lieutenant General Albert Wedemeyer, Donovan's aide, Colonel Willis Bird, flew to Mao's headquarters in Yenan to strike a monumental deal with the Chinese Communists involving arming several divisions of Communist troops and massive intelligence cooperation with the Communists, including training the Communists for assassinations, demolitions, and all sorts of sabotage skills. As Colonel Bird later reported to Wedemeyer, the OSS reached a deal with the Communists in the following terms:

> a. To place our S.O. men with their units for purposes of destroying Jap communications, air fields and blockhouses, and to generally raise hell and run.
> b. To fully equip units assisting and protecting our men in sabotage work.
> c. Points of attack to be selected in general by Wedemeyer. Details to be worked out in co-operation with Communists in that territory.
> d. To provide complete equipment for up to twenty-five thousand guerrillas except food and clothing.
> e. Set up school to instruct in use of American arms, demolitions, communications, etc.

f. Set up intelligence radio network in co-operations with 18th Route Army.

g. To supply at least one hundred thousand Woolworth one shot pistols for People's Militia.

h. To receive complete co-operation of their army of six hundred fifty thousand and People's Militia of two and a half million when strategic use required by Wedemeyer.[62]

Secret inflow of arms and intelligence initiatives on such a large scale would have great consequences to America's war efforts, in addition to the obvious political storm it surely would cause in Chungking. Miles's team inside SACO had been closely monitoring OSS's radio traffic and discovered this plot and promptly informed the U.S. ambassador, Major General Patrick Hurley, who had been kept in the dark and who understandably grew furious and famously suppressed this Army-led OSS initiative by sending following cable to President Roosevelt on 14 January 1945:

It has taken from the 1st of January until now to find the fundamental cause of the break [between Chiang Kai-shek and the Communist Party]. Here it is:

During the absence of General Wedemeyer from Headquarters, certain officers of his command formulated a plan for the use of American paratroops in the Communist held area. The plan provided for the use of Communist troops led by Americans in guerilla warfare. The plan was predicated on the reaching of an agreement between the United States and the Communist Party bypassing completely the National Government of China and furnishing American supplies directly to the Communist troops and placing the communist troops under the command of an American officer. My directive of course was to prevent the collapse of the national Government, sustain the leadership of Chiang Kai-shek, unify the military force of China, and as far as possible to assist in the liberation of the Government and in bringing about conditions that would promote a free unified democratic China. The military plan as outlined became known to the Communists and offered them exactly what they wanted, recognition and Lend-Lease supplies for themselves and destruction of the National Government.[63]

Yet, Hurley's primary feud was with the U.S. Army and its political advisers from the State Department. Consequently, he generously spared OSS in his rage on account of his renowned friendship with Donovan. But OSS's key role in this episode should not be discounted. Colonel Ivan Yeaton, the commanding officer of the Dixie Mission under General Wedemeyer, pointed out, "History may show that the O.S.S. exerted more influence on Chinese Communist Party policy than any other units of the 'Dixie Mission'"[64]

With all these conflicts on concepts of operations, command, and politics, Miles and Donovan failed to reach even a modicum of agreement. In December 1943, Donovan flew to Chungking for the first time to meet Tai Li and Miles in an effort to resolve Miles's "double loyalty" problem. In a great outburst of anger and profanity, Donovan fired Miles from the post of OSS chief inside SACO and announced that he would set up a different OSS command in SACO to directly deal with Tai Li. Miles was happy that he would no longer represent OSS as long as Tai Li was satisfied with a separate OSS command inside SACO. He willingly accepted Donovan's dismissal without protest. Yet, the Navy Department was incensed with Donovan's lordly behavior and would have liked to keep OSS under control lest the entire SACO efforts go wasted. Admiral Purnell angrily cabled Miles in Chungking. "In view that Stilwell agreed only to a special setup under Tai Li and you, what led you to indicate by your letter to Tai Li that you recognized a setup [of OSS] that I have no reason to believe was approved by the JCS, Admiral King or Stilwell?"[65] Purnell bluntly told Miles, "General Donovan cannot relieve you of O.S.S. obligations without my approval."[66]

A few weeks later, the Joint Chiefs of Staff officially rejected Donovan's order to relieve Miles by declaring "Donovan's orders of December 5 1943 were without authority. All intelligence under SACO to be procured and evaluated by O.S.S. is not acceptable. Cutting off O.S.S. funds without warning injured Captain Miles and the whole project by losing face for Captain Miles and destroying the faith of the Chinese in reliability of promises made by accredited U.S. authorities."[67]

The Chinese, of course, were confused about this American infighting all along. When Donovan stormed to Chungking to fire Miles in December 1943, Tai Li royally treated the OSS chief in an effort to patch up his relationship with Miles. An elaborate scheme was worked out by Tai Li, who, after Donovan, Miles, and he himself had done enough shouting and arguing, adeptly arranged an opera to be performed for his American partners. The selected opera was about three brothers in Chinese history who did not get along and fought a lot, but in the end they all realized what was at stake, and out of brotherly love, they mended their differences and, with great gallantry and sacrifice, transcended trivialities, and went on to achieve glory and prominence.[68]

During one of the meaningless fights over command, Colonel Xiao (Hsiao) Bo got drunk in great frustration and had this conversation with an OSS officer inside SACO:

Colonel Hsiao: "Things do not go well. Too many factions. There is the Navy and O.S.S."
Devereux: "Both are really the same."
Hsiao: "They *should* be the same but are not."
Devereux: "We are all fighting Japan, and in Franklin's words, we ought to hang together lest we all hang separately." [This quotation apparently struck Colonel Hsiao, who applauded it and repeated it over and over again.]
Hsiao: "I can do no more than bring boy and girl together. The rest is up to them. I got drunk tonight in order to bring boy and girl together. I cannot marry them, they must marry by themselves."
Devereux: "They are already married, are they not?"
Hsiao: "But they don't get along. I got drunk trying to get them together, but I can do no more."
Devereux: "A friend of the family can often reconcile a quarreling husband and wife. I had the impression everything was going along well. You realize I am only a lieutenant [jg] and no one tells me anything."
Hsiao: "Are you Navy or O.S.S.?"
Devereux: "I am on temporary duty [from the Navy] with O.S.S."[69]

But the command paralysis continued. In utter frustration, Lieutenant Commander Robert Larson, one of Miles's man inside the SACO, poignantly observed, "The China theater was just simply filled with petty international and inter-service rivalries and jealousies which made the job of a Navy commander in the area very difficult."[70]

In the fall of 1944, a senior American naval intelligence officer lamented, "The diffusion of our intelligence activity in China is hopelessly inefficient from our own standout and the confusion incident to so many agencies and sub agencies operating in the theater is making us look ridiculous to Chinese officials and most likely to the British as well. It is extremely desirable to end this state of affairs and integrate our intelligence operations in China"[71]

Yet, despite all these seemingly insurmountable problems Miles and Tai Li faced, SACO proved a highly effective wartime operation that dealt the enemy heavy blows. Camp One was established in March 1943 in Weng Country, Anhui, near Shanghai. Altogether, nine classes, or some sixteen thousand guerrillas, graduated from this camp. Most of them belonged to Tai Li's quasi-military organization, "the Loyal Patriotic Army," behind the enemy lines. In June 1943, Camp Two was established in Nanyue, Hunan, in central China, with three classes, or twenty-two hundred guerrillas, graduated. After the Japanese took over that area, Miles moved his people to Jiangxi in Eastern China behind the enemy line to continue Camp Two. Renamed the Yangtze Work Unit, another thousand trainees graduated from there. Camp Three was run by the OSS in Linru, Henan, and then moved to Xian. Established in October 1943, it had five classes altogether, with three thousand graduates.

In the spring of 1944, Camp Four was set up in Shanpa, Shuiyuan Province. This was the northernmost reach of SACO, close to the Communist region and the Soviet-dominated Mongolia. In addition to training Tai Li's guerrillas, it was an important weather intelligence-gathering post for the U.S. Navy. Four classes were graduated, totaling about nine hundred trainees, from this camp. Camp Five was situated in the southern city of Nanning, Guangxi, with yet another nine hundred or so graduates.

In May 1944, Camp Six was set up in Anhua, Fujian, near the Taiwan Strait. This was deep inside the enemy line, yet it was Miles's most interested project, because it was directly related to Admiral King's order to survey a possible amphibious landing area for a planned invasion from the Pacific. With great difficulty in logistics and fending off enemy penetration and attacks, two large classes, with some sixteen hundred of Tai Li's cutthroat guerrillas, were graduated. Most of them remained active until the very end of the war. For the same purpose, SACO set up Camp Seven in Jianou, Fujian, near the sea coast, which trained another fifteen hundred guerrillas in three classes.

Camp Eight was located in the eastern province of Zhejiang, behind the enemy line. Four classes of eighteen hundred went through the training routine. Camp Nine was based in the SACO headquarters in Chungking, but it had a workshop in faraway Xifeng, Guizhou Province, which was often called Camp Ten. Both were essentially one entity devoted to counterintelligence, with much of its instructors from the FBI.

Toward the end of the war, much of the Camp One personnel and equipment were transferred to another site closer to Shanghai in July 1945, which trained another 920 guerrilla specialists. About the same time, Camp Twelve went up in Mei County, Guangdong, near Hong Kong, which graduated some twelve hundred demolition and special operation experts.[72] Those were remarkable undertakings by the standard at the time and under the circumstances in China.

In the end, as the historian Oscar P. Fitzgerald observed:

SACO guerrillas killed more Japanese and destroyed more enemy material with a smaller expenditure of men and supplies than any other force in the Far East. . . . In little more than a year of combat, SACO guerrillas reported over one thousand engagements in which nearly twenty-seven thousand [Japanese and puppet] soldiers were killed, eleven thousand wounded and five hundred eight captured. . . . [SACO] destroyed eighty-two railway engines, three hundred forty-three railroad cars, sixty-four railroad bridges and tore up nearly four thousand sections of track . . . two hundred sixty motor vehicles, one hundred nineteen highway bridges, thirty-five river steamers, one hundred fifty-eight sampans and two hundred twenty-one warehouses.[73]

Colonel David Barrett, head of the U.S. Dixie Mission, is warmly welcomed by Mao Zedong and Zhu De in Yenan, 1944. *Courtesy of David Barrett*

General Alexander von Falkenhausen, senior German military adviser to China, 1935–38, is pictured here in 1942 as military governor of Belgium. *Courtesy of Dai Houjie's* The Biographies of Foreign Advisers (*Hebei People's Press, 2004*)

130

Marshal Vasily Ivanovich Chuikov
was senior Soviet military adviser to
China, 1938–41. *Courtesy of Harold
Shukkan's* Stalin's Generals *(Phoenix
Press, 2002)*

Generalissimo
Chiang Kai-shek was
China's wartime leader.
*Chinese Government
Information Office*

George C. Marshall confers with Mao Zedong during the failed Marshall Mission. *U.S. Army photo*

A Flying Tigers P-40 gets ready to take off. *U.S. Army photo*

General Joseph "Vinegar" Stilwell poses with the Chiangs in a grand façade of harmony. *U.S. Army photo*

Chiang Kai-shek inspects SACO headquarters escorted by General Tai Li (left) and senior U.S. naval officers. *Estate of Rear Admiral Milton Miles*

Chiang Kai-shek gives General Claire Chennault, forced to retire on the eve of V-J Day, a farewell dinner together with General Albert Wedemeyer (bald man with back to camera). *U.S. Army photo*

The vintage scene of the meandering Burma Road leading to China.
U.S. Army photo

General Stilwell dines with one of his favorite Chinese officers, Admiral Yang Xuanchen, along with U.S. Ambassador Patrick Hurley (right). *U.S. Army photo*

Leaflet dropped by the 14th Air Force over occupied zones depicting a downed U.S. pilot being rescued by the Chinese locals, with caption saying "One Harvests What One Has Planted," and a reminder of how to identify the Americans by uniform symbol. *U.S. National Archives*

136

Leaflet dropped by the 14th Air Force over occupied zones depicting a downed U.S. pilot on parachute. The caption says, "This is a pilot forced to parachute. He is fighting for you. Please help him." *U.S. National Archives*

Leaflet dropped by the 14th Air Force over a Japanese-held railroad hub to be bombed by allied planes. The caption urges civilians to escape the bombardment: "Railroad worker friends, run for your lives." *U.S. National Archives*

First Lady Eleanor Roosevelt sits with Madame Chiang Kai-shek in the Rose Garden,1943. *Chinese Government Information Office*

William Joseph Donovan, director of the Office of Strategic Services, was photographed in his law office. *U.S. National Archives*

Chinese trainees stand inside SACO headquarters, with military dogs. *Estate of Rear Admiral Milton Miles*

Chinese soldiers from one of the German-trained divisions march toward the front line in the defense of Shanghai, 1937. *Chinese Government Information Office*

Mao Zedong enjoys a photo opportunity provided by an OSS officer in Yenan, 1944. *U.S. National Archives*

This was the emblem of the Flying Tigers. *Personal collection of the author*

U.S. Presidential Envoy Wendell Wilkie pays a visit to the Chiangs in Chungking, 1944. Standing top left is FDR's White House aide in charge of China affairs, Lauchlin Currie. *U.S. National Archives*

Mao's able lieutenant Zhou Enlai as photographed by an OSS officer in Yenan, 1944. *U.S. National Archives*

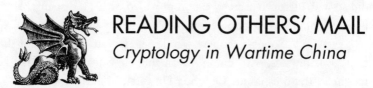

Chapter 8

READING OTHERS' MAIL
Cryptology in Wartime China

LIKE THE REST OF THE WORLD, gentlemen in China do read each other's mail. In the tumultuous and bloody twentieth century, knowing your enemy and what is on your enemy's mind in this war-torn nation had become a doubly serious business. In the hush-hush realm of code breaking, amongst a flock of contenders, Chiang Kai-shek and his Nationalist government stood out as the indisputable leader, far ahead of the numerous warlords who stood in the way of Chiang's relentless quest for national unification under the Nationalist ideals.

How did China's modern code breaking get started? Here again, a salient tradition of the East proved vital: family ties do matter. Modern code breaking was brought to China by Chiang's brother-in-law, T. V. Soong, who, in a certain sense, was more American than Chinese. T. V. Soong spent much of his adulthood in the United States and received his PhD in economics from Harvard in 1915. A financial genius, Soong proved indispensable to Chiang Kai-shek during the arduous Northern Expedition between 1926 and 1928 when Chiang tried to unify China. Soong was able to co-opt, cajole, and coerce the Shanghai capitalists to provide Chiang with large sums of money to sustain the revolutionary armies. With Soong's key help in finance, Chiang unified China in 1928 by defeating virtually all the warlords, who soon pledged their loyalty to Chiang and his newly established central government in Nanjing.

But old habits die hard, and warlord revolts constantly challenged the new regime throughout the early years of the Republic. From 1929 onward, a series of warlord revolts led to bloody "pacification campaigns" by the central government against the Guangxi warlord, Li Zongren (1929); the North China hegemon, Yan Xishan, and the "Christian general," Feng Yuxiang (1930); the Southeast warlords, Li Jisheng and Chen Mingshu (1933); and a number of other minor rebels. Chiang's central armies won all the major campaigns and did so with a crucial secret weapon provided by his indispensable brother-in-law, T. V. Soong—a group of codebreakers led by Wen Yuqing (Y. C. Wen).

Wen, T. V. Soong's nephew, was also a Harvard PhD, except that his specialty was physics, with emphasis on the "high tech" of the day, radio. Wen taught at the prestigious Qinghua University (China's MIT) as a professor and helped Soong in managing the Kuomintang's (KMT's) finances by serving as the superintendent of the Beijing Tax Academy (*Beijing shuiwu xuexiao*).[1] Soong discovered that Wen's genius belonged not to taxation but to snooping in the air. When the warlord revolts started, Soong swiftly appointed Wen to head a group to decode the secret radio traffic of the rebellious warlords, with full financial backing by Soong himself. Signal intelligence security was seldom a concern to most warlords, whose codes were simple and rudimentary. The codes were easily broken by Wen. The decoded intercepts of enemies' radio messages proved vital to Chiang's military campaigns and strategies. T. V. Soong's political stock in the KMT rose rapidly. Years later, when serving as Chiang's foreign minister and plenipotentiary to Washington, Soong proudly boasted to President Franklin Roosevelt that he himself was "something of a cryptographer" and that "I have won two civil wars for Chiang Kai-shek by setting up an efficient decoding service which kept him posted about movements of his enemies."[2]

Yet in the end, cryptography as a viable military instrument in China owes a lot to one single individual, Major General Tai Li.

After 1935, when Japanese militarists sped up their provocative actions in North China, the central government of China began to shift its focus from the Chinese Communists, who had just been defeated if not annihilated, to the Japanese. In March 1936, Chiang Kai-shek ordered Wen Yuqing to tackle a new target—the Japanese codes. Wen now was authorized to establish and lead an office called the Inspection and Decoding Office of the Secret Telegrams (*midian jianyi suo*). Wen and his colleagues spent several months figuring out the Japanese code system, and by the summer had broken a low-grade code of the Japanese foreign ministry.[3]

But there were two problems with regard to the KMT's code-breaking operations. First, there was always the issue of control of signal intelligence: Chiang Kai-shek treated Wen's decrypts as a family monopoly. Only Chiang and his two brothers-in-law were allowed access to them.[4] The Chiang family's monopoly of cryptanalysis only encouraged a fierce competition among the myriad factions in the KMT for control of this important activity. Second, what China needed desperately after 1937, when all-out war between China and Japan broke out, was access to Japanese military as well as diplomatic codes. Unfortunately, no one in China could read Tokyo's military systems. Against the background of these controversies, Tai Li emerged as the principal force behind the creation of a serious signal intelligence program in China.

In the early 1930s, China's radio surveillance was managed by another KMT intelligence agency commonly known as the Zhongtong (the Bureau of Investigation and Statistics of the KMT Party's Organization Department). It was charged mostly with internal security against various "deviant parties" (*yidang*), especially the Chinese Communist Party. After a humiliating scandal in 1931 in which Zhongtong was revealed to have been infiltrated by the Chinese Communists in 1931, Tai Li stepped into the business of intelligence by setting up the Group of Investigation and Communication of the KMT Military Council, also known as the Ten Men Group (*shiren tuan*).[5] The first thing Tai Li wanted to do was to establish his own radio network independent of other KMT agencies. But Tai Li did not have any experienced radio experts to operate his signal intelligence. Extensive training was necessary. During the 1932 Sino-Japanese military skirmish in Shanghai, KMT general Hu Zongnan recommended a young radio expert by the name of Wei Daming to Tai Li.

Wei may have been the best radio operator China had at the time. He had worked for the warlord-controlled government in Beijing as a radio expert. For three years he had worked as the top radio man on the pilot ship *Linkong* as that flagship of the British-managed Shanghai Pilot Association guided several dozen ships in and out of Shanghai harbor every day. Wei's skills were such that he could easily identify the nationalities of all the ships in Shanghai by noticing the special ways each ship's radioman tapped the keys.[6]

In March 1927, when Chiang Kai-shek's Northern Expedition Army moved into Shanghai, Wei joined the Nationalist cause and was appointed the chief of Chiang's shortwave radio station in Shanghai.[7] What Tai Li wanted Wei Daming to do for him was simple: to train an elite core of radio intelligence experts. Starting in March 1933, Wei embarked on this arduous training mission at Tai Li's Police Academy in Hangzhou, Zhejiang. The first class of twelve students graduated with high marks.[8] To expand the pool of recruits, Tai Li ordered Wei to set up a secret recruiting station in cosmopolitan Shanghai, where younger, more technically minded youths could be admitted. The cover was a commercial radio training school, where the best and the brightest would be identified and then secretly recruited as Tai Li's agents and sent to the Police Academy for further training in radio intelligence. Wei's training program in Hangzhou lasted until July 1937. A total of eleven classes graduated.[9]

With an elite core of radio experts, Tai Li began to place his assets in various corners of the KMT organization. The Revival Society served as a good conduit for this penetration. The first success came when Tai Li joined hands with the Chinese air force. A fledgling service, with a mere three hundred aircraft, China's air force was then under the tight control of Madame Chiang Kai-shek, who was known to be Tai Li's prime opponent in the ever-fierce KMT factionalism. Yet, the Air Force Academy was located not far from Tai Li's Police Academy, and Generals Zhou Zhirou and Jiang Renjian, superintendent and dean of the Air Force Academy, respectively, happened to be staunch members of Tai Li's Revival Society.

When the war broke out with Japan in July 1937, Tai Li and the Air Force Academy immediately set up air and sea observation stations along the coasts of Zhejiang and Fujian provinces south of Shanghai. The chief targets of reporting were the Japanese ships and airplanes traveling within the triangular area defined by Formosa (Taiwan), a Japanese colony with strategic airfields; Eastern China; and the Japanese home islands. These stations were efficient and were able to report from the coast to Tai Li's headquarters within three to five minutes on the nationalities, types, numbers, directions, speed, and, for aircraft, altitudes of all the passing ships and airplanes.[10]

The glory of Tai Li's radio intelligence came on 14 August 1937, when eighteen Japanese heavy bombers took off from Taiwan en route to destroy the Chinese heavy concentration of aircraft at the Air Force Academy's base. The Chinese planes from this base had bombarded the Japanese warships in Shanghai the day before. Tai Li's agents spotted the enemy planes at his observation stations in Wenzhou and Heishan thirty minutes before they reached their destination. The Chinese air force used this crucial intelligence report and prepared an ambush from a higher altitude. The Japanese were caught completely by surprise, and the Chinese planes slaughtered the enemy. The air battle destroyed six Japanese heavy bombers, with several severely damaged and dropped to the ground on the way back to their base in Taiwan. And the Chinese, with much-inferior planes, suffered only two losses.[11] This triumph makes 14 August China's Air Force Day, which is still observed by the Chinese government in Taiwan. And Tai Li's intelligence was given much credit for this victory, but far more important, the role of Tai Li's radio intelligence gained respectable recognition.

The high point in China's cryptography came when Tai Li broke the Japanese military code. Until 1938, China wasted its radio intelligence resources by using trained operators as mere code clerks and telegraphers who transmitted encrypted cables. A Japanese diplomatic code had been broken with relative ease by the Chinese in 1936, but what really mattered were the Japanese army codes used in the China theater. Many attempts were made against the latter, to no avail. Wei Daming was still in charge of radio intelligence for Tai Li, but no breakthrough had been made. Then an irresistible idea hit upon Tai Li: China should get help from others who knew more about Japanese codes. One person, an American, enjoyed a particular reputation in this area. Herbert Yardley had directed the cryptanalytic services of the United States between 1917 and 1929. He dramatically revealed the American success against Japanese codes and ciphers in a book, *The American Black Chamber*, that brought him fame and the abiding hostility of American intelligence officers.

In 1938 Yardley was wasting his talents in a variety of business schemes and the pursuit of personal pleasure. That summer, Major Xiao Bo (Hsin Ju Pu Hsiao) of the Chinese embassy in Washington, who was, in fact, Tai Li's station chief in the United States, approached Yardley in Queens, New York, and offered him an annual salary of $10,000 to organize a Chinese Black Chamber. Yardley accepted the offer and, traveling under the name "Herbert Osborne," arrived at Chungking, China's wartime capital, in November 1938.

Yardley's experience was less than a resounding success. The codes used by Japan in China in 1938 were different from those he had studied in the 1920s. Yardley did not understand the Japanese language. The dozen or so Japan experts Tai Li provided to work with Yardley understood Japanese well, but they knew little about secret codes. For the time being, Yardley could only provide guidance on the principles of cryptography. Yardley was also profoundly unhappy with the personal arrangements Tai Li had made for him. Undisciplined and decadent, Yardley was prohibited from bringing his girlfriend to China and thus caused constant trouble to Tai Li.[12] Nevertheless, during his stay of one year and a half in China, Yardley did accomplish for Tai Li the advanced training of about two hundred agents in the art of cryptography.

What made the solution of Japanese military codes ever more imperative was the ferocious bombing of Chinese cities, especially Chungking, by Japanese airplanes. The Chinese air force and Claire Lee Chennault's mercenary Flying Tigers (the American Volunteers' Group, AVG) were severely outnumbered and outgunned by the superior Japanese air force. In early May 1939, the bombing of Chungking by the Japanese claimed the lives of forty-four hundred civilians, wounded another thirty-one hundred, and destroyed much of the city. The Chinese air defense and air warning were pitifully inadequate. After wreaking havoc on Chungking, the Japanese planes continued on to the nearby metropolis of Chengdu to drop bombs. During this attack, an enemy plane was shot down and the tail gunner, Oishi Shinzo, who was also the code handler, was captured alive. Wei Daming rushed to Chengdu and took possession of the POW, who showed a willingness to cooperate.[13]

With Yardley's general guidance in the principles of cryptography and with Oishi Shinzo's specific debriefing on the Japanese system, Wei Daming and his team finally broke the Japanese air force code in the late summer and early fall of 1939. The Chinese now knew that the Japanese air force in China used a chart of a hundred groups of kana letters that could easily be decoded despite constant minor changes by Japanese cryptographers.[14] This was a marvelous achievement for Tai Li, who was now able to provide air-warning intelligence more than one hour ahead of the arrival of the Japanese planes. Coded radio traffic to/from Japanese air force bases in Wuhan and Yuncheng, and in-air communications among planes were all promptly intercepted and decoded by Wei Daming's team. The Chinese masses were then able to effectively evacuate into the legendary caves in the hilly city of Chungking, and China's small air force could adopt corresponding tactics.

Yet overall, China's air defense was far from enough, despite extraordinary heroism by the enthusiastic pilots. For example, on 13 September 1940, over the sky of Chungking, thirty-four Chinese aircraft encountered sixty-six invading Japanese planes. The dogfight was nasty, and the Chinese loss was heavy, with twenty-four shot down.[15]

In June 1941, China bought 100 P-40 planes from the United States, but they were still technically inferior to the Japanese Zero planes. Pressured by Chiang Kai-shek to win an air battle, General Mao Bangchu, the Chinese air force commander in chief, in early September 1941, decided to use China's advantage in signal intelligence to deal a blow to the Japanese. P-40 planes were slower than the Zeros, and conventional chase-and-shoot tactics would give the Japanese an advantage by a large margin. General Mao decided to use a head-to-head encounter to directly confront the invading Japanese planes, thus making speed a less important factor in the dogfight. But this required exact and highly accurate air intelligence about Japanese planes' positions, altitude, intentions, targets, and so forth. Wei Daming did not disappoint the general. With accurate signal intelligence, China's P-40s carried out the semisuicidal mission with heroism and won a decisive, albeit rare, victory over the Japanese air force over the sky of Chungking. Once beaten, the Japanese seldom came back again.[16]

By now Tai Li's Bureau of Investigation and Statistics (BIS) enjoyed a commanding lead among various KMT intelligence agencies in decoding Japanese communications. In theory, the central government had five agencies charged with breaking different Japanese codes. The Office of Technological Research (*junweihui jishu yanjiu shi*), created by Wen Yuqing, had the specific target of the Japanese diplomatic code. Facing Tai Li's often-unsubtle challenge, Wen was unhappy in the KMT bureaucratic infighting. He soon found an excuse to go to Hong Kong and never came back. Wen's sudden departure was not taken lightly in Chungking, and he was regarded as a persona non grata and his office became ineffectual.[17]

The Second Division of the Military Operations Department (*junlingbu di-er ting,* the Chinese equivalent of American G-2) under Admiral Yang Xuanchen was supposed to work on the code of the Japanese army, but it in fact was a shadow intelligence agency without much strength. The air force had the Air Intelligence Group (*Hangweihui zhenkong dui*), which was entirely staffed with Wei Daming's radio experts under the complete control of Tai Li. The Zhongtong, under the Organization Department of the Chinese Nationalist Party, also had a group of decoders to tackle the Chinese and Soviet Communist secret codes, but their strength and budget were severely limited. Although in theory BIS was only charged with working on the Japanese-controlled puppet's radio codes, its influence permeated every intelligence agency in the government.

In the SACO enterprise after the Pearl Harbor attacks, one of Tai Li's primary interests was in getting help from the United States about cryptography. Article 18 of the SACO Agreement specifically stipulated that China and the United States would share cryptographic technology. Camp Six of SACO was mainly set up for this purpose. This further enhanced Tai Li's dominant role of code breaking within the KMT. By March 1943, when the central government surveyed every major intelligence agency's budget, Tai Li's BIS received ten times more than its close contender, Zhongtong—$4.8 million versus $0.47 million.[18]

China's most meaningful international cooperation in code breaking was with the British, toward whom the Chinese had ambivalent feelings. As previously mentioned, on the one hand, the British had long adopted an appeasement policy toward the Japanese that culminated in the three-month closure under Japanese pressure of the vital war supply line from Burma to China. On the other hand, since the summer of 1940, Japan had signaled a strong intention of moving southward to threaten Britain's colonial empire in Southeast Asia. The fall of France in June was followed by the entry of Japanese troops into French Indochina in September. At the same time, Germany, Italy, and Japan had officially formed a military alliance. War in East Asia seemed imminent. The British were then forced to approach the Chinese for military cooperation to face a possible Japanese attack on the British colonial empire in the region.

In the fall of 1940, Generals Shang Zhen and Zheng Jiemin led a military delegation to visit British military strongholds in Hong Kong, Burma, and Singapore. Among the most coveted help the British wanted from the Chinese was Tai Li's signal intelligence on the Japanese. After much hesitancy, China agreed to send a cryptanalytic team to Hong Kong. In October 1940, Tai Li's agent, Chen Yibai, went to Hong Kong to make arrangements. The British would be the sole recipient of the decrypted Japanese traffic and would be responsible for local logistics. To protect their methods, the Chinese excluded British personnel from their work spaces. Contact was maintained through a British liaison. In November, a team of fifteen Chinese codebreakers led by Wang Huimin flew from Chungking to Hong Kong. Code named Group 8 (*diba gongzuo dui*), it had eight interception sets and one Chinese-made deciphering machine.[19]

For the next thirteen months, this Chinese team provided the British military authorities in Hong Kong with daily decrypts of Japanese air force, and less frequently navy, traffic to and from Japanese air bases in Swato (Shantou), Fuzhou, Sanzhao Island, and, after April 1941, Canton (Guangzhou).[20] One unexpected result was the interception of communications between British merchants and the Japanese military forces in dealings over contraband. Group 8 provided accurate intelligence on these illicit activities and pressured the Hong Kong government to suppress such trade, which it did.[21]

At 6:00 AM on 8 December 1941, Group 8 intercepted messages ordering Japanese planes to attack Hong Kong. The Chinese promptly passed the decrypts to the British. Within the hour, planes began bombing the city. At the same time, Pearl Harbor was also attacked. For over a week, fierce aerial bombardment never ceased. Hong Kong was thrown into total chaos. During this trying time, Group 8 served as the only air-warning intelligence source in Hong Kong. But on 12 December, the sole British liaison officer was killed during a bombing raid, and contact with the British military authorities was cut off. Group 8 was then forced to relay all decrypts to Chungking. Five days later, Hong Kong surrendered to the Japanese. The members of Group 8 destroyed their equipment and sneaked back to China disguised as refugees.[22]

The tenuous relationship between the British and Chinese in signal intelligence contributed to a major military fiasco on 10 December 1941. Around 10:00 AM that day, BIS's monitoring stations in Chengdu and Chungking intercepted and decoded messages between a Japanese base in Saigon and a Japanese scout plane. The scout plane reported that two large enemy battleships were about one hundred nautical miles off the coast of Singapore. At 11:00 AM, the Chinese heard the message that three groups of Japanese bombers were taking off to destroy the ships. At 1:50 PM, a message from the scout plane reported that the two ships were fatally hit by the Japanese bombers and were gradually sinking and that the names of the two ships were HMS *Prince of Wales* and HMS *Repulse*. Wei Daming promptly reported this to Tai Li, who went immediately to Chiang Kai-shek. Chiang summoned the British ambassador and informed him of the unfortunate news. The ambassador was dumbfounded and refused to believe the news until next morning when London confirmed it.[23] Had there been close intelligence sharing between Britain and China, the British military authorities might have been able to organize some form of air defense and the two capital ships might not have been lost on that fateful day.

The sinking of the two British capital ships and the subsequent surrender of Hong Kong to the Japanese alerted the British to the urgent task of defending the remaining British colonies in Asia. At the time, Singapore and Burma seemed in the greatest danger. For twelve years, the British had been building Singapore into the most valued military stronghold in Southeast Asia. It was absolutely vital to keep it from the Japanese. After the defeat in Hong Kong, London requested that the Chinese send yet another air intelligence team to Singapore. However, the poor performance of the British troops in Hong Kong and elsewhere had raised doubts in Chinese circles. While Zheng Jiemin agreed in principle to the British request, Tai Li insisted on an unexpected condition—he would send the additional team of Chinese codebreakers to Singapore only if the British would give China a coveted new gadget—a set of radar equipment.

The negotiations went back and forth for weeks without agreement. And then, suddenly, the British unconditionally surrendered Singapore and its eighty thousand troops to the Japanese on 15 February 1942. The fall of

Singapore was the most humiliating defeat of the British military in Asia, and, as Winston Churchill put it, constituted "the worst disaster and largest capitulation of British history."[24]

The defense of Burma became yet another thorny issue. China had a vital interest in fending off the Japanese from Burma, which was the only meaningful link to the outside world for military supplies after the fall of Hong Kong. Once again, the British asked the Chinese to contribute an air intelligence team. Tai Li wasted no time and dispatched a twenty-four-man unit of codebreakers, code named Group 6, led by Ni Naibing, to Burma. On 19 January 1942, they flew from Chungking to Lashio and a train took them from there to Rangoon, where they started work immediately. Daily intercepts were given to the British military authorities.[26]

Yet, the British were in complete chaos in Burma, and by mid-February, all signs indicated that the British lines were about to collapse. Worse yet, Chinese air intelligence was tragically ignored on many occasions, which made the Chinese team highly critical of the British command. On 14 March, for example, the Chinese codebreakers read Japanese air force messages indicating that the RAF planes at Magwe airfield were the target of an imminent Japanese bombing sortie. This was immediately relayed to the British headquarters, but no action was taken and the Japanese bombers destroyed the ten RAF planes on the ground.[27] In sharp contrast, the Chinese/American air command in the region under Claire Lee Chennault of the American Volunteers' Group (AVG) had complete confidence in the Chinese Sigint effort and used the intelligence to the fullest extent. To the members of the Chinese cryptanalytic team in Burma and to many other Chinese generals, "AVG" came to mean "Americans Very Good," and "RAF" to mean "Rotten Air Force."[28]

The loss of Burma in April contributed to yet another schism between the Chinese and the British. To the latter, one thing became clear: the Chinese were good at breaking Japanese codes but were nevertheless highly critical of British military performance. Thus, the British concocted a new scheme. After the Chinese codebreakers retreated to Kunming, China, in May 1942, the British asked Tai Li to send a team to India, the last stronghold of British defense in Asia against Japan. Again, the Chinese consented. In October, eighteen cryptanalysts were sent to India. This time the British showed unusual warmth and hospitality. All mechanical equipment was provided by the British, who received the Chinese decrypts with much appreciation. But there was an angle unknown to the Chinese: the British had set up their own interception station in Calcutta and received the same Japanese secret messages the Chinese team did. By comparing the Chinese reports with the encoded Japanese traffic, it did not take long for the British to figure out the keys used by the Chinese to decode the Japanese messages.[29] By the end of 1942, the Chinese team had lost its usefulness to the British. Wei Daming and Tai Li figured out the Anglo scheme and were confirmed in their already strong anti-British sentiment.[30]

What about Chinese cooperation with the Americans in code breaking? The SACO Agreement obliged the two countries to cooperate in this arena. Article 18 of the agreement stipulated that the United States share cryptographic skills and results with the Chinese. This provision was adamantly resisted by the U.S. Army, especially General George C. Marshall, in order to protect the secrecy of the MAGIC endeavor.[31] Throughout the war, the Chinese never received any meaningful cooperation from the United States in this regard.

This profound distrust of Chinese capability to maintain cryptographic secrecy had far-reaching consequences. First, it put an ominous cloud over virtually all major joint intelligence projects between the United States and China. Tai Li and Wei Daming became highly doubtful of American intentions and raised this issue again and again with American high officials. Even William Donovan, the director of the OSS (Office of Strategic Services), was quite embarrassed by the discrepancy between American signature and American commitment on this particular issue. He apologetically admitted to Tai Li in Chungking in 1943 that "not only as a signer of that Agreement, but also as an American citizen, [he] felt that the United States [had not done] its duty with respect to their promise to the Chinese [with regard to Article 18 on cryptographic cooperation]."[32] Secondly, this distrust of Chinese cryptographic security assumed monumental political significance when the British and Americans used this very issue as the most important reason to exclude the Chinese from participating in joint Allied strategic and political planning, especially the fateful meeting in February 1945 at Yalta when the Chinese had much at stake but were curiously absent.

What can we conclude about the code-breaking operations in wartime China? The Chinese cryptological effort testifies to the paramount importance of interservice cooperation. The lack of this cooperation within the bureaucratic maze of the Nationalist government greatly undermined the effectiveness of China's cryptanalysis enterprise. The intriguing international relations and racial politics in East Asia, however, further hampered the usefulness of the Chinese cryptanalysis achievement as a means of Allied war operations. The fundamental distrust and suspicion between colonial British and Nationalist

Chinese famously obviated the strategic value of China's code-breaking skills to the Allied war effort, resulting in lamentable losses both in land battles as well as on the high sea.

While the Chinese achieved remarkable results in code breaking, the overall accomplishment did not assume any meaningful strategic value as did the ULTRA and MAGIC effort. The importance of signal intelligence was vital to the growth of Tai Li's intelligence empire, and he was quick to recognize its value. Yet, in the absence of a modern, mechanized, and consolidated military and industrial might that could deal the enemy a decisive and fatal blow, any excellent intelligence system would lose its relevance and usefulness. In today's world, we often forget that what ultimately wins a war is not intelligence operations alone, however good they may be. This supplementary role of intelligence is often ignored by empire builders, who thereby lay the foundation for their own demise.

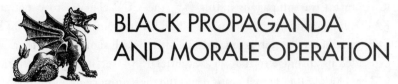

Chapter 9

BLACK PROPAGANDA
AND MORALE OPERATION

WORLD WAR II USHERED IN AN AGE of mass media in China that functioned as a potent instrument of war fighting. Total war in nature, the eight-year conflict in China created an outpouring of mass mobilization through media for the single purpose of defeating the enemies. It was also during World War II that the media in China became a critical part of military operations in the form of war propaganda and intelligence gathering. Yet, in the meantime, the war provided an excellent opportunity for various political and bureaucratic factions in China to publish partisan media outlets to engage in internecine infighting within their own rank.

The outbreak of war in July 1937 tremendously boosted the national unity of China, which had been greatly divided between the Nationalist central government of the Kuomintang Party (KMT) and the Chinese Communist Party (CCP). This national spirit of unity was most pronounced in the sudden surge in numbers of the new publications, all of which carried the central theme of "Resisting Japan." This outpouring of new publications further diversified the formats of Chinese media as well, with a wide variety of dailies, weeklies, fortnightlies, or monthlies. In the Chinese northern city of Tianjin, for example, before the war there had been no more than half a dozen regular publications of all kinds. Within a year and a half, the publicly circulated new publications mushroomed to more than thirty.[1]

However, this unity was also misleading. Under the façade of a national united front against Japan, the Nationalist central government lost control over a significant part of the media publications, because now its rival, the CCP, had a legitimate reason to expand its control over new publications. In fact, it was during the war that the CCP for the first time was able to use such newspapers as the *New China Daily* to propagandize its party line and gained national recognition. In the case of Tianjin, more than half of the new publications were controlled by the CCP.

Furthermore, the war stimulated the great need to set up radio stations to drum up war propaganda. This gave the CCP chances to penetrate the KMT propaganda organizations. The KMT-run Central Broadcasting Radio Station, which was established in 1928 with the call sign XGOA, for example, expanded its coverage to remote areas after 1937. Yet, its key stations nationwide, including the Shanxi Station and the more important Kunming Station, were virtually taken over by the CCP underground agents.[2]

Arguably, part of the reason the KMT lost to the CCP in 1949 was because the CCP was able to gain sizeable control over mass media as propaganda tools during World War II, while the KMT's otherwise rigid press control eroded greatly during the war. In the struggle between unity and disunity, the CCP triumphed sub rosa, which laid the foundation for the demise of the KMT government in 1949.

Never before in Chinese history had mass media become a potent method of war as it did during World War II. On the KMT government side, a vast newspaper enterprise was operated by the intelligence apparatus for the single purpose of gathering intelligence and spreading disinformation to destabilize the enemy's will to fight. Both Wang Pengsheng's Institute of International Research and Tai Li's Bureau of Investigation and Statistics (BIS) ran newspapers and other media outlets for intelligence purposes.

After the Pearl Harbor attacks and the Americans' entry into the China theater, it was the Americans who used the media as a regular method of war on a massive scale. The first American organizations that legitimized the use of media as a war-fighting method were the Office of War Information (OWI) and the OSS (Office of Strategic Services). Both agencies share a common bureaucratic origin. On 11 July 1941, President Franklin Roosevelt authorized the creation of an overall information-gathering organization under William Joseph Donovan. Designated as coordinator of information (COI), Donovan was immediately drawn into two major tasks: war propaganda and intelligence collection on behalf of the U.S. government. For war propaganda, COI began to vigorously recruit agents from the circles of the established media outlets. The National Broadcasting Company (NBC), for example, was tasked to provide technical equipment for COI to set up radio stations on the U.S. West Coast to transmit war propaganda programs to the East Asian theaters of war.

A large number of newspaper reporters answered the call from COI and joined the organization. But before long, a major problem arose among the rank and file of the newly created propaganda and intelligence agency—

propaganda could include two totally different kinds of material. One could be factually accurate and therefore "white," while the other kind of propaganda under wartime exigencies could be fabricated and therefore "black." Both were promoted by Donovan as legitimate means of war fighting. But a significant number of COI employees were uncomfortable with the "black" propaganda and openly challenged the moral ground for conducting factually false wartime propaganda by COI as a U.S. government entity. To solve the dispute, President Roosevelt on 22 June 1942 split the COI into two separate agencies. The Office of War Information would be solely responsible for "white" propaganda, and the Office of Strategic Services would be responsible for "black" propaganda.

But "white" propaganda was to be strictly conducted for the purpose of winning a war. In other words, it was purely an instrument of war fighting, to be closely coordinated with the U.S. military authorities both in Washington and on the battlefields in China. President Roosevelt's directive defines the mission and organization of OWI as follows:

> The Office of War Information will plan, develop and execute all phases of the Federal program of radio, press publications and related foreign propaganda activities involving the dissemination of information. The program for foreign propaganda in areas of actual or projected military operations will be coordinated with military plans through the planning agencies of the War and Navy Departments, and shall be subject to the approval of the Joint Chiefs of Staff. Parts of the foreign propaganda program which are to be executed in a theater of military operations will be subject to the control of the Theater Commander.[3]

In the China theater, OWI operated radio stations at various locations, most prominently Chungking and Kunming, where 50-kilowatt medium-wave broadcasting devices were set up. Radio programs included shows produced and relayed from San Francisco and Hawaii. There were also "live" programs beaming into Japan, Taiwan, and Japanese-occupied areas in China.

Yet, the most notable unit of OWI/China was its Language, Art, and Leaflets Unit, first based in Chungking, and then Kunming. In close collaboration with the U.S. 14th Air Force in Kunming, which was commanded by Major General Claire Lee Chennault, the unit employed a considerable number of artists and writers to produce leaflets for aerial drops in occupied areas. Many millions of psychological warfare leaflets were mass produced and dropped in the China theater by this unit. One unique feature of these leaflets was bombing warnings for the Chinese civilians living near the target areas. A typical leaflet would read something like this example from a bombing warning message to the people of the city Nanchang, Jiangxi Province:

> Friends of Nanchang: Our air forces are going to bomb your city. As you well know the Japanese are making valuable use of Nanchang and we must blast them out. That is war. We do not wish to harm a single Chinese. Therefore, friends of Nanchang, we ask you to evacuate the city. Get as far away as possible. Our planes will come again and again. They will keep coming until they have flattened the Japanese and all rail and storage places that are vital to the Japanese in their war against China. Friends of Nanchang, act quickly. Leave the city. The bombings are coming![4]

In light of the large-scale collaboration with the Japanese, vigorous propaganda was also conducted against the puppet troops. "Soldier, if you continue to serve the Japanese," one leaflet reads, "you will be throwing yourselves into an abyss. You will be considered enemies by both loyal Chinese and Americans. The line between friend and foe has become sharply drawn." To make the purpose of such propaganda perfectly understood, the leaflet continues, "Soldiers, now is the time for you to make your choice. Now is the time to change sides. Leave the Japanese or go down with them to destruction. Make your choice swiftly—time is short!"[5]

Of course, one of the most serious problems in wartime China was the protection and rescue of downed American pilots. For this, the "white" propaganda produced an inordinate amount of material to educate the Chinese population in the areas of aerial operations to identify and protect the downed American pilots. "The American airman is a comrade in arms," one leaflet reads, "Before his arrival, the Japanese bombed your towns and villages at will. Then came the pilots of the A.V.G—Chennault's Flying Tigers—and later the hard-hitting 14th Air Force, and the 20th [Bomber Division under Curtis LeMay]. The Japanese planes were driven away. Few American airmen are shot down . . . yet those few men are dear to their country, and invaluable for the protection of China." Specific instructions are also given in this leaflet. "If any [American airmen] parachute down in your vicinity hide them quickly so the Japanese won't learn about them. Then cautiously get in touch with reliable men who will help the Americans to safety. Your reward will be great."[6]

While all the "white" propaganda conducted by the OWI was to be traceable to an American source and reflected the official policies of the United States government, the "black" propaganda conducted by OSS was strictly and deliberately to be misleading and psychologically damaging so as to affect the enemy's will to fight. From the beginning of the war, Donovan had argued, successfully, that during a war, it was absolutely justifiable to use the media to "fabricate propaganda, rumor and news, and to disseminate the same, whether true or false, to promote or incite resistance, revolution, and sabotage of all kinds."[7] As such, a wartime organization was set up and became active in China during the war when the Americans were involved. It was called the Morale Operation (MO) branch of the OSS, the function of which was purely to engage in "black propaganda," that is, to make up rumors and other disinformation to confuse and affect the Japanese morale in China.

Based in Chungking and Kunming, the MO branch employed mostly journalists and artists, including the long-time *Wall Street Journal* Tokyo correspondent, Raymond Cromley; the journalist Elizabeth MacDonald; and the cartoonist William Smith. An OSS MO report to Washington in November 1944 lists many examples of the rumors made up by its China operatives and spread to the Japanese occupied areas. They include "parody of [Japanese] battlefield code—exact facsimile of captured [Japanese] code book with text satirizing the foolishness of [Japanese] ethics in demanding sacrifice for insincere and selfish leaders;" and "faked [Japanese] leaflet—purporting to come from [Japanese] Army, leaflet telling of coming of southern Burmese troops into Burma [distasteful to northern Burmese] distributed by O.S.S. agents behind [Japanese] lines."[8] The same report also states the establishment of MO bases in Kandy (in today's Sri Lanka), Delhi, Nazira, Kweilin, and Chungking, and the fact that "Chinese agents [were] trained and organized into 2 MO teams sent to Canton and Macao to establish intelligence network and acquire printing facilities for creation and distribution of subversive propaganda."[9]

The Japanese Communist Party chief, Sanzo Nozaka, or as the Americans called him, Okano Susumu, was staying with the Chinese Communist Party leadership in Yenan throughout most of the war. He became an adviser to the OSS MO operations and helped the Americans operate black propaganda radio stations beaming at the Japanese homeland as well as the Japanese occupation army in China. The Japanese Communist chief earnestly advised the OSS MO personnel that OSS's propaganda texts were often written in too haughty a tone, which would not be very effective on the Japanese soldiers. In addition, Sanzo Nozaka volunteered to help the OSS in facilitating intelligence penetration into Japanese-occupied zones, especially Manchuria.[10]

For his help, Sanzo Nozaka demanded that the Americans pay him $400,000 in the Japanese Federal Reserve Currency for North China.[11]

The most elaborate wartime newspaper enterprise used as a military operation was the *Shanghai Evening Post and Mercury*. First established by American expatriates in Shanghai in 1929, this publication grew into a respectable and influential newspaper in China. Initially, it was published in English. Its Chinese edition began publishing in 1933, with great success. In December 1937, the Japanese military authorities in Shanghai tried to close down the Chinese edition, but it was owned by American interests. As a result, the *Shanghai Evening Post and Mercury* was allowed to publish inside Japanese-occupied Shanghai until 8 December 1941, when the Japanese military moved into the foreign settlements and closed down both the English- and the Chinese-language editions of the paper at a time when its Chinese-language edition alone enjoyed a circulation of forty thousand.

One year later, in December 1942, C. V. Starr, the principal owner of the *Shanghai Evening Post and Mercury*, offered his newspaper to the OSS as a cover to gather intelligence and conduct MO operations against the Japanese. As a senior OSS special intelligence officer reasoned, "Newspapermen everywhere are expected to stick their noses into everybody's business. No suspicion attached to their curiosity. A newspaper is therefore automatically almost indestructible cover for the collection of information."[12]

On 1 January 1943, the OSS took on Starr's offer and started the New York edition of the *Shanghai Evening Post and Mercury* as an intelligence-gathering operation. On 31 October 1943, the Chungking edition was also started. These two newspapers were to last until the end of the war as an OSS intelligence project. By July 1944, the OSS had spent $350,000 on these two publications. Veteran journalists were sent to Chungking to collect information for the OSS. By July 1944, eighteen months after its initiation as an OSS project, the *Shanghai Evening Post and Mercury* was able to boast great success: "Data on over 5,000 individuals has been assembled and carefully edited—covering Japanese, Koreans, European and American suspects, Chinese, Indo-Chinese, Thais, Malays, Burmese and Indian puppets and collaborators." Also accomplished was a huge body of intelligence reports and analysis—fifteen hundred papers in all—on a variety of subjects ranging from "Japanese Americans in China," to "Japanese Gendarmerie," to "Currency Warfare in China," and to "Penetration of Christian Church by Japanese."[13]

Media serving as war propaganda and intelligence operations can also have its problems. As is normal in many societies, the most talented and most effective elements in conducting consciousness-raising propaganda are the radicals of different extreme ideological persuasions. In wartime China, many of those hired by the propaganda units of the military turned out to be radical leftists who were talented in the art of making people excited and who had unequivocally pro-Communist sentiments. During the war and immediately afterward, as reported by the U.S. naval attaché in China, "it is a commonly held belief among Chinese newspapermen that many of the Chinese staff of the USIS [the United States Information Service, of which the OWI was the predecessor] are definitely pro-Communist and Leftist, from the Chief Chinese editor . . . on down the line."[14]

Another problem was the amateurish approach by the media professionals to intelligence gathering, causing frequent headaches to the military authorities. Occasionally, these embarrassments rocked the high commands in both Washington and Chungking. One notorious example is the case of Theodore White of *Time Magazine*, who was sent to China during the war. White served General Joseph Stilwell as his top civilian media person for political intelligence in the intriguing world of Chungking officialdom. General Stilwell regarded the recapture of Burma and the planned reconstruction of the Burma Road to China as his top military priorities, while many of his colleagues and superiors, noticeably Chiang Kaishek, had serious doubts about Stilwell's agenda. Understandably, Stilwell was extremely sensitive about Washington's attitude toward his top priorities. White had developed a large pool of informants within the Chinese government at the time. In February 1944, when Stilwell was most anxious to get Washington's firm support for his plans, Theodore White furnished Stilwell with an astonishing piece of "intelligence" that the Chinese ambassador, Wei Daoming, had just come back from the White House carrying a personal letter from the president to Chiang that said President Roosevelt believed the Burma road was not worth getting. "Even if the Burma Road were reopened it could not truck in one tenth the supplies needed to reequip the Chinese Armies for a large offensive. . . . We hope that by the end of 1945 we can finish off Japan. Perhaps the Burma Road will never need be reopened."[15]

Stilwell loudly protested to Washington, which led President Roosevelt to a state of absolute fury. "I have carefully checked the files," the president angrily wrote to Admiral William Leahy, the chairman of the Joint Chiefs of Staff, "and find that I have no letter even remotely resembling the information given out by Ambassador Wei. Frankly, in view of this, I think that we should run down this story, verify it, and get a denial from Ambassador Wei."[16] The U.S. Army immediately conducted a frantic investigation and concluded that "[Theodore] White attached too great importance to his informant's story of his conversation with Wei and erroneously assumed that this was the factual contents of the letter."[17] Thus, a potentially serious diplomatic crisis was quietly dropped. Unfortunately, incidents such as this caused by media professionals' amateurish intelligence-gathering attempts were numerous.

Newspapers reporters, columnists, or radio program editors are people of connections. They feed each other stories and information as a way of life. When a significant number of these newsmen joined intelligence agencies in China, they often caused a major security problem. In the OSS-run *Shanghai Evening Post and Mercury*, for example, a gossip column on 16 October 1943 disclosed the identity of two of the active agents working in Chungking at the time. This incident prompted an alert within the counterintelligence branch of OSS's Washington headquarters.[18] Another glaring example concerns the appalling leak of intelligence reports to the widely read columnist, Drew Pearson, which led to a scathing protest from the Chinese informant who provided this intelligence, accusing the American intelligence officials of endangering the informant's life.[19]

World War II/China was remarkable for its fierce internal bickering among various factions. The CBI theater officially stands for China-Burma-India theater, but instead was widely depicted as "Constant Bickering Inside." To advance partisan causes and bureaucratic turf claims, all sides used media as a weapon of self-promotion and intentional leaking, through newspapers aimed to denigrate others or sabotage other's policies. The top U.S. commanders in China, General Joseph Stilwell and General Claire Chennault, were hostile toward each other on almost every issue and deeply despised each other personally. To enhance their personal images, both Stilwell and Chennault used veteran correspondents to promote themselves in China and in the United States. Surrounding Stilwell were partisan reporters such as Theodore White and Jack Beldon, who wrote countless dispatches glowingly praising the very controversial general. Equally media conscious was Chennault, whose primary image maker was the very powerful journalist, Joseph Alsop, working inside Chennault's Kunming headquarters.

But the most partisan role the media played in wartime China involved the promotion of the Chinese Communists by foreign journalists. Contrary to popular perception, the wartime media control by the KMT-ruled government was quite ineffective for the most part. The press office in charge of media censorship and wartime reporting was under Chiang Kai-shek's confidante, Hollington Tong. He was publicly resented by the foreign journalists who had flocked to China during the war. Many of them were pro-Communist and disliked the KMT ideologically. Israel Epstein, Agnes Smedley, Anna Louise Strong, Ilona Ralf Suess, and Gunther Stein, among others, were vigorous promoters of the Chinese Communist Party in their partisan reporting for major newspapers in the Western democracies. Yet, others not predisposed to be ideologically strident, such as Tilman Durdan, Harrison Foreman, James Young, Brooks Atkinson, and Maurice Votaw, were frequently unhappy about any wartime restrictions on news reporting. Such resentment against the Nationalist central government finally created a dramatic episode in June 1944, when a large delegation of journalists visited Yenan, the CCP stronghold in North China. This was a windfall for the CCP, and it was thoroughly exploited as a propaganda event to champion the CCP's "democratic reforms" and the Communists' "love" of President Roosevelt's "Four Freedoms."[20]

In addition to these visiting journalists praising the CCP, there were also a few permanent media personnel in Yenan promoting partisan causes. The Soviet TASS news agency had its permanent reporter in Yenan, which is not surprising. But the more interesting case is Michael Lindsay, who had been the press officer in the British embassy in China previously, but who went to Yenan in early 1942 and stayed there until the war's end. Lindsay, a British aristocrat soaked with blue blood, vociferously championed Mao's guerilla war against the Japanese.[21] In fact, a senior KMT press officer admits that the wartime management of foreign reporting in China had been mostly a failure and was by no means effective.[22]

The partisan nature of wartime media in China can also be seen through the countless incidents of intentional press leaking designed to influence the policymaking process. Much top secret information was given to influential newspaper men for publication. Drew Pearson, the most powerful gossip and political columnist in the United States during World War II, often dished out astonishingly embarrassing details of bureaucratic infighting related to the China theater.[23] Perhaps the ultimate climax of this pernicious partisan manipulation of media in order to influence government policy is the *Amerasia* case, in which many top secret U.S. government documents were illegally provided to the pro-Communist magazine for publication. This case serves as a good point to usher in a new war, that is, the Cold War, both in China and the in the United States.

Chapter 10

AN ARMY OF ONE
Stilwell's Chinese Vinegar

THE MISSION OF GENERAL JOSEPH STILWELL to China was the single most contentious issue of all U.S. policies in East Asia during the entire war. From the very beginning of this appointment, trouble was brewing. This gradually snowballed into the biggest fiasco of Sino-American relations during this period and fundamentally affected the postwar development of China.

Weeks after the Pearl Harbor attack, plans were under way in Chungking and Washington to send an "eminent American general" to China to take charge of the American side of military affairs in the China-India-Burma theater of war and, in particular, to be in charge of distributing the Lend-Lease materiel to the Chinese. Initially, the very eminent General Hugh Drum was chosen to go to Chungking and was already in the process of packing for departure. Yet in America, while politics may be local, military affairs often tend to be personal. The U.S. Army chief of staff, General George C. Marshall, strenuously objected to Drum's appointment to China for personal reasons. Marshall instead forced Secretary of War Henry Stimson to replace General Drum with Marshall's old subordinate, a much lower-ranking officer, Brigadier General Joseph Stilwell.

A bilious curmudgeon with long experience in China, mostly as a military intelligence officer in the capacity of military attaché in various provinces, Stilwell had long developed an utter contempt for Chinese Nationalist leaders, especially Chiang Kai-shek. In addition, Stilwell, widely known by his nickname "Vinegar Joe" for his acid tongue, was perhaps not the best one to choose to be posted in China at a time when diplomatic finesse was required as the prerequisite in dealing with the Chinese, the British, and various other hard-to-get-along-with elements.

Perhaps the most crucial part of the Stilwell appointment to China was the granting to Stilwell of control over the China-bound Lend-Lease materiel, which was a crucial event in the U.S. military aid to China during the war.

It came about as a result of a series of negotiations involving T. V. Soong. As China's chief representative in Washington, Soong became Chiang's plenipotentiary in mapping out the role and functions of Stilwell's China mission. Before the Pearl Harbor attack, one of the persistent problems China had with regard to the Lend-Lease materiel had been interdiction of the China-bound materiel by the British in Rangoon. This was illustrated by the SS *Tulsa* incident, in which the British took the defense materiel in Burma on the SS *Tulsa* that were originally part of the China allotment of the Lend-Lease program.[1]

Soong had been wistfully hoping the U.S. government would more actively intervene in such disputes and send someone to Asia to make sure the British would not develop this behavior into a pattern. Furthermore, the timing of the Stilwell appointment was extraordinary, because it was during the days when the U.S. government had just approved a generous loan of $500 million for China. In a fit of momentary giddiness, profoundly grateful to the Americans, T. V. Soong in late January 1942 agreed to a fateful set of documents specifying Joseph Stilwell's role in his new mission to China, put forward to him by General George Marshall through Henry Stimson. As recorded by Soong himself in a memo to Stimson on 30 January, "I wish to confirm our understanding that the functions of the U.S. Army Representative [Stilwell] are to be generally as follows: To supervise and control all U.S. defense aid affairs for China; to command under the Generalissimo all U.S. Forces in China and such forces as may be assigned to him; to represent the U.S. Government on any international war council in China and act as Chief of Staff for the Generalissimo."[2]

This was a monumental decision when it comes to military aid to China. Stilwell had his mind set on one ultimate goal: to wrest command of the entire Chinese army from Chiang Kai-shek and place it under his control. He wanted to control the Chinese army, reform it, and command it. Though Chiang was Stilwell's superior on paper, in reality, Stilwell was hoping to exert de facto control. As Stilwell put it himself, "In carrying out Chiang Kai-shek's instructions, I carry out command." When asked by Marshall and Stimson to go to China, Stilwell immediately announced his condition for taking this job, "Either they [the Chinese] refuse and I don't go, or they accept [his command over the entire Chinese army]."[3] This was a highly inappropriate demand, especially considering that in early 1942 the Americans, British, and Dutch were being soundly defeated by the Japanese and that China had stood alone against the Japanese for more than four years.

To satisfy Stilwell's demand, an elaborate scheme was worked out to ensure that Stilwell would ultimately get his command of the Chinese army. The central part of the scheme was to give Stilwell complete control over the China-bound Lend-Lease materiel as bargaining leverage over Chiang Kai-shek. Consequently, throughout his tenure until his unceremonious recall in late October 1944, Stilwell used his control over the Lend-Lease materiel to force Chiang into doing whatever Stilwell wanted done and used his power to satisfy his desire for command by granting favors to one particular Chinese commander over the others. In the end, Stilwell's inattention and chaotic management style over the Lend-Lease materiel prevented much larger amounts of American military aid from going to China. In other words, in the internecine struggle for command power between Chiang and Stilwell, the U.S. military aid program to China became a victim, which greatly contributed to the scanty quantity and variety of the military hardware that was requested and specified by the Chinese military authorities.

That Stilwell was given such enormous power as the ultimate authority over the China-bound Lend-Lease materiel was quite unusual. In theory, all Lend-Lease materiel, once shipped outside of the U.S. border, belonged to the recipient country, which then had the sole power of distribution. If at the beginning Chiang Kai-shek and T. V. Soong failed to realize how powerful Stilwell had become as the Lend-Lease czar, it took them only a few months of Stilwell's using his power as a club dangling over China's head to realize that he had to be separated from his military duties.

But before T. V. Soong's efforts could have any effect, there was another major factor that predetermined Stilwell's stormy tenure in China: the contentious issue of strategic priority of the war efforts. As we have seen, from the beginning of the Sino-Japanese war in 1937, the bulk of China's foreign military hardware was related to air force materiel. These supplies were the most urgent items China received from the Soviet Union. The core of Soviet military involvement in combat in the China theater was Soviet air force personnel. When the Americans began to replace the Soviets as China's major source of foreign military aid, China continued to place its priority on building a strong air defense. Especially with Claire Lee Chennault's coming to China early in the war, and the brilliant performance of Chennault's American Volunteers' Group (AVG) before and after the Pearl Harbor attack, air force gained a prominent place in China's strategic thinking. Throughout his cooperation with the United States in the war, Chiang Kai-shek persistently asked that more American aircraft be sent to China. More important was Chiang's unfettered confidence in Chennault as an able commander.

As discussed earlier, the importance placed on airpower and Chennault's role in the war profoundly disturbed the War Department's plans for the China theater. On strategy, the War Department had come to an overwhelming decision even before the Pearl Harbor attack with regard to the most crucial war effort in China: to keep the Burma Road open so that American weapons could move into China in large volume.

The Army did have a valid point in emphasizing recapturing the Burma Road. The extraordinary scantiness of Lend-Lease materiel China received during World War II was not entirely the result of a lack of will on the part of the Allies, especially the United States. Throughout China's epic struggle for survival and for victory, China was plagued with one particularly acute problem—how to defeat Japan's grand strategy of cutting off China's lifeline connecting it to the outside world. China had virtually no defense industry of its own when the war broke out in 1937. Its entire modern equipment of arms had to be imported from the outside. When the Japanese realized they could not break China's will to fight, they soon resorted to securing the key routes that had been supplying China with arms and other war materiel. And the Burma Road was the most crucial link to China's war efforts at the time.

General Stilwell arrived in China in February 1942 with this Burma Road obsession, only to be met with a humiliating rout in Burma by the Japanese. The agony of defeat in Burma further tied the War Department's Burma obsession to Stilwell's personal glory in regaining Burma. Until his final recall in October 1944, Stilwell, who alone controlled the crucial Lend-Lease materiel, focused his military efforts on retaking Burma with a vengeance.

Consequently, Chiang's emphasis on airpower and Stilwell's emphasis on building China's ground forces to retake Burma became a central point of contention when it came to the acquisition and distribution of the Lend-Lease items. While Stilwell tried strenuously to allocate the maximum amount of materiel for the "X" forces in India and the "Y" forces in Yunnan for the Burma campaign, and cared about little else, Chiang Kai-shek relentlessly pushed Stilwell and lobbied the White House to give emphasis to strengthening airpower in China. As General Marshall bitterly complained to President Franklin Roosevelt toward the end of the war, " From the beginning of the war, we have insisted on the necessity for building up the combat efficiency of the Chinese ground forces as the only method of providing the necessary security for our air bases in China. The pressure on us from the Generalissimo throughout the war has been to increase the tonnage over the hump for Chennault's air in particular, with the equipment and supply for the ground forces as incidental only."[4]

Before the loss of Burma in April 1942, Stilwell had an ambitious plan of equipping sixty divisions of infantry troops for China.[5] After the loss of Burma, Stilwell became single-mindedly determined to take back Burma and would not give much Lend-Lease tonnage to other services, especially Chennault's air force in China. In fact, when Washington time and again tried to redeploy air components already stationed in China to other theaters of war, Stilwell barely registered any protest to keep them while Chiang became furious over these deployments. As far as the Lend-Lease materiel was concerned, Chiang wanted Stilwell to devote most of the tonnage to strengthen Chennault's air force. When Stilwell persistently stonewalled Chiang's numerous requests, Chiang took the issue directly to Washington, which further antagonized Stilwell. Time and again, at the highest level of Sino-U.S. decision making, Chiang's demands for more Lend-Lease tonnage for Chennault's air force came through loud and clear. Almost every telegram or cable Chiang sent to Roosevelt carried a central plea—give more aircraft and more airpower to Chennault.

In a somber and sad way, it was almost as if the U.S. Army represented by Generals Marshall and Stilwell, and the Chinese armed forces, represented by Chiang Kai-shek and General Chennault, were fighting two different wars, each demanding control over the limited delivery of the Lend-Lease military hardware. It is fair to say that the clash between Chiang and Chennault's obsession with airpower, and Marshall and Stilwell's obsession with the Burma campaign and ground troops, defines the essence of the Sino-U.S. military cooperation during World War II. Chiang's relentless push for airpower backfired in Washington, providing the basic background for Stilwell's harsh demand for immediate takeover of the Chinese army in the summer and fall of 1944, which itself backfired, resulting in the bitter recall of Stilwell.

This bureaucratic and military disagreement over strategy and service priority greatly aggravated personal feelings among the leading figures in the wartime alliance. Stilwell became virulently defiant of his superior commander, Chiang Kai-shek, while Chiang was seriously doubtful of Stilwell's military judgment and command capability, Chennault remained loyal to Chiang and turned eternally hostile to Washington's stonewalling against his military plans.

Yet overall, with direct orders from Roosevelt and the Joint Chiefs of Staff, and as a result of Chiang Kai-shek and T. V. Soong's vigorous lobbying, Stilwell was forced to provide 70 percent of the overall Lend-Lease materiel to Chennault's air force in China, with Chennault constantly demanding more. But the total amount was very small and did not constitute anything significant—the entire Hump airlift sent to China throughtout the war was 650,000 short tons of materiel, mostly gasoline and oil, with about 60 percent of it shipped to China after Stilwell's recall. As Arthur Young put it in perspective, "This was only about equal to the cargo capacity of 70 Liberty ships, and was small relative to China's need. Shortages greatly limited the fighting that could be done in and from China."[6]

In the end, Stilwell abandoned his ambitious plan to equip and train sixty Chinese armies with the American equipment. Instead, he focused on his "X" force of two Chinese divisions in India for the Burma campaign and refused to provide any weapons and other armaments to Chiang's other forces, with the exception of the "Y" force of several divisions in Yunnan, also allocated to the Burma campaign. With Stilwell's recall, the Chennault/Stilwell internecine fight was finally over in China, which provided an impetus for both increasing Chennault's airpower and enhancing the training programs of the Chinese ground forces. While Stilwell was only able to essentially train and equip several Chinese divisions, General Albert Wedemeyer, Stilwell's successor from November 1944, was engaged in, with complete Chinese cooperation, training and equipping more than thirty divisions of the Kuomintang (KMT) forces.[7]

How Stilwell was fired from his China job was symbolic of the nature of the wartime Sino-U.S. relationship. The central figure in the general's downfall was Chiang's brother-in-law, T. V. Soong. As we have seen earlier, Soong particularly regretted that he had initially agreed to Stilwell's job description. If his initial compliance with Marshall and Stimson's proposal concerning Stilwell's role and function in January 1942 constituted an "original sin," Soong very quickly began a saga of redeeming himself by engaging in a vigorous recall campaign against Stilwell. The first salvo from Soong was fired in July 1942, only six months after Stilwell's appointment. At that time, Stilwell was demanding direct control of the Chinese army and Chiang strongly objected. This led to acrimonious hairsplitting interpretations of the January 1942 Stimson/Soong Memorandum specifying Stilwell's China mission. Soong seized on the military fiasco at Burma, with which Stilwell was closely associated, as well as Stilwell's bad reputation for arrogance and a foul mouth to launch a campaign to recall Stilwell, with the central request that the American military commander in China be disassociated from control over the Lend-Lease materiel. With Chiang's acquiescence, in mid-July 1942, Soong started consultation sessions with the War Department in Washington to recall Stilwell.[8]

General George Marshall reacted violently to Soong's recall request and drafted a harshly worded cable for President Roosevelt, backing Stilwell and stressing the point that even if Stilwell were to be recalled, his successor would still be granted control over the Lend-Lease materiel. Startled by the War Department's hostile reaction, Soong appealed to President Roosevelt not to send the Marshall-drafted cable to Chiang Kai-shek to prevent a diplomatic blowup. Roosevelt agreed to Soong's plea, with the condition that Soong would not tell Chiang about the War Department's angry reaction. Sensing the timing was bad, Soong complied and dropped the issue quietly, for the time being.[9]

Soong's redemption efforts to recall Stilwell and salvage the Lend-Lease program to China resurged with much stronger force in September 1943. On 8 September, Soong sent a proposal to Chiang to request a recall demand. Along with the proposal, Soong included a document called "the China Theater Reorganization Plan," which contemplated the idea of adding a "deputy supreme commander" under Chiang, which would be Stilwell. The role of Chiang's chief of staff currently held by Stilwell would be a Chinese officer, with his deputy being an American officer. China would also be represented in the Combined Chiefs of Staff and the Lend-Lease armaments distribution committee, where Chinese representation had been excluded.[10] Chiang agreed to Soong's proposal, because this would either make Stilwell a titular "deputy supreme commander" without any real command power or lead to Stilwell's recall.

On 15 September 1943, Soong sent a memo to Harry Hopkins in the White House to make the proposal. The idea went around the White House and the War Department, with the president and General Marshall tempted by Soong's reasoning. Yet, when Soong accompanied Lord Admiral Louis Mountbatten and the U.S. Service of Supply chief, General Brehon B. Somervell, to Chungking to meet Chiang in early October 1943, Stilwell's almost certain recall was suddenly halted because Chiang Kai-shek had unexpectedly changed his mind. Historians have speculated on the complicated reasons, but they generally agree that three factors led to Chiang's about-face. First, Stilwell had gotten wind of his approaching recall and panicked. He turned to Chiang and pleaded for mercy, promising future cooperation and friendliness; second, Madame Chiang and, her sister, Madame H. H. Kung, became profoundly jealous of the possible takeover by T. V. Soong of Stilwell's power over the Lend-Lease materiel distribution. As the women closest to Chiang in Chungking, the two Soong sisters vigorously lobbied Chiang on Stilwell's behalf and changed Chiang's mind; third, the planned Cairo Conference was in sight, and Chiang did not want to dampen the good spirit of an important Allied summit by demanding the recall of America's top military officer from China.[11] Consequently, Soong's effort to recall Stilwell was thwarted again.

But the problem of command and control of the Lend-Lease materiel continued. In the Spring of 1944, the Japanese launched the Ichigo campaign, which was aimed at immobilizing the Allied air bases in East China. Yet, Stilwell and Chiang clashed on basic strategies. Stilwell wanted to drive the Japanese out of Burma and regain control over the Burma Road, while Chiang saw the danger of fighting alone in Burma without large-scale Allied amphibious landing in southern Burma. Chiang also believed that if a significant number of troops were redeployed to aid the Burma campaign, the Japanese would certainly seize the opportunity to attack the rest of the fronts on China's mainland, causing the collapse of the entire Chinese theater. Fundamentally, this was a classic struggle between a general obsessed with one particular battle and a generalissimo concerned with the overall war situation.

Here again, the Americans showed extraordinary heavy-handedness in forcing a reluctant Chiang to comply with a campaign in Burma that he did not believe worth fighting. Stilwell and Marshall played key roles in the rude treatment of Chiang and directly used Stilwell's power with the Lend-Lease materiel as a weapon against Chiang. On 3 April 1944, General Marshall drafted a cable for Roosevelt to be sent to Chiang Kai-shek. This extraordinarily blunt cable, signed by Roosevelt, includes the following passage:

> It is inconceivable to me that your "Y" forces, with their American equipment, would be unable to advance against the Japanese 56th Division in its present depleted strength. . . . To take advantage of just such an opportunity, we have, during the past year, been equipping and training your "Y" forces. If they are not to be used in the common efforts, to fly in equipment and to furnish instructional personnel have not been justified. They should not be held back on the ground that an amphibious operation against the South Burma Coast is necessary prior to their advance. Present developments negate such a requirement.[12]

When this Marshall-drafted cable was sent to Chungking verbatim, Madame Chiang Kai-shek was shocked by the condescendingly harsh tone and had to tone down the wording before showing it to Chiang Kai-shek.[13]

Clearly, the essence of the clash between China and the United States was over who was really in charge of the Allied forces in China. Chiang Kai-shek envisioned the importation of the American Lend-Lease materiel to support military actions under his command and direction, while the Americans viewed the military aid only as a means to force China to accept American

military strategies in the China theater irrespective of Chiang's own judgment. The explosive nature of this relationship was fully illustrated when the
showdown finally came in the summer and fall of 1944.

After repeated failures to steamroll Chiang into sending more troops to
northern Burma, Stilwell mobilized all his lobbying power in Washington,
especially Army Chief of Staff George Marshall, to force Chiang to comply
with his demands. The first attempt to prod Chiang into action was the threat
of using the Chinese Communist military forces in the North, which resulted
in the dispatch of the Dixie Mission to Yenan. Then on 4 July 1944, Stilwell
and his political advisers, most notably John Paton Davies, drafted a series of
proposals and used the War Department and Joint Chief of Staff channel to
have them presented to President Roosevelt. The essential demand as reflected
in these proposals was the immediate handover of Chiang's command of the
entire Chinese army to Stilwell. Again, President Roosevelt signed the cable
prepared by the Army and sent it to Chiang. Chiang was shocked by the blunt
demand but could do little about it, because of China's abject need for the
U.S. Lend-Lease materiel that was under Stilwell's control. On 8 July, Chiang
replied to Washington, agreeing to give Stilwell the command, with two pleas:
let the transfer of this command to Stilwell be gradual and send to China
a presidential envoy "with farsighted political vision and ability" to "constantly collaborate with me" and to adjust the relations between me and General
Stilwell so as to enhance the cooperation between China and America."[14]

It must be pointed out that General Marshall, in Washington, played a
crucial role during the so-called "Stilwell Incident." He was the man who
drafted all the presidential memos to Chiang Kai-shek with strong and harsh
tones, for which the president often felt embarrassed and constantly tried to
tone down. Roosevelt was deeply struck by Chiang's statement in his 8 July
reply to Washington's demand, which summed up the root of the problem
between China and the United States: "Military cooperation in its absolute
sense," Chiang declared to Roosevelt, "must be built on the foundation of
political cooperation." About this, Roosevelt believed "there is a great deal in
what the Generalissimo says."[15]

Yet, Marshall did not think much of what Chiang had to say. On 8 August
1944, Marshall drafted a memo in the name of the president for Chiang Kai-
shek, demanding that Chiang immediately hand over to Stilwell complete
command of the entire Chinese armed forces. This time Roosevelt handled
it with more care, personally penciling out all the offensive wording in the
memo and waiting three days before it was sent to Chungking.[16] But while
the president was busy in Quebec with the Anglo-American strategic confer-

ence, Stilwell, in Chungking, fed the War Department inflammatory cables accusing Chiang Kai-shek of intentionally delaying actions and insisting he should be held personally responsible for losing East China to the Japanese. Again, Roosevelt signed all the cables to Chiang Kai-shek prepared by the War Department.

Chiang grew furious over the flurry of insulting cables with hostile tones, all signed by the president from the White House. But this time, Chiang Kai-shek was going to win this showdown with the U.S. Army. Two persons proved crucial in the final downfall of Stilwell. The first person was T. V. Soong, who was now back in Chungking at Chiang's side. Soong pointed out to Chiang how the White House presidential documents were prepared and convinced Chiang of one important fact: Roosevelt's harshly worded cables in recent months were most likely written and prepared by the War Department and did not necessarily represent Roosevelt's actual thoughts. Therefore, Soong told Chiang, China should stand absolutely firm this time to get rid of Stilwell, and President Roosevelt might actually back this.[17]

Any doubt of Soong's wisdom was cast away when on 18 September 1944, a spectacular cable written by the president himself was sent to Chiang directly from Quebec at the conclusion of the Allied strategy session. In this cable, Roosevelt glowingly praised Chiang and the Chinese efforts in fighting the Japanese, a tone sharply different from the series of cables Chiang had been receiving lately. "The heroic effort of your forces," Roosevelt wrote Chiang, was most admired and appreciated by the Allies. The president further informed Chiang that the British, led by Lord Louis Mountbatten, would launch an amphibious attack from South Burma in aid of China.

Chiang was elated by this friendly and encouraging cable from FDR and was further convinced that the president might not be a firm backer of Stilwell after all and that he might still be willing to listen to him. On 25 September 1944, Chiang Kai-shek dropped a bombshell by informing the president that he had changed his mind and would resolutely refuse to give command of the Chinese army to Stilwell. Both Stilwell and Marshall were stunned by Chiang's bluntness. Ten days later, President Roosevelt agreed to Chiang's request and suggested that Stilwell be relieved of duties as the overall overseer of the U.S. Lend-Lease materiel to China and as Chiang's chief of staff.[18] But the president also accepted General Marshall's desperate plea to keep Stilwell as the commander of all the Chinese forces in Yunnan and Burma, to which Chiang Kai-shek flatly refused on 9 October 1944. Again, Roosevelt agreed with Chiang and announced the total recall of Stilwell from China on 25 October 1944.

The second person who proved instrumental in helping Roosevelt gain the Chinese perspective, which led to Stilwell's downfall, was Patrick Hurley, who was sent to China at Chiang's request as the U.S. presidential special envoy in the summer of 1944. There was a particularly peculiar system of communications and file keeping in the Roosevelt White House. The supersecret nerve center of the American high command was the White House Map Room, created in 1942 to coordinate the war. Roosevelt wished to prevent the Army and the Navy from controlling communications channels, so he decided that all the outgoing presidential communications would go through the Navy channel and all the incoming communications from the field in various theaters to the president would go through the Army channel. Only the White House Map Room would have a complete copy of every piece of communication on a particular issue.[19]

This system, however, had become a major culprit in souring Sino-U.S. wartime relations, because the U.S. Army was able to control all the messages from China to the president, including Stilwell's as well as Chiang Kai-shek's. Thus, we see a repeated pattern of manipulation of facts and partisan views on the China theater from the Army channel. Virtually every cable to the president from Chiang Kai-shek had to go through Stilwell and Marshall, and often with the Army's attached backgrounders and interpretations of Chiang's intentions and even flat refutations of what Chiang had to say in his messages to the president. There was no effective alternative reporting channel to the White House under this system. Worse, there was virtually no way for Chiang Kai-shek to express his candid views to Roosevelt on Stilwell and his disagreements with the temperamental general. As Chiang later bitterly complained to Hurley on the dire consequence of this situation, "Both the President and the War Department are dependent on General Stilwell for information concerning the military situation in China. Thus the President may not be aware that I not only have no confidence in General Stilwell, but also lack confidence in his military judgment."[20]

When Hurley reached China, the first thing he changed was his method of communicating with the White House—he decided to use the Navy channel instead of the Stilwell channel. For the first time in the war thus far, Chiang Kai-shek was able to convey his unfettered views on Stilwell and the China situation through Hurley and the Navy channel directly to Roosevelt. In fact, Chiang's most complete explanation to Roosevelt as to why he wanted Stilwell relieved was addressed to Hurley, who sent it to the White House as an attachment. In this memo, undoubtedly Chiang's most important one of the war, Chiang pointed out Stilwell's military incompetence as a theater commander, his obsession with the Burma campaign at the expense of the overall China theater conditions, and his arrogance and narrow mindedness.[21]

In particular, Chiang Kai-shek was most bitter against Stilwell on one issue—his use of his power over American military aid to China to serve his own tactical interests by ignoring the urgent needs of other components of the war efforts. "Prior to June 1944," Chiang wrote to Roosevelt via Hurley, "with the exception of the Yunnan Expeditionary Forces, the entire Chinese Army did not receive a single rifle or piece of artillery from American Lend-Lease. It was not until the first week of June 1944, that General Stilwell at last visited Chungking to discuss the east China situation with me. When the enemy's offensive was already well on the way to its objectives, General Stilwell finally consented to give a small quantity of equipment to the Chinese armies in east China, and to facilitate more effective air support." Then Chiang Kai-shek delivered a stinging line that would reverberate loudly in Washington, "In all, excepting the Yunnan Expeditionary Forces, the Chinese armies have received 60 mountain guns, 320 anti-tank rifles and 506 Bazookas."[22]

With Chiang Kai-shek's devastating charges against Stilwell, Hurley provided the crucial official recommendation to the president that ultimately prompted Stilwell's recall. Hurley advised the president as follows:

> I have been in almost constant conference with the Generalissimo. I spent last week end with him in the country. Our discussions of the Stilwell matter have been continuous. Before I left Washington, you told me that your overall purpose is to prevent a collapse of China and keep the Chinese Army in the war. As a part of your plan to do this, you had decided to sustain the leadership of Chiang Kai-shek. In studying the situation here I am convinced that there is no Chinese leader available who offers as good a basis of cooperation with you as Chiang Kai-shek. There is no other Chinese known to me who possesses as many of the elements of leadership as Chiang Kai-shek. Chiang Kai-shek and Stilwell are fundamentally incompatible. Today you are confronted by a choice between Chiang Kai-shek and Stilwell. There is no other issue between you and Chiang Kai-shek. Chiang Kai-shek has agreed to every request, every suggestion made by you except the Stilwell appointment.[23]

Ten days later, the White House announced the recall of Stilwell, relieving him of all duties associated with the war effort in the China-Burma-India theater. A power struggle that had devastated the China theater's war efforts was finally over. But the damage had been done. Stilwell, in trying to regain

Burma and obtain command of the Chinese armed forces, used his control of the Lend-Lease materiel as the ultimate bargaining chip against Chiang Kai-shek. In the process, America's military aid to China in the most crucial years of the war became effectively inconsequential to the overall war situation. Great fights broke out constantly over fair shares of each party in the China theater of the extremely limited war materiel carried to China through the famed Hump flight from Asam, India, to Kunming, China. And the political fallouts from this infighting would haunt the troubled Sino-U.S. relations for a long time and would also play a remarkable role in the U.S. partisan politics for decades to come.

Chapter 11

MISSION IMPOSSIBLE
*Last Chance for the U.S. Military
Operations in China, from
Wedemeyer to Marshall*

AT THE TIME OF GENERAL JOSEPH STILWELL'S RECALL in October 1944, the China theater was a mess for the Allies. In fact, until the very day of the Japanese surrender, this area was plagued by problems and headaches. Admiral William Leahy, chairman of the Joint Chiefs of Staff, always regarded it as "that confused Oriental environment."[1] General Albert Wedemeyer, Stilwell's successor as the U.S. commanding officer in the China theater from November 1944, stated only two days before the Japanese capitulation that he had been operating in a land of "confusion, intrigue, and indecision."[2] And he was not only talking about the Chinese.

By the time Wedemeyer took over, the Allies in China were hindered by two major obstacles: lack of a unified command structure and the inability to deal with the growth of Communism in China. Preoccupation with overcoming these two mounting problems defined the final months of the war on the vast Chinese mainland.

In the last months of the war, the Allies in China were not heavily engaged in offensive attacks on the Japanese. Instead, a rigorous housecleaning was carried out to rectify the problems of a confusing and loose command structure imbued within the American forces. These problems were part of the Stilwell legacy.

When the temperamental General Vinegar Joe Stilwell was recalled, Wedemeyer soon realized what a messy situation Stilwell had left behind. Aside from the obvious tensions between the headquarters of Stilwell and that of Chiang Kai-shek, the U.S. forces in China themselves were, in Wedemeyer's words, internally "rife with dissention and disorganization," and most of the theater staff members were "imbued with a defeatist attitude, noncooperative spirit, and ideas of suspicion in their relations with other Headquarters."[3]

There were more than twenty U.S. agencies in China completely unconnected with each other, and each wanted to win the war single-handedly.

General Claire Chennault's 14th Air Force and Admiral Milton Miles's Naval Group China inside the Sino-American Special Technical Cooperative Organization (SACO) were operating virtually independently of the theater commander. Turf competition among U.S. agencies was extraordinarily tense. Within U.S. intelligence alone, there were more than a dozen independent American intelligence branches congested in Chungking and competing for trivial crumbs of information. The U.S. embassy; Joint Intelligence Collection Agency (JICA); the Army, Navy, and Air Corps attachés; Theater Command; the 14th Air Force; the Office of Strategic Services (OSS); the Counter Intelligence Corps of the Army (CIC); and the Naval Group China were all organizationally unconnected, each with separate command links to individual governmental departments in Washington.

Wedemeyer's housecleaning of the China theater was drastic in the final months of the war. He first completely reorganized Army headquarters, and despite hostile resistance, the entire senior staff of Stilwell's command was forcible removed.[4]

Wedemeyer next tried to consolidate his command over the famed 14th Air Force under the command of Claire Chennault, who was anything but close with the regular Army. Chennault viewed Wedemeyer as a staff officer deeply tied up with the War Department in Washington, which Chennault disliked with extraordinary passion. In April 1945, Wedemeyer decided to move Major General George Stratemeyer's 10th Air Force into China and put the 14th Air Force under Stratemeyer's command. Chennault was outraged, because he would "no longer be the senior airman in the area, where he enjoyed prestige and complete control from an air viewpoint as in the past several years."[5]

But Chennault had no other choice but to accept Wedemeyer's decision, because by this time, Chennault's ultimate supporter, President Franklin Roosevelt, had died. Furthermore, Wedemeyer reduced air priority in the Asian mainland to enhance ground forces.[6] Chennault's relevance in the China theater under Wedemeyer's command continuously diminished. Only days before the war finally ended, the famed airpower advocate and China's all-time American hero was forced to board a plane back to the United States and officially retired from the 14th Air Force. As Chennault recorded, "I left China full of anger and disappointment,"[7] Nevertheless, the biggest obstacle to the unity of command under an Army general was gone, despite much bitterness.

Much of the ineffectiveness during war in China came from a lack of coordinated allied war efforts. In the final months of the war, the Theater

Command, under Wedemeyer, redressed this problem. Under a major initiative proposed by the U.S. Army, regular Chinese-U.S. high-level staff meetings routinely took place. Chinese and American war planners, for the first time since the war began, were able to engage in meaningful exchange of information and coordination of actions. The most significant act taken by Wedemeyer and his boss, Chiang Kai-shek, was the trimming of China's enormous, ill-fed, insufficiently equipped, and undertrained 327 divisions of ground troops.

The most difficult consolidation of command was in reorganizing Allied intelligence. "One outstanding weakness in allied war effort in China," Wedemeyer reported to his boss, General Marshall, "is the fact that there are so many different agencies operating independently and uncoordinated, running at cross purposes, competing for limited Hump tonnage and altogether confusing the situation."[8] In the last months of the war, Wedemeyer took drastic action. He first appointed Colonel Richard Heppner of the OSS to be his intelligence czar in charge of merging various intelligence agencies under a single command.

The thorny issue of Naval Group China in SACO naturally came to fore. Under the Stilwell regime, the Navy contingent was the only American military group under a joint Sino-American command. This was made possible largely because of the cordial personal relationship between General Stilwell and Commander (later Rear Admiral) Milton Miles. With Stilwell gone, Wedemeyer was determined to pull Naval Group China out of Chinese command and put it directly under the U.S. theater command. But this proved to be a seemingly insurmountable task, because SACO's command structure was protected by a document sanctioned by President Roosevelt and Chiang Kai-shek, with the firm support of Admiral Ernest J. King. Wedemeyer directly appealed to the JCS for a revised version of the SACO Agreement.

In March 1945, while going back to see President Roosevelt for further instructions on America's policy toward post–World War II French Indochina, Wedemeyer brought the issue of command over Americans inside SACO to the Joint Chiefs of Staff. The Navy was alarmed by this and called Miles back from China to Washington to argue his case. The issue was heatedly debated in the Joint Chiefs of Staff. Admiral King was outvoted by Generals George Marshall and Hap Arnold. As a result, the SACO Agreement was amended to the effect that Miles's Navy Group China would be under the theater commander, meaning Wedemeyer's command. The wording of the amendment was unmistakable:

The Commanding General, U.S. Forces, China Theater [China and Indochina] will exercise command and operational control over all personnel and material belonging to American military, quasimilitary, and clandestine organizations which are operating or will in the future operate in or from the China Theater. Agreements whether written or oral entered into by American personnel of the Sino-American Special Cooperative Organization shall be considered binding insofar as they are in consonance with the present, future and projected policies of the Commanding General, U.S. Forces, China Theater, in his implementation of directives from higher authority.[9]

But Tai Li disagreed with this change and, according to SACO Agreement, the consent from the director was required to make any changes with regard to command. Also, Admiral King was perturbed by the JCS decision and protested loudly about this change, "I am in complete agreement that the Commanding General, U.S. Forces China Theater, should be in a position to coordinate the activities of all U.S. forces in the theater," King defiantly wrote, "I do not, however, feel that it is necessary to modify the Sino-American Special Technical Cooperative Agreement to accomplish this end."[10] As a result, even though on paper Wedemeyer had the command over Miles, the admiral kept direct communication with Miles in Chungking and had firm operational control over Naval Group China inside SACO. For all practical purposes, the Army-Navy game continued in China unabated.

In the last days of the war in East Asia, there was also another high drama unfolding in the China theater—a fierce struggle between the British and Americans over their respective China policies, as concretely demonstrated in the issues of who should have overall control of French Indochina and whether British intelligence should operate in China independently of the Chinese authorities. "We Americans," Wedemeyer reported to the War Department, "interpret United States policy as requiring a strong unified China and a China fighting effectively against the Japanese. There is considerable evidence that British policy is not in consonance with United States policy. The British Ambassador personally suggested to me that a strong unified China would be dangerous to the world and certainly would jeopardize the white man's position immediately in the Far East and ultimately throughout the world." In conclusion, Wedemeyer asserted, "in the case of the British I strongly suspect that their activities may be undermining the very United States policy that I am striving so hard to implement."[11]

The clash came when Lord Louis Mountbatten, the supreme Allied commander of the Southeast Asia Command, insisted on the British operating intelligence activities in French Indochina without notifying Chiang Kai-shek and Wedemeyer. Wedemeyer argued that Chiang was the recognized supreme Allied commander for China, French Indochina, and Thailand. As such, the Chinese should be notified before any British intelligence actions were taken. It was obvious to Americans that the British intention in French Indochina was to restore European colonial rule after the war and was purely motivated by political reasons.[12]

Wedemeyer was so adamant that when he ran out of ammunition in his fight with the British over French Indochina, he flew back to Washington in April 1945 to solicit support from President Roosevelt. But at the White House, Wedemeyer saw an appallingly pale and feeble president, whose intention to keep European colonialism out of Asia was clear but who lacked the energy required to implement this policy. When the British won the upper hand in operating a French-led intelligence group, the Gordon-Bernard-Tam Team, the Americans in China decided to organize a Vietnamese intelligence net to operate in French Indochina. In the spring of 1945, the American intelligence agency, Air Ground Aid Service (AGAS), which was primarily charged with rescuing downed allied pilots, hired a Vietnamese national in Kunming, China, to lead an intelligence team for the Allies. That man's name was Ho Chi Minh. The feisty Wedemeyer/Mountbatten dispute thus gained added complexity.

When the war in Europe was finally over on 8 May 1945, Wedemeyer was optimistic that a concerted Allied effort would finally bring down the Japanese. Following his efforts to streamline and unify the Allied command, large numbers of Americans were transferred from the European theater to China immediately after the German surrender. OSS agents formerly active in France and Yugoslavia were sent all across China.[13] Several senior military commanders in Europe, including George Patton and General William Simpson, the commander of the Ninth Army in the European Theater, were ordered to China to help Wedemeyer.[14] In June 1945, Wedemeyer and Simpson made a grand inspection trip of the China theater and found that "the splendid cooperation" prevailing between American and Chinese in the field is very heartening.[15] On 1 August 1945, Wedemeyer wrote in an exuberant spirit to Washington that he was ready to launch a major credible offensive in September and establish seaports in South and Southeastern China to finally break China's isolation imposed by the Japanese. But nine days later, on 10 August, Tokyo Radio announced Japan's readiness to accept the Potsdam Declaration. The war was essentially over.

But, for the Allies, this was not a time for joy, because in East Asia, peace can be more frightening than war. As Wedemeyer warned Washington on 1 August 1945, "Frankly, if peace should come within the next few weeks we will be woefully unprepared in China."[16] Wedemeyer was speaking of the specter of Communist expansion.

During the eight years of Japanese aggression in China, the Chinese Communists expanded greatly. The armed forces of the Chinese Communist Party (CCP) grew by more than twenty-five times, from barely forty thousand in 1937 to more than one million in August 1945; during the same period, the CCP-controlled population in China increased by almost seventy times, from 1.5 million to more than 100 million; and the CCP membership reached 2.7 million, controlling a vast area of 950,000 square kilometers of China.[17] By the time the Japanese surrendered, the CCP had become the biggest challenger to national power held by the Kuomintang under Chiang Kai-shek.

In the waning days of the war, the relationship between the American military forces in China and the Chinese Communists suddenly became intense. If the CCP's goal in the war was always to subvert the Kuomintang (KMT) regime, Mao Zedong's policy toward the U.S. forces in China underwent major changes. Before the Yalta Conference in February 1945, the CCP policy was to neutralize the United States in its struggle against the KMT. With the assurance at Yalta of the Soviet Union's entrance into the war with Japan, the CCP changed its policy from actively persuading the United States to form a military/political alliance to isolate the KMT to a policy of hostile resistance against U.S. military operations in North and Central China. In April 1945, the CCP convened its historic seventh party congress, in which Mao Zedong's ten-year tenacious internal struggle for absolute power within the CCP against Moscow-dominated rivals was officially over. Joseph Stalin recognized Mao's supreme leadership in the CCP, because he needed a strong and consolidated Chinese Communist Party to cooperate with his imminent invasion of Manchuria, as promised in Yalta. In response, the CCP's attitude toward the United States changed to a hard-lined aggressive one.

The first confrontation came on 28 May 1945, when four American intelligence officers were suddenly and surreptitiously captured in Fuping, Hobei Province, in Northern China. The capture of these four Americans, known as the Fuping Incident, was a turning point in CCP-U.S. relations. The CCP Central Committee in Yenan issued a directive days after the Fuping Incident to all Communist headquarters throughout China instructing them to arrest, disarm, and hold all unauthorized Americans encountered anywhere.[18]

Wedemeyer was duly alarmed, because this incident marked the first fundamental clash between U.S. military forces and the Chinese Communists on the concept of authority in North China, where both the Communist forces and the Japanese troops had coexisted. This American intelligence team had reported to Wedemeyer before they were captured that "the amount of actual fighting being carried on by the 8th Route Army [the Communist army] has been grossly exaggerated. It was their policy to undertake no serious campaign against the Japanese or Puppets. There were occasional ambushes and hit and run raids."[19]

But far more serious a problem to Wedemeyer as the China theater commander was whether he had the authority to send American military personnel to North China, which had been officially declared as occupied by both the Japanese and the Communists, without the Communists' permission, as insisted by Mao Zedong. Wedemeyer directly challenged Mao in a special meeting by stating that getting prior permission from the Communists to fight the Japanese in the Communist- and Japanese-occupied area was "not always feasible. In fact [it was] generally impossible to do. I have Americans operating all over the China Theater. I do not send information out to other commanders concerning such operations. Americans would contact them when and where possible. They are recognized and accepted as friends and co-workers. Commanders take them right in and treat them kindly."[20]

What truly defined the nature of the CCP-U.S. Military relationship in the summer of 1945 in China was the killing of a U.S. intelligence officer, Captain John Birch, of the OSS, under Wedemeyer's command. On 25 August 1945, in Shandong Province, Birch was murdered by a special interception team belonging to the West Shandong District, 11th Subdistrict, 12th Regiment, of the Chinese Communist Eighth Route Army. Birch was killed by the Communists because the Communists tried to keep all American influence out of the geographically important Shandong Peninsula and Northern Jiangsu, which guard the entrance in the Gulf of Chihli (Bo Hai Gulf) to Port Arthur (Lu Shun) and Dairen (Da Lien)—both under Soviet occupation since mid-August 1945. It was also because the CCP troops were actively searching for the Birch party to prevent it at any cost from meeting the person Captain Birch was instructed to see, General Hao Peng-ju, formerly a puppet collaborator, with whom the CCP was conducting a hasty and most secret negotiation.

An investigation conducted by the U.S. judge advocate of the China theater, dated 13 November 1945, concluded, "Although Capt. Birch's conduct immediately prior to his death indicated a lack of good judgment and failure to take proper precautions in a dangerous situation, nevertheless the actions taken by the Chinese Communist Army personnel fell short of according the rights and privileges due even to enemy prisoners of war and constituted murder. . . . The shooting was done maliciously . . . the killing was completely without justification."[21]

General Wedemeyer was incensed by the Birch killing. On 30 August 1945, he directly protested to Mao Zedong and Zhou Enlai in person. "This is a very serious and very grave incident. . . . When the American people learn about Captain Birch's death it will have a very disturbing effect."[22] Wedemeyer further pointed out to Mao and Zhou, "I cannot have Americans killed in this theater by Chinese Communists or anyone else."[23]

During this tense encounter, Wedemeyer took the opportunity to bring up the four Americans still detained by the Communists at Fuping, "I have not told the American people that Mr. Mao has retained four Americans as prisoners at Fuping since last May."[24] Wedemeyer then exploded in front of Mao. "Why did they [the Communists] capture these men—why did they take them as prisoners? You [Mao] should have had the courtesy to at least wire me and say, 'Wedemeyer, who are these people that just came into this area?' Do I have the assurance that these four men will be sent to me immediately?" To which Zhou Enlai grudgingly answered in the positive.[25]

The war ended in East Asia abruptly. As Colonel Richard Heppner of OSS/China pointedly remarked, "We have been caught with our pants down."[26] While Wedemeyer was still preparing for a breakthrough of the Japanese naval encirclement of China in the South, the entire Japanese military forces of approximately two million troops in the Asian mainland, including French Indochina, China proper, and Manchuria, were suddenly to be surrendering to Generalissimo Chiang Kai-shek and to be repatriated back to Japan. Instantly, all potent political forces in the Asian mainland became active in accepting the Japanese surrender. Despite the fact that according to the Potsdam Declaration, the only authority the Japanese had to surrender to was Chiang Kai-shek in China and northern Indochina, many challenges remained. Some warlords who had enjoyed wartime expansion became openly hostile to Chungking and to the U.S. forces in China. Lung Yun, the governor of Yunnan, harbored the biggest ambitions, and thus was most dangerous to Chungking. Chiang Kai-shek spared no time in taking decisive action to restrain Lung. Chiang first gave Lung the ostentatious glory of accepting the Japanese surrender in the northern part of French Indochina. When Lung dispatched his one hundred and eighty thousand troops into north Vietnam,

Chiang staged a coup by arresting him, who he then isolated from his army.

But the most serious challenge in dealing with accepting the Japanese surrender came from the Chinese Communists. On 11 August 1945, General Zhu De, the commander in chief of the one million-strong Chinese Communist military forces, announced that the Chinese Communists should and would accept the Japanese surrender without authorization from the central government of Chiang Kai-shek. The CCP's surrender policy was firm. Chiang Kai-shek's antagonism against this CCP policy was equally strong and adamant. A civil war between the CCP and KMT seemed dangerously inevitable unless the U.S. authorities exerted quick and decisive action to prevent a civil war from happening in the immediate wake of victory over Japan.

Unfortunately, Washington, at the critical month of August 1945, was intoxicated with the euphoria of victory and failed to adequately realize the new danger in the China theater, despite Wedemeyer's desperate pleas from Chungking. The War Department had already developed a priority list on occupation matters on which Japan was the first, then Korea, and the occupation policy over China was placed third. Wedemeyer protested this decision strongly. In his 12 August 1945 cable to Marshall, Wedemeyer reasoned:

> It is my considered opinion that the American contingents contemplated in occupational plans . . . must arrive as promptly as possible in China. WARX 47945 places Japanese archipelago in first priority, Korea in second, and China in third or last priority. As I view overall situation in Far East upon surrender of Japanese, the Japanese archipelago will present no immediate problems relative to control, repatriation, disarmament, or disturbances of revolutionary character; whereas, on the Asiatic mainland we are confronted with two serious possibilities requiring prompt action on part of Allies. First, Chinese Communist forces may precipitate civil war in China; Second, the Japanese army remaining on the mainland, approximately two million strong, may continue to fight either in force or in isolated areas, requiring continued employment of air and land forces. The area of China is so vast and communications so limited, the problems posed by the above two conditions obviously require timely and appropriate disposition of Allied forces, American and Chinese. Definitely, China Theater's minimum requirements for American occupational forces should be given first priority.[27]

But Wedemeyer's plea came to no avail. To prevent a possible outbreak of a bloody civil war in China, Wedemeyer proposed a second-best solution to Washington: to send as many American troops as possible to China immediately to occupy key Chinese points and preclude the Communists from launching a civil war. According to this proposal, two divisions of American troops would be sent to Shanghai, another two divisions would be sent to the Taku area in the strategic Peking-Tientsin (Tianjin) region, and one division would go to the Canton area in the South.[28] However, Wedemeyer's proposal was flatly refused by General Marshall.[29]

Much credit should go to Wedemeyer for his insight at this critical juncture that the key to the KMT-CCP conflict was in Moscow and Washington. What was about to happen in China, to Wedemeyer, was not merely a Chinese "civil war;" it was instead part of the Soviet-U.S. power game being played out in China. In light of the escalated military confrontations between the KMT and CCP in the waning days of the war, Wedemeyer boldly suggested to General Marshall that "the only sure method of avoiding a civil war between the Communist and Central Government forces, with all of its potentially explosive consequences throughout the Far East, is to apply strong outside pressure from the United States and Russia."[30]

Fearful of the horrific, yet realistic, prospect of a third world war ignited by the KMT-CCP confrontation, both Washington and Moscow took Wedemeyer's suggestion seriously, at least on paper, and each exerted pressure on Chungking and Yenan, respectively, to come to the table for peace negotiations. While increasing military skirmishes continued, Chiang Kai-shek was quick to respond to Washington's pressure and on 14 August 1945 issued an invitation to Mao Zedong to come to Chungking for peace talks. Mao adamantly refused to talk and held out for a military solution. Chiang sent a second and third invitation via telegrams to Mao on 20 and 23 August; all were ignored by Mao Zedong.[31] At this critical moment, Stalin dispatched a telegram to Mao Zedong in Yenan ordering the Chinese Communist Party to sit down with Chiang Kai-shek for peace talks to avert a civil war.[32] Mao was displeased with Stalin's stance, but upon receiving a second telegram from the Kremlin demanding that Mao go to Chungking, Mao grudgingly agreed to meet Chiang in Chungking for face-saving "peace talks."

On 27 August 1945, American ambassador Patrick Hurley flew to Yenan to escort Mao Zedong to Chungking.[33] Two weeks later, a Soviet military plane carrying a liaison officer for the Soviet military commander in chief in Manchuria, General Malynovski, landed on the Yenan airstrip.[34]

The prospect of Soviet involvement in Manchuria fundamentally affected the Allies' war strategy against Japan in East Asia during the last days of the war. At Yalta, Stalin agreed to declare war on Japan three months after Germany was defeated, on the condition that the Soviet Union would have dominant influence over the Chinese territory of Manchuria. Perhaps the most telling aspect of the Yalta deal on Manchuria was the fact that none of the high officials of either Chinese high command or U.S. authorities in China, including Chiang Kai-shek, Ambassador Hurley, and General Wedemeyer was informed of the secret deal. When the news leaked out, Chiang was outraged; Hurley flew to Washington, only to find that FDR was too exhausted to be helpful on the China situation. The ambassador then went straight to London and Moscow in an effort to secure promises from Churchill and Stalin to guarantee Chinese territorial integrity. Both Churchill and Stalin gave Hurley cynical replies.[35]

Soviet participation in defeating the Japanese was regarded by Washington as so necessary that the U.S. military's planned advance toward the Japanese homeland encountered political obstacles. In April 1945, soon after the Yalta Conference, the United States scored a major victory in the Pacific and launched the successful Okinawa campaign. This brought the U.S. military closer to the Japanese homeland and also raised the question as to whether Soviet participation was still necessary. The Allied war planners were split on this issue. Instead of striking directly at the heart of Japan from Okinawa while possessing momentum, General Douglas MacArthur proposed to attack the distant target of Borneo instead. Admiral Chester Nimitz also avoided a direct attack on Japan and proposed a series of subsidiary operations that would encircle the Japanese homeland.

But by doing so, the United States lost its victorious momentum. To have done otherwise, warned Lieutenant General Stanley Embick in the War Department, the Soviets would have been upset, because "Russia may retard her contribution against Japan if [she] is led to believe that the U.S. regards the time factor as of overriding importance, regardless of cost to America."[36]

Wedemeyer, the commanding general in the China theater, was outraged by such a war strategy and chastised MacArthur's Borneo plan as "eccentric to sound strategic advance against the enemy."[37] He urged Washington to avoid diverging from the effort to concentrate and deploy for a decisive thrust at the heart of the Japanese war effort and proposed immediate "early large scale operations against Japanese homeland."[38] Wedemeyer's pleas were never taken seriously in Washington.

Most inexplicable of all was the fact that, as commanding general of the U.S. Forces in China, Wedemeyer was kept entirely in the dark as to the terms of the Soviet presence in Manchuria. One day after the Russians declared war on Japan, Wedemeyer was still asking Washington a basic question: "Have any agreements been made with Russia as to what parts of Manchuria, if any, Russian forces will occupy?"[39]

This lack of policy guidance regarding Manchuria became ever more dangerous when one hundred thousand Chinese Communists quickly slipped into Soviet-occupied Manchuria and poised for a final showdown with the Nationalist troops that were supposed to take over Manchuria from the Soviets three months after the invasion. The situation in Manchuria grew so intense, Wedemeyer reported to Washington, that Chiang had completely abandoned any serious effort at all to repatriate the two million Japanese military personnel from China and instead was devoted to conducting a campaign against the Chinese Communists.[40]

In the meantime, Manchuria had become a hotbed of the new "Cold War" in East Asia. The Soviets were adamantly opposing any U.S. presence in that area. When the Soviets declared war on Japan, General William Donovan of the OSS, who was in China with Wedemeyer at the time, immediately pointed out, "The entry of the Russians into Manchuria points up my urgent petition that we be no longer delayed in the northern penetration. If we are not in Korea and Manchuria when the Russians get there, we will never get in."[41]

In the name of rescuing American POWs in Manchuria formerly detained by the Japanese, Wedemeyer sent two intelligence teams into Manchuria on 12 August 1945. Colonel Richard Heppner, Wedemeyer's intelligence chief, instructed his agents, "take every step at your disposal . . . to get agents placed with utmost dispatch in key points in Manchuria . . . you know the reasons for this and I leave it to your discretion to take best methods for speedy implementation."[42] An urgent request to airlift agents into critical areas of Manchuria was made so that "we may be on ground before arrival of Russians."[43] One of the two teams, code-named Flamingo, was designated for Harbin. But it never reached there because of the sweeping Russian advance and the hostile attitude toward Americans in that area. The other American team, code-named Cardinal, finally parachuted down at its destination in Mukden on 16 August 1945 and soon discovered a Japanese POW camp that incarcerated 1,321 Americans, 239 British, and some Australian, Dutch, Canadian prisoners.

The Soviets occupation troops were particularly irked by American presence in Manchuria. Wedemeyer's intelligence team reported back that "Americans are by no means immune from Russian mistreatment, many having been robbed at tommy gun point of their watches, and sometimes of their rings and money. . . . [There were also] stabbing a B-24 tire, drunken abuse of 'Americanski's,' flagrant insults to American flags, etc."[44] The Soviets had reasons to harass the American intelligence officers in Manchuria, because many unannounced Communist activities were observed and reported back to Chungking, such as the covert influx of thousands of Chinese Communist soldiers into Soviet-occupied Mukden (Shenyang) on 7 September 1945.[45] Finally, at 3 PM on 3 October 1945, Major General Kavqun Stankevich, the Soviet war commandant at Mukden, issued an ultimatum to the Americans: "This is to inform you that since you do not have a visa from the Government of the U.S.S.R, your papers may not be regarded as official documents. It is therefore ordered that by 5 October 1945 you be outside the boundaries of Manchuria."[46] Thus marks the complete withdrawal of the brief American military presence in Manchuria after World War II.

The situation in Manchuria reached a boiling point in the fall of 1945. The CCP and KMT both stationed huge numbers of troops in the strategic areas of Manchuria by the end of the year. A bloody civil war, which would inevitably lead to a Soviet/U.S. military confrontation, had become imminent. In desperation, Wedemeyer proposed an immediate total withdrawal of all U.S. troops from China to avoid U.S. involvement in a war with the USSR in East Asia, and he further called for a trusteeship by the United States, Great Britain, the Soviet Union, and China over Manchuria and Korea.[47]

However, none of Wedemeyer's suggestions was favorably received in Washington. Instead, President Harry Truman dispatched the recently retired U.S. Army chief of staff, General George Marshall, to China in late December 1945. The Marshall Mission tried to transcend the international Cold War tinge on the CCP/KMT conflict by persuading the two warring factions to enter into a peaceful settlement.

On 14 August 1945, General Wedemeyer warned the Joint Chiefs of Staff in Washington, "I view Asia as an enormous pot, seething and boiling, the fumes of which may readily snuff out the advantages gained by Allied sacrifices in the past several years and may also definitely preclude realization of the objectives of the Atlantic Charter and the Teheran, Yalta, and Potsdam agreements."[48] Tragically, Wedemeyer was right.

For Washington, the Marshall Mission was the last act in China. Many of the difficulties Marshall faced in China were not without irony. The military and political mishmash caused by the CCP and KMT was regarded by most in Washington as the result of failed nobility and internecine fight of parochial nature. China was in deep trouble precisely because Chinese politicians and military leaders were unable to transcend partisan triviality, to put national unity and the general well-being of the people above narrow personal and

political differences. It was believed in Washington that Patrick Hurley's mediation efforts notably failed not because he lacked passion for peace and unity
of China, but because Hurley did not possess a personality grand enough to
command a moral authority over the quarreling CCP and KMT leaderships.
A great man of enormous prestige such as Marshall, a major architect of the
victory over fascism, an esteemed military hero and a trusted public figure of
the world, now traveled to China with a glowing White House halo to salvage
peace and prosperity. His primary concern was understandably how he would
be regarded by all squabbling sides as impeccably honest and noble, without
any stained hands in any ignoble businesses of secret nature. America was to
be thought of as motivated by nothing but an altruist spirit for the genuine
peace and democracy in postwar China and, more important, America's means
to reach such a goal would be absolutely aboveboard.

Unfortunately, this obsession with openness and transparency became one
of Marshall Mission's own undoings, because by so doing, the mission volun-
tarily gave away the most important means of ascertaining correct military and
political intelligence from the vast areas of contention between the Chinese
government and the Communists. Intelligence is, by nature, secret and furtive.
To prove his motivations and integrity, Marshall decided to sacrifice efficient
intelligence operations. The tragic consequence, however, is that, without efficient intelligence operations in a murky situation like China, good intentions
and personal nobility, however crucial and important they might be, were subject not only to constant frustration of lack of precise information for proper
and timely action, but also to shrewd manipulation of warring factions, and to
ruthless disinformation, intelligence penetration, and hostile propaganda.

The conflicting nature of intelligence analysis on China convinced
Marshall, upon his arrival in China in late December 1945, to ignore the
existing intelligence services altogether and to form his own team afresh. The
person he chose to lead the intelligence affairs for the mission went to a novice
in the China scene, Walter Robertson, chargé d'affaires at the U.S. embassy.[49]

To a certain extent, the Robertson's role was crucial to the success of the
entire mission. The structure Marshall set up for the mediation was a two-
layered one. On the upper level was the "Big Three Committee," consisting of Zhou Enlai on the CCP side; Xu Yongchang (later Zhang Zhizhong
and Zhang Chun), representing the KMT; and Marshall himself. This was
the "gentlemen's committee" of diplomacy and nobility, which dealt primarily with policy issues. On the lower level, however, was the much-more
important Executive Headquarters, composed of three commissioners—all

sophisticated intelligence chiefs in their own right. On the KMT side was General Zheng Jieming (Cheng Kai-min), the number two man in KMT intelligence; on the Communist side, major intelligence and security chiefs in Yenan were dispatched into the Executive Headquarters. Leading the CCP team was Lieutenant General Ye Jianying (Yeh Chien-Ying), the chief of staff for the CCP armed forces and frequently in charge of military intelligence, with Li Kenong (Kang Sheng's deputy at the Social Affairs Department, which was CCP's version of the NKVD—the People's Commissariat Internal Affairs) and Luo Ruiqing (later the PRC's public security chief of many years) serving as aides. Robertson was Marshall's choice as the U.S. commissioner in the Executive Headquarters. His savvy on intelligence had been amply demonstrated in many of his highly acclaimed and well-balanced intelligence surveys in the short time since he arrived in China.[50]

The intelligence operations on both sides of the CCP and KMT surrounding the Executive Headquarters were a classical farce of deliberate distortion and disinformation, designed to manipulate public opinion—a blatantly merciless blame game. By March 1946, Marshall was able to convince the warring sides to agree to the principle of a cease-fire all across China. But the seemingly rosy picture was deceptive. By that time, the Executive Headquarters was operating more than twenty field teams composed of three sides in the hot spots of fighting all over China. Yet, both the CCP and KMT intelligence agents sent voluminous reports to the headquarters charging the opposing side of violating the cease-fire agreement. Each time a charge was filed, the temperature in the controlled media and propaganda machines increased. Robertson's team thus faced an enormous task of verifying those false and exaggerated reports from the field. On 20 March 1946, Robertson forced Ye Jianying and Zheng Jiemin to jointly issue an order entitled "Measures to Stop the Submission of Misleading Reports." The order stipulates:

> This Headquarters and the Executive Headquarters Field Teams have received many reports of violations of the "cease-fire" and other directives. Many of these reports have been so exaggerated as to be very misleading. In order for the field team to be able to complete their essential work, the submission to them of these misleading messages must cease. The responsibility for screening these reports must be on the Commanding General of the area rendering the report. Most of the minor reports may be taken up with the liaison officer from the opposing force and settled on the spot. The remaining reports must be submitted to include the following information:

1. Time of alleged violation of "cease-fire" orders or directives.
2. Place of violation, together with approximate latitude and longitude, or by location in respect to a large city.
3. Nature of the offense to include the approximate number of attackers, what they did and to what organization they belonged.
4. Name of the officer submitting the report together with the name of the liaison officer with whom the report has been cleared. The name of the liaison officer should be of assistance in establishing which organization made the attack or other violation.[51]

One of Robertson's methods to show the American teams' absolute impartiality to both sides was to listen carefully to complaints and negotiate a middle-of-the-road solution. When complaints were about the U.S. personnel, Robertson showed no hesitation in taking action rectifying them as quickly and practically as possible. The KMT had been consistently complaining about the secret dealings of American military intelligence agencies with the Communists. To allay any suspicion on part of the KMT officials, Robertson ordered the Army to compile a complete list of all U.S. personnel, military and civilian, who had been stationed at or had visited the Dixie Mission in the Communist headquarters in Yenan since July 1944 up to April 1946 and showed it to Zheng Jiemin as a gesture of impartiality.[52]

In the meantime, in response to the Communist charge of U.S-KMT connivance, Robertson insisted, obviously with Marshall's blessing, on avoiding employing any U.S. personnel Zhou Enlai might not like. Together with Hurley, Wedemeyer had been labeled by the CCP as "reactionary," because of the American general's increased disdain for Communist tactics in the field and on the negotiation table, particularly since the stormy confrontation between Wedemeyer and Mao Zedong in Chungking the previous summer over the murder of OSS agent John Birch by the Communists. Not surprisingly, all of Wedemeyer's staff members, including senior intelligence officers, were carefully avoided. Instead, the Executive Headquarters was packed with stalwarts of the generally pro-CCP staff of Stilwell's disbanded command—most prominently Generals T. S. Timberman and Henry Byroade.

Wedemeyer was understandably bitter; so were many of his subordinates. Colonel Ivan Yeaton, Wedemeyer's handpicked chief to the Dixie Mission, officially known as the U.S. Army Observer Group, since July 1945, and later his chief of G-2, was particularly cold shouldered by Marshall and his team. Shortly after his arrival in China, Marshall, upon Wedemeyer's recommendation, held a meeting in his house with Yeaton, who was then stationed in Yenan.

Marshall asked for Yeaton's opinion on the nature of Chinese Communists from an intelligence officer's viewpoint. Yeaton had been an assistant military attaché in the U.S. embassy in Moscow, with the advantage of observing world Communist movements firsthand for years. At the meeting with Marshall, Yeaton dutifully reported that the Chinese Communist Party was not composed of "agrarian reformers" but "pure Marx, Lenin and Mao" and that Mao's headquarters had maintained busy radio communications between Yenan and Moscow. Yeaton further told Marshall that the CCP's only hope for weapons was to receive captured Japanese arms from the Soviets in Manchuria. However, Yeaton's words fell on Marshall's deaf ears. "If he had heard a word I said," Yeaton complained in his memoirs, "he did not show it. As he finished tying his bow tie, he said, 'Thank you,' and showed me the door."[53]

But all of Marshall's balancing acts would come to no avail in the end, because neither the CCP nor the KMT wanted the mission to succeed. There was an intrinsic irony in Marshall's objective in China. "On the one hand," the historian Mark Stoler explains, "he was supposed to be the impartial mediator. On the other he was supposed to support and build up Chiang Kai-shek while minimizing Soviet and Chinese Communist influence." This conflicting role, of course, as has been said by many, created a self-destructive mechanism for Marshall's endeavor. "The second mission made his impartiality suspect for successful completion of the first, while American unwillingness and inability to intervene militarily meant he did not possess the power to fulfill the second if the first failed."[54]

As Claire Lee Chennault aptly put, "Well equipped with trucks, artillery, machine guns, and mortars they began a systematic mop up of Communist troops wherever they could be found. The Generalissimo's offensive was well under way and progressing successfully when General George C. Marshall reached China in November 1945 as a special emissary."[55] Eventually, Chennault charged, "the truce sponsored and pushed by Marshall . . . forced the Generalissimo to halt his anti-Communist offensive at a time when it was on the verge of wiping out large bodies of Chinese Communist troops."[56]

The fate of the Marshall mission was a foredoomed one. Regarded as a chief architect of the Allies' victory during World War II, George Marshall was sent to China to prevent an already ongoing civil war between the Chinese government and the Chinese Communists from escalating. In the end, the civil war was not prevented by Marshall, and it ended up with a total Communist victory.

Thus marks the completion of Allied military and intelligence operations in wartime China.

EPILOGUE

FOREIGN OPERATIONS IN WARTIME CHINA occurred in two phases during the eight long years of military campaigns. The first phase covers the period between July 1937, when the all-out war between China and Japan broke out, and December 1941, when the attacks at Pearl Harbor and other strategic points in the Pacific brought Britain and the United States officially into the China theater as full-time allies against a common enemy. The second phase covers the period from December 1941 and September 1945, when Japan formally surrendered. For the purpose of continuity, this book has extended the second phase to early 1947, when the last foreign military operation under the aegis of the Marshall Mission ended, and when all military and intelligence operations thus went sub rosa in China with the creation of the Central Intelligence Agency and the Cold War in full gear in the vast Asian country.

In the first phase, the Soviet Union provided the most meaningful military aid to China and conducted direct military and intelligence operations in China on a large scale. Between September 1937, when the first Soviet armaments arrived in China, and June 1941, when all Soviet military aid to China finally stopped because of the Nazi blitzkrieg, the Soviet Union provided the Chinese with 900 aircraft, 1,140 artillery sets, 82 tanks, 10,000 machine guns, 50,000 rifles, 2,000 trucks, 2 million hand grenades, 31,160 airborne bombs, 2 million shells, 180 million bullets, and other materiel. During this period, Moscow also gave China three major loan packages totaling $250 million at a very low interest. Before the Pearl Harbor attack, almost every major and minor campaign in China involved the participation of the Soviet military advisers. There were seven hundred Soviet "voluntary" pilots and aircraft mechanics who were directly involved in combat, downing about two hundred Japanese planes, with more than two hundred Soviet pilots killed in combat.

Yet, the Soviets and Chinese were allies of convenience during this phase. In August 1937, the Soviets and the Nazis signed a nonaggression pact, which led to a significant reduction of Soviet involvement in China against Japan, Hitler's ally in Asia. By April 1941, the Soviets signed a Neutrality Pact of its own with Japan, practically ending all Soviet operations in China against Japan.

During the first phase, the Chinese also had small but meaningful military and intelligence cooperation with the British and the French; both of the latter had vast colonial possessions in Asia that were directly threatened by Japan's military advances in China and elsewhere. It was in Britain's and France's colonial interests to see Japan bogged down, or even defeated, in China by the Chinese army. Since China bordered on French Indochina and British Burma, Hong Kong, and India, the Chinese government depended on the British and the French to keep the land lines for weapons transportation into China open via these colonial territories. Much of the military and intelligence cooperation with the British and the French was about keeping these routes open.

The first phase also witnessed small-scale American military involvement. The most significant was China's mercenary air force, which was entirely manned and operated by the Americans. Famously known as the Flying Tigers and led by the legendary Claire Lee Chennault, who resigned from the U.S. Army's Air Corps as one of America's leading advocates for fighter-oriented air strategy, this small but remarkable air force served the Chinese war efforts with distinction. It not only had a glorious combat record, but it also exerted indelible influence on the Chinese high command for an air force–heavy strategy, which would gravely influence Chiang Kai-shek's command decisions a few years later when he was given a deputy from the U.S. Army, General Joseph Stilwell.

The second phase (December 1941–January 1947) witnessed the rapid, comprehensive, and large-scale increase in foreign military and intelligence involvement in China. While the Soviets, who were relatively active in China during the first couple of years of the war, were completely out of the picture in China, the Americans, the British, and the Free French all quickly established formal military and intelligence organizations and programs to operate in China.

For the British, the prewar organization China Commando Group, the largest London-backed intelligence and special operations project in China, now came directly under the aegis of the SOE (Special Operations Executive), with a headquarters inside the British embassy and a direct communications line with the War Office in London. Although the training and weapons inflow aspects received an encouraging leap right after the Pearl Harbor attack, the British and the Chinese had developed profound distrust of each other in areas of strategic objectives, intelligence sharing, and especially, the control over cryptoanalytical methods and decrypts. Within months, the China Commando Group was ousted by the Chinese, and all major British military and intelligence operations had to continue under semiunderground circumstance in China until the war's end.

During the second phase, the French resistance elements also made significant efforts to operate inside China. However, intriguing politics inside the French resistance, mostly between Charles de Gaulle's faction and General Henri Giroud's North African faction, played out in dramatic fashion in China, with large numbers of French nationals squabbling with each other over turf and resources while being trained and lodged in the Chinese military barracks.

Yet, the overwhelming weight of foreign military and intelligence operations in China during this phase came from the United States. Within several months of America's entering the war with Japan, and throughout the rest of the war, tens of thousands of American military and intelligence personnel, representing dozens of American military and bureaucratic organizations, flocked to China to conduct various activities. They include the Office of Strategic Services (OSS), the Office of War Information (OWI), the Bureau of Economic Warfare (BEW), the general headquarters of General Joseph Stilwell, the headquarters of the 14th Air Force (formerly the Flying Tigers, still under Chennault, now a major general in the U.S. Army), the Military Intelligence (G-2) of the War Department, the Naval Intelligence of the U.S. Navy, the intelligence arms of the U.S. State Department, the Treasury Department and the Commerce Department, the U.S. Army-run Dixie Mission to the Chinese Communist Headquarters in Yenan, the postwar Marshall Mission, and above all, the Sino-American Special Technical Cooperative Organization, or SACO, the overarching intelligence mammoth jointly operated by the Chinese military intelligence organization (the Bureau of Statistics and Investigation) and the U.S. Navy that ran nine major bases all across China.

Foreign military and intelligence operations significantly changed the nature of wartime Chinese nationalism. During the first phase of the war when foreign operations were few and scant, the war in China was as much about beefing up Chinese nationalism as about military campaigns. China's nationalism under the leadership of Chiang Kai-shek, who only united China fewer than ten years before, now enjoyed a new peak as a result of the Japanese invasion. Facing the war, the Chinese were unprecedented in unity under Chiang Kai-shek's leadership. Unmatched by Japan's military power, China was nevertheless defiant, and the Kuomintang's prestige and legitimacy were further solidified by the war in the first phase.

However, with the sudden influx of foreign operations during the second phase, Chiang Kai-shek failed to control widespread, uncoordinated foreign operations that were disorganized and ripe with internecine infighting for turf and command control.

While in the first phase of the war Chiang Kai-shek could concentrate on fighting the Japanese and gaining respect from the Chinese people for doing so, he and his government during the second phase were dragged into endless policy debates, disputes over strategies, and turf wars with his foreign allies. The most famous of such was the Chiang Kai-shek/Stilwell debacle over the strategy in Burma and Eastern China, which pitted virtually all senior military and civilian officials such as Chennault and Stilwell against each other.

As a result, foreign operations served to weaken Chiang Kai-shek's prestige in the eyes of the Chinese and thus reduced the Kuomintang's legitimacy. This was especially the case when most foreign military and intelligence organizations in the second phase strenuously demanded to run operations independent of the Chinese Nationalist government, thus making Chiang and his Nationalist government irrelevant and weakening his claim as the leader of a sovereign state.

Consequently, Chiang Kai-shek's grip over various potent political factions inside China began to slip. While the Chinese Communist Party was more or less compliant with Chiang's leadership position during the first phase, it became actively engaged in dismantling his legitimacy to rule. Adding to this assault to the Nationalist government was the fact that China's various otherwise dormant political forces—former warlords, disenchanted academics, local vigilantes, secret societies, and so forth—began to join hands with various partisan foreign military and intelligence organizations such as the British SOE, the Soviet NKVD (People's Commissariat Internal Affairs), and the American OSS and OWI, to make Chiang's central government much less relevant as a sovereign authority. In the end, Chiang's regime lost the respect and confidence of its international allies, which led to the dramatic fragmentation of the Chinese society as a whole, severely shattering the Nationalist government's confidence and ability to rule.

In sum, it can be argued that it was the failure of the Nationalist government under Chiang Kai-shek to successfully control foreign military and intelligence operations during World War II that greatly contributed to its own demise fours years after the war ended.

 NOTES

PREFACE

1. Most historians in East Asia tend to accept the point that World War II began in China with the Marco Polo Bridge Incident on 7 July 1937. For a Western reference, see Donald Detwiler, "World War II Began at Wanping: Why the Lu-Kou-Chiao Incident Marked the Beginning of the Second World War," conference paper at Yangmingshan, Taipei, Taiwan, 1987.

CHAPTER 1

1. Chen Cungong, "minchu lujunjunhuo zhi shuru" [Arms Imports to China during the Early Years of the Republic of China] *Journal of Modern Chinese History* 6 (June 1977). Also see Zhang Baijia, "China's Experience in Seeking Foreign Military Aid and Cooperation for Resisting Japanese Aggression," conference paper for Harvard University Conference on World War II in China, Hawaii, January 2004.

2. Ma Zhendu and Qi Rugao, *dihu? Youhu?—Deguo yu zhongguo kangzhan [Enemy or Friend?—Germany and China's War of Resistance against Japan]* (Guilin, China: Guangxi Normal University Press, 1997), 100-101.

3. William Kirby, *Germany and Republic of China* (Palo Alto, CA: Stanford University Press, 1984), 40–41.

4. Zhang Baijia, "China's Experience in Seeking Foreign Military Aid and Cooperation for Resisting Japanese Aggression," unpublished conference paper, January 2004, 3.

5. The Chinese National Archives II, *zhongde waijiao midang, 1927–1949 [Secret Archives in Sino-German Relations, 1927–1949]*, 136–51; also Zhang Baijia, "China's Experience in Seeking Foreign Military Aid," 3.

6. Zhang Baijia, "China's Experience in Seeking Foreign Military Aid," 3.

7. Dai Houjie, "ta chouhua le guomin zhengfu kangzhan chuqi de zhuozhan lantu—jiangjieshi de di si ren deguo junshi zhong guwen fakenhaosen" [The German Who Wrote China's War Plans in the Early Days of the War of Resistance against Japanese Aggression—Chiang Kai-shek's Fourth

German Military Adviser Alexander von Falkenhausen], in Dai Houjie, ed., *The Biographies of Foreign Advisers in Modern China* (Hebei, China: Hebei People's Press, 2004): 275–97.

8. Xin Damo, "fakenhaosen jiangjun huiyi zhong de jiang weiyuanzhang yu zhongguo," [Memoirs of General Falkenhausen: My Years with Generalissimo Chiang Kai-shek and China] *zhuanji wenxue [Biographical Literature]* 19, no. 5.

9. Dai Houjie, "The German Who Wrote China's War Plans," 280–81.

10. Letter, Hans Klein to Weng Wenhao, secretary general of the Executive Yuan, ROC, 29 October 1935, National Government Resources Committee files, Chinese National Archives II, cited in Dai Houjie, "The German Who Wrote China's War Plans," 283.

11. Zhang Baijia, "China's Experience in Seeking Foreign Military Aid," 6.

12. Ma Zhendu and Qi Rugao, *Enemy or Friend?*, 316–17.

13. Zhang Baijia, "China's Experience in Seeking Foreign Military Aid," 6.

14. Qin Xiaoyi, ed., *zhonghua minguo zhongyao shiliao chubian—dui ri kangzhan shiqi [The Preliminary Compilation of the Important Historical Documents of the Republic of China—the War Against Japan]*, Volume III, Wartime Diplomacy (2), 687.

15. Dai Houjie, "The German Who Wrote China's War Plans," 297.

16. Yue Qianhou, *guweijun yu zhanshi waijiao [Wellington Koo and Wartime Diplomacy]* (Hebei, China: Hebei People's Press, 1998), 278.

17. Ibid., 280.

18. Tang Zong, ed., *zai jiangjieshi shenbian—sicong shi gaoji muliao tangzong riji [Diaries: My Eight Years as Chiang Kai-shek's Confidential Secretary]*, Archives of the Ministry of Public Security, entry, 12 January 1942.

19. Ibid., 314.

20. For the heated exchanges of views on India between Chiang Kai-shek, Roosevelt, and Churchill, see Map Room Files, box 10, folder 1, in the FDR Library, Hyde Park, New York.

21. Li Shian, *taipingyang zhanzheng shiqi de zhongying guanxi [Sino-British Relations during the Pacific War]* (Beijing: Chinese Social Sciences Press, 1994), 12.

22. The Tolstoy-Dolan mission, the OSS files, Record Group 226, entry 146, U.S. National Archives II.

23. Tang Zong, *Diaries*, entry, 12 January 1942, 285, 313.

CHAPTER 2

1. Blücher would become Stalin's most senior military officer, the first of the five field marshals, in 1935 when the Red Army initially adopted the military ranking system, only to be killed by Stalin three years later during the Purge for "treason." See A. N. Kartunova, *General Galens in China*,

1924–1927, translated from Russian into Chinese, Beijing: Chinese Social Science Academy Press, 1983; also, Wang Zhiliang, "dongzheng beifa de chouhua zhihui zhe" [The Commander of the Eastern and Northern Expeditions—The Overall Military Adviser General Galens during the Great Revolution], in Dai Houjie, ed., *The Biographies of Foreign Advisers in Modern China*, 109–44.

2. Li Jiagu, "jiuyiba shibian hou zhongsu guanxi de tiaozheng" [On the Readjustment of the Sino-Soviet Relationship after the Manchuria Incident of 18 September 1931), in *Journal of War with Japan* 2 (1992).

3. Liu Zhiqing, *enyuanlijinhou de fansi—zhongsu guanxi qishi nian [Seventy Years of Sino-Soviet Relations—Reflections after Tumultuous Experiences, 1917–1991]* (Jinan, Shandong, China: The Yellow River Press, 1998), 236.

4. Ibid., 238.

5. Li Jiagu, *hezhuo yu chongtu—1931–1945 nian de zhongsu guanxi [Cooperation and Confrontations—Sino-Soviet Relations between 1931 and 1945]*, 82.

6. Yang Jie, *Yang Jie Riji [Yang Jie's Diaries]*, in Li Jiagu, *Cooperation and Confrontations—Sino-Soviet Relations between 1931 and 1945*, 82.

7. Qin Xiaoyi, ed., *The Preliminary Compilation of the Important Historical Documents of the Republic of China—The War against Japan*, Volume III, Wartime Diplomacy (2), 486–91; also Liu Zhiqing, *Seventy Years of Sino-Soviet Relations*, 242.

8. Zhang Baijia, "China's Experience in Seeking Foreign Military Aid," 9.

9. The figures vary by Chinese and Russian accounts, but the variations are inconsequential. The key document is the Chinese government's 4 March 1941 ledger listing all the weapons inflow from the USSR. See Li Jiagu, *Cooperation and Confrontation*, 85–99; also Liu Zhiqing, *Seventy Years of Sino-Soviet Relations*, 242–43.

10. For example, Stalin let the Chinese use the loan to buy Soviet aircraft for $50,000 apiece, a remarkable bargain for the Chinese indeed. See Wellington Koo, *Gu Weijun huiyilu [The Memoirs of Wellington Koo]* (Beijing: Zhonghua Books, 1985), 136; Zhang Baijia, "China's Experience in Seeking Foreign Military Aid," 10.

11. Wu Jingping, *Song Ziwen pingzhuan [A Critical Biography of T. V. Song]* 311–18; also Wu Dongzhi, *zhongguo waijiaoshi [A History of Chinese Diplomacy, 1919–1949]* (Henan, China: Henan People's Press, 1990), 457; Peng Yulong, "sulian dui zhonguo kangri zhanzheng de junshi yuanzhu" [The USSR's Military Aid to China's War of Resistance against Japan], *Junshi Lishi [Journal of Military History]* 2 (1991).

12. Liu Zhiqing, *Seventy Years of Sino-Soviet Relations*, 241.

13. Li Jiagu, *Cooperation and Confrontations*, 78–81.

14. Peng Yulong, "The U.S.S.R.'s Military Aid to China's War of Resistance against Japan"; Liu Zhiqing, *Seventy Years of Sino-Soviet Relations*, 245, 250.

15. Liu Zhiqing, "kangri zhanzheng qijian zulian zaihua junshiguwen jiqi zhuoy-
    ong" [The Soviet Military Advisers in China during the War of Resistance
    against the Japanese and Their Role], *Junshi lishi [Journal of Military History]*
    4 (1991).

16. Ibid.

17. Liu Zhiqing, *Seventy Years of Sino-Soviet Relations*, 249.

18. There are no definite statistics for the total number of downed Japanese
    airplanes attributable to the Soviet pilots, as with any such claims by any
    air force units in most countries. The KMT government documents dated
    in 1941 estimate the total number of Japanese planes shot down by both
    the Chinese and Soviet pilots in China between August 1938 and 1941 at
    1,049; yet recent scholarship in Taiwan calculates that the Soviet pilots par-
    ticipated in no fewer than twenty-five major campaigns in China and were
    directly responsible for a hundred or so downed Japanese planes, and sank
    more than seventy Japanese ships. The number I have used here is based
    on a careful comparison of the Russian documents and Chinese statistics
    and has been regarded as most creditable by most historians in this field.
    See Zhang Baijia, "China's Experience in Seeking Foreign Military Aid,"
    11; Wang Zheng, *dongdang zhong de tongmeng—kangzhan shiqi de zhongsu
    guangxi [An Alliance in Turmoil—the Sino-Soviet Relationship during the War
    of Resistance against Japan]* (Guilin, China: Guangxi Normal University
    Press, 1993), 124; Liu Zhiqing, *Seventy Years of Sino-Soviet Relations*, 251.

19. Liu Zhiqing, *Seventy Years of Sino-Soviet Relations*, 252–53.

20. Ibid., 252.

21. Qin Xiaoyi, ed., *The Preliminary Compilation of the Important Historical
    Documents of the Republic of China—The War against Japan*, Volume III,
    Wartime Diplomacy (2), 335.

22. Liu Zhiqing, *Seventy Years of Sino-Soviet Relations*, 278, 289.

23. Memo, H. T. Jerrel to the director of naval intelligence, subject: "Some Notes
    on Foreign Diplomatic Representation in Chungking," 27 August 1945,
    Record Group 38, Alusna Letters—1945, ONI-FE-China/Malay Desk, U.S.
    National Archives II.

24. Liu Zhiqing, *Seventy Years of Sino-Soviet Relations*, 249.

25. Shi Zhe, *zai lishi juren shengbian—shi zhe huiyi lu [Alongside the Great Men
    in History: Memoir of Shi Zhe]* (Beijing: Central Documents Press, 1991),
    131–32. She Zhe served as an NKVD officer in the Soviet Union for nine
    years and came back to China to be Mao Zedong's Russian interpreter and
    intelligence aid for much of the 1940s and 1950s.

26. Cable of ECCI to the Central Committee of the CCP, 9 September 1939,
    quoted in Niu Jun, *cong yanan zouxiang shijie [From Yenan to the World]*
    (Fuzhou, China: Fujian People's Press, 1992), 64.

27. For a detailed account of this military campaign, see Alvin Coox, *The*

Anatomy of a Small War—Soviet-Japanese Struggle for Changkufeng/Khasan, 1938 (Westport, CT: Greenwood Press, 1977).

28. The Chinese Communist newspaper, *Xinhua Ribao (New China Daily)*, published in Chungking, provided daily detailed accounts of the conflict, with total editorial support for the Soviet actions. See Liu Zhiqing, *Seventy Years of Sino-Soviet Relations*, 266.

29. Ibid.

30. Ibid., 286.

31. Zhang Baijia, "China's Experience in Seeking Foreign Military Aid," 14.

32. V. I. Chuikov, *Memoirs—My Mission to China*, New Jersey: Eastbridge Publishers, 2003), 57–58.

33. For details on this episode, see John Garver's *Chinese-Soviet Relations, 1937–1945—Diplomacy of Chinese Nationalism* (New York: Oxford University Press, 1988).

34. Qin Xiaoyi, ed., *The Preliminary Compilation of the Important Historical Documents of the Republic of China—The War against Japan*, Volume III, Wartime Diplomacy (2), 363–70.

35. Liu Zhiqing, *Seventy Years of Sino-Soviet Relations*, 267.

36. Chuikov, *Memoirs—My Mission to China*, 35.

37. Ibid., 36.

CHAPTER 3

1. Claire Lee Chennault, *Way of a Fighter—Memoirs of Claire Lee Chennault*, ed. by Robert Hotz (New York: G. P. Putnam's Sons, 1949), 29.

2. Ibid., 21.

3. Ibid., 20.

4. Ibid.

5. Ibid.

6. Wanda Cornelius and Thayne Short, *Ding Hao: America's Air War in China, 1937–1945* (Gretna, LA: Pelican Publishing Co., 1980), 46.

7. Chennault, *Way of a Fighter*, 21.

8. Ibid.

9. Ibid., 23.

10. Ibid., 22.

11. Ibid., 17.

12. Ibid., 30.

13. Ibid.

14. Ibid., 34–35.

15. Xi Xia, "riben feiji de kexing, hangkong weiyuan hui guwen, feihudui dui-zhang chen na de" [The Nemesis of Japan's Airplanes—A Biography of Claire Lee Chennault as the Adviser to the National Aviation Council and the Leader of the Flying Tigers], in Dai Houjie, ed., *The Biographies of*

Foreign Advisers in Modern China, 334–35.

16. James McHugh, *Memoirs,* chapter 4, box 1, *The James McHugh Papers.*

17. Xiao Ming, "xian shibian de woxuan zhe—jiang jieshi zhang xueliang de guwen duan na" [The Mediator of the Xian Incident—Adviser to Chiang Kai-shek and Zhang Xueliang], in Dai Houjie, ed. *The Biographies of Foreign Advisers in Modern China,* 33–69.

18. Li Shushan, and Wang Yehong, *zhongguo kongjun zhanshi [A Military History of China's Air Force]* (Guangzhou: Huaxia Press, 1996,) 16–18.

19. Ibid.

20. Chennault, *Way of a Fighter,* 34.

21. Xi Xia, "The Nemesis of Japan's Airplanes," 336–37.

22. Chennault, *Way of a Fighter,* 37.

23. Xi Xia, "The Nemesis of Japan's Airplanes," 337.

24. Chennault, *Way of a Fighter,* 39.

25. Ibid.

26. Li Shushan and Wang Yehong, *A Military History of China's Air Force,* 29–30.

27. Xi Xia, "The Nemesis of Japan's Airplanes," 338.

28. Ibid., 341.

29. Robert B. Hotz, et al., *With General Chennault: The Story of the Flying Tigers* (New York: Coward-McCann, Inc., 1943), 90–91.

30. Chennault, *Way of a Fighter,* 98.

31. Xi Xia, "The Nemesis of Japan's Airplanes," 342.

32. Chennault, *Way of a Fighter,* 99.

33. Ibid., 100.

34. Ibid., 101.

35. John Earl Haynes and Harvey Klehr, *VENONA: Decoding Soviet Espionage in America* (New Haven, CT: Yale University Press, 1999), 145–50.

36. Lauchlin Currie, "Report on Some Aspects of the Current Political, Economic and Military Situation in China," 15 March 1941, *The Lauchlin Currie Papers,* Box 4.

37. Ibid.

38. Ibid.

39. Ibid.

40. Chennault, *Way of a Fighter,* 99.

41. Ibid.

42. Ibid., 102.

43. Dick Rossi, *A Flying Tiger's Story,* unpublished manuscript, 22 July 2005.

44. Ibid.

45. Chennault, *Way of a Fighter,* 104.

46. Dick Rossi, *A Flying Tiger's Story.*

47. Chennault, *Way of a Fighter,* 112.

48. Ibid.

49. Ibid.

50. James Howard, *Roar of the Tiger* (New York: Orion Books, 1991), 122.

51. Xi Xia, "The Nemesis of Japan's Airplanes," 345; also Robert Hotz, *With General Chennault*, 21. Note that Hotz claims nine Japanese planes were shot down.

52. The origin of the phrase "Flying Tigers" has been vague. Recent documents from China indicate that it probably came from the Chinese Manchuria warlord Zhang Zuolin, who assembled the first real Chinese air force squadrons in 1923. At the time, Zhang named three of his squadrons "Flying Tigers," "Flying Dragons," and "Flying Eagles." See Li Shushan and Wang Yehong, *A History of China's Air Force*, 17.

53. Chennault, *Way of a Fighter*, 134.

54. James Howard, *Roar of the Tiger*, 103.

55. For the statistics, see Xi Xia, "The Nemesis of Japan's Airplanes," 345.

56. Ibid., 345–46.

57. George Marshall and Sherman Miles to John Magruder, 11 July 1941, The U.S. Army, AMMISCA File, RG 493, U.S. National Archives II.

58. Albert C. Wedemeyer, *Wedemeyer Reports!*, 197.

59. Chennault, *Way of a Fighter*, 142.

60. Report, Magruder to War Department, 24 December 1941, RG 493, AMMISCA Mission, *The Magruder Files*.

61. Chennault, *Way of a Fighter*, 170.

62. Ibid.

63. Ibid.

64. Chennault, *Way of a Fighter*, 171.

65. Ibid., 172.

66. Ibid.

67. Chennault, *Way of a Fighter*, 174.

68. Ibid., 174–75.

69. Ibid., 174.

70. Correspondence, Chennault to Milton Miles, 4 March 1958, box 1, folder 4, *The Milton Miles Papers*.

CHAPTER 4

1. Minute of meeting, Chiang Kai-shek, Kerr, and McHugh, Chungking, 4 November 1938, box 11, folder 17, *The James McHugh Papers*.

2. For example, in March 1939, Herbert Yardley, the dissolute American code-breaking master, who had been secretly hired by the Chinese secret police on a $10,000 yearly salary to organize a Chinese Black Chamber in Chungking to break Japanese codes, was somewhat puzzled as to why Japanese spies and prisoners of war under hot pursuit by the Chinese secret

police would, by their first instinct, seek sanctuary in the British embassy in Chungking. Yardley was also amused by a curious British bombing escape method in Chungking: whenever the Japanese bombers flew over Chungking and dropped bombs, the British "ran up the Union Jack," hoping not to be harmed by Japanese bombers. Herbert Yardley, *The Chinese Black Chamber* (Boston: Houghton Mifflin, 1983), 76–78, 95–96.

3 . Chinese News Service, *After Five Years of the War,* a report in English published by the Chinese government in New York, 1941, vi.

4. Fan Chengkang, *Zhongguo Zhujie Shi [A History of Foreign Concessions in China]* (Shanghai, Shanghai Social Sciences Academy Press, 1991), 455.

5. Chinese News Service, *After Five Years of the War,* vi.

6. Memo, most secret, Dennys to Director, Military Intelligence, the War Office, etc, subject: Anglo-Chinese Cooperation, 7 February 1941, FO, 371/27615.

7. Liao Yaoxiang and Du Jianshi, "women suo zhidao de guanyu mei jiang goujie de neimu qingkuang" [What We Know about the Secret Deal between the U.S. and Chiang Kai-shek], in *wenshi ziliao xuanji [Selected Culture and History Material]* issue 29, 1–2.

8. Ibid.

9. Memo, most secret, Dennys to Director, 7 February 1941.

10. Report, Keswick to MEW, 12 April 1942, box 2, folder 1, *The James McHugh Papers.*

11. Ibid.

12. Intelligence Report, McHugh to the Office of Naval Operations, Ibid.

13. Ibid.

14. Charles Cruickshank, *SOE in the Far East,* (New York: Oxford University Press, 1983), 77.

15. By the time whatever remnants in the original Detachment 204 finally emerged in Yunnan after the Pearl Harbor, it was a group of emaciated, fatigue-ridden, jungle-tortured British soldiers.

On 14 March 1942, a DC-2 airplane en route to Chungking mysteriously crashed and burned at Kunming airport. A total of thirteen people on board were killed. Among them was Major General L. E. Dennys, the director of Detachment 204 and the most senior British military person in China at the time. (See United States Army, AMISCA File, The Magruder Mission to China, July 1941 through June 1942, War Diary, #459, Microfilm, Government Documents, Library, University of California, Berkeley.) One month later, Clark Kerr was given a new assignment by Churchill as the British ambassador in Moscow, and he remained there throughout the war, thus finally concluding the first attempt of the British to operate clandestine activities in China. Detachment 204 was quickly forgotten.

16. Cruickshank, *SOE in the Far East,* 4–5.

17. John Keswick Report, box 2, folder 1, *The James McHugh Papers.*
18. Cruickshank, *SOE in the Far East,* 61.
19. Ibid., 5.
20. Ibid., 61–77.
21. "History of S.O.E Oriental Mission—May 1941–March 1942," PRO, HS 1/207.
22. Keswick Report, box 2, folder 1, *The James McHugh Papers.* A slightly different version of this proposal can also be found in "A Report of the China Commando Group," Chungking, 9 April 1942, PRO, HS 1/349.
23. Memo, O to AD/O, O/FE/790, 20 February 1942, PRO, HS 1/164.
24. Keswick Report, box 2, folder 1, *The James McHugh Papers.*
25. Memorandum, "Sabotage in China," most secret, January 1942, PRO, HS 1/164.
26. Keswick Report, box 2, folder 1, *The James McHugh Papers.*
27. Tai Li was a pivotal figure in the KMT empire, yet he was merely a major general in the hierarchy.
28. Jonathan Spence, *To Change China—Western Advisors in China, 1620–1960,* 198; also, Shen Yuan, *Tai Li of Jiangshan County (Jiangshan Daili),* (Beijing: Tuanjie Press, 1992), 3–6.
29. G-2 Report, #89-d-45, the Naval Group China Files, RG 38, box 39, U.S. National Archives.
30. Herbert Yardley, *The Chinese Black Chamber,* 38.
31. Milton Miles, *A Different Kind of War* (New York: Doubleday, 1967), 129–34.
32. Cruickshank, *SOE in the Far East,* 78.
33. Keswick Report, box 2, folder 1, *The James McHugh Papers.*
34. Ibid.
35. Official History Manuscript, RG 38, *The Milton Miles Papers,* box 1, folder 1, 19, U.S. National Archives.
36. Tang Zong, *Diaries,* 250.
37. McHugh Report, box 2, folder 1, *The James McHugh Papers.*
38. Official History Manuscript, RG 38, *The Milton Miles Papers,* box 1, folder 1, 20, U.S. National Archives.
39. Ibid.
40. Ibid.
41. Meeting memo, 8 December 1941, by Magruder, *The John Magruder Papers.*
42. Meeting memo of Ho, Magruder, and Dennys, 10 December 1941, *The John Magruder Papers.*
43. Cruickshank, *SOE in the Far East,* 160.
44. Meeting memo, 23 December 1941, *The James Magruder Papers.*
45. Meeting memo, 26 December 1941, *The James Magruder Papers.*

46. Meeting memo, 16 December 1941, *The James Magruder Papers*.

47. Intelligence Report, Donovan to FDR, #427, 20 April 1942, President's Safe Files, box 148, the FDR Library, Hyde Park, New York.

48. Qiao Jiacai, *Selected Writings of Qiao Jiacai*, Vol. 2, *daili jiangjun he tade tong-zhi [General Tai Li and His Comrades]* (Taipei: Chongwai Press, 1981), 309.

49. Tang Zong, *Diaries*, 267.

50. *New York Times*, 19 April 1942.

51. Report, 0.100 to London, subject: O.M., China, 29 April 1942, PRO, HS 1/164.

52. Intelligence Report, Esson Gale to Donovan, Record Group 226, entry 99, box 78, folder 55, 55.

53. "Capt. Mohan Singh to Major Fujiwara Iwaichi for the Willingness of the Indian Prisoners of War to Join Hands with Japanese Forces and to Form the I.N.A. to Fight the British," 31 December 1941, in T. R. Sareen, ed. *Select Documents on Indian National Army* (Delhi: Agam Prakashan, 1988), 4.

54. Tang Zong, *Diaries*, 255.

55. Official History Manuscript, Milton Miles Files, Record Group 38, box 1, folder 1, 20, U.S. National Archives.

56. Intelligence Report, Esson Gale to Donovan, Record Group 226, entry 99, box 78, folder 55, 92.

57. Tang Zong, *Diaries*, 260–61.

58. Memo, 0.100 to London, 29 April 1942, "O.M.—China, Commando Group," PRO, HS 1/164.

59. Meeting Memo, 10 December 1941. *The John Magruder Papers*, in AMMISCA Files, RG 493, U.S. Military Mission to China, Brigadier General Magruder Files, U.S. National Archives.

60. Secret Memo, 0.100 to London, 29 April 1942, "O.M.—China, Commando Group," PRO, HS 1/164.

61. Official History Manuscript, *The Milton Miles Papers*, RG 38, box 1, folder 1, 20, U.S. National Archives.

62. Tang Zong, *Diaries*, 266.

63. McHugh Report, box 2, folder 1, *The James McHugh Papers*.

64. Ibid.

65. Fu would later be surrounded by Chinese Communist agents, including his own daughter, and he eventually betrayed Chiang and switched over to the Communists in 1949.

66. McHugh Report, box 2, folder 1, *The James McHugh Papers*.

67. Ibid.

68. Bradley Smith, *The Shadow Warriors—OSS and the Origins of the CIA* (New York: Basic Books, 1983), 44.

69. Tang Zong, *Diaries*, 266.

70. McHugh Report, box 2, folder 1, *The James McHugh Papers*.
71. Ibid.
72. Keswick Report, box 2, folder 1, *The James McHugh Papers*.
73. Cruickshank, *SOE in the Far East*, 154.
74. Ibid.
75. McHugh Report, box 2, folder 1, *The James McHugh Papers*.
76. Interview with Eddie Liu, 29 June 29 1992, Mountain View, California. Eddie Liu (Liu Cheng-fang) was Tai Li's agent and throughout the war served as the chief interpreter for Tai Li, first in the China Commando Group then the Sino-American Cooperative Organization (SACO).
77. Official History Manuscript, RG 38, *The Milton Miles Papers*, box 2, folder 1, U.S. National Archives, 21. Also, Keswick Report, box 2, folder 1, *The James McHugh Papers*.
78. Cruickshank, *SOE in the Far East*, 78.
79. Keswick Report, box 2, folder 1, *The James McHugh Papers*.
80. Cruickshank, *SOE in the Far East*, 78.
81. Keswick's letter to Nyholm, see Cruickshank, *SOE in the Far East*, 79.
82. Interview with Eddie Liu, 29 June 1992, Mountain View, California.

CHAPTER 5
1. Milton Miles, *The Navy Launched a Dragon*, unpublished manuscript, 1.
2. Ibid.
3. Edgar Snow, "The What-the-Hell Pennant," *Saturday Evening Post*, 10 November 1945.
4. *Official History Manuscript*, Miles Files, chapter 1, 2 RG38, box 1, folder I, "Personal," U.S. National Archives.
5. For detailed discussion on this, see Maochun Yu, *OSS in China* (New Haven, CT: Yale University Press, 1997), 50–51.
6. *Official History Manuscript*, Miles Files, chapter 1, 2 RG38, box 1, folder I, 4, "Personal," U.S. National Archives.
7. Ibid.
8. Ibid.
9. Chief of Naval Operations Serial 0302823, 11 March 1942, Naval Historical Center, Navy Yard.
10. Milton Miles, *A Different Kind of War*, 18.
11. Letter, McHugh to Knox, "Secret and Personal," 1 August 1942, box 1, folder 9, *The James McHugh Papers*.
12. Minute of talk between Harry Hopkins and T. V. Soong, *T .V. Soong Papers*, box 29, folder "H. Hopkins."
13. Roy Stratton, *The Army-Navy Game* (Falmouth, MA: Volta Company, 1977), 26–27.
14. COI had split into Office of Strategic Services, the OSS, and the Office of

War Information, the OWI, in June 1942.

15. Milton Miles, *The Navy Launched a Dragon*, chapter 5, 58.
16. Ibid., 58–59.
17. Ibid., 61.
18. Stratton, *The Army-Navy Game*, 61.
19. Ibid., 71.
20. Ibid., 67–68.
21. Ibid.
22. Memo, Miles to Tai Li, 19 December 1942, RG 38, *The Milton Miles Papers*, box 2, U.S. National Archives.
23. Miles, *The Navy Launched a Dragon*, 62.
24. Stratton, *The Army-Navy Game*, 47.
25. Ibid., 100.
26. Ibid., 71–72.
27. Ibid.
28. Miles, *The Navy Launched a Dragon*, 62.
29. Stratton, *The Army-Navy Game*, 13.
30. Ibid., 68–69.
31. Ibid., 69.
32. Ibid., 76.
33. Miles, *A Different Kind of War*, 48.
34. Yu, *OSS in China*, 67–68.
35. Miles, *A Different Kind of War*, 50–51.
36. Ibid., 53.
37. Miles, *The Navy Launched a Dragon*, 63.
38. Stratton, *The Army-Navy Game*, 49.
39. Ibid.
40. Ibid., 49–50.
41. Ibid.
42. Metzel to Miles, 3 January 1943, RG 38, *The Milton Miles Papers*, box 2.
43. Cable, Purnell to Tai Li, 27 January 1943, RG 38, *The Milton Miles Papers*, box 2.
44. Cable, War Department to AMMISCA, NR.2146, 16 February 1943, RG 38, *The Milton Miles Papers*, box 2.
45. Cable, King to Miles, 16 February 1943, RG 38, *The Milton Miles Papers*, box 2.
46. Ibid., 21 February 1943.
47. Ibid.
48. Stilwell to AGWAR, 21 February 1943, RG 493, Record of China-Burma-India Theater of Operations, U.S. Army, Record of Commanding General, Personnel Message File, box 1, Suitland Record Center, U.S. National Archives.

49. Secret memo, William D. Leahy to Miles, attached to the official English version of the SACO Agreement signed on 15 April 1943, RG 226, entry 148, box 2, folder 51, "Chungking-OSS-Op-1," U.S. National Archives.

50. Memo, Miles to Purnell, Metzel, and Legget, 1 January 1943, RG 38, *The Milton Miles Papers*, box 2.

CHAPTER 6

1. For the arduous and painful negotiations with the United States for these loans, see Wu Jingping, *A Critical Biography of T. V. Song*, 311–18.

2. Arthur N. Young, *China and the Helping Hand, 1937–1945* (Cambridge, MA: Harvard University Press, 1963), 142.

3. Ibid., 144.

4. Cable, T. V. Soong to Chiang Kai-shek, 15 April 1941, in Qin Xiaoyi, ed., *The Preliminary Compilation of the Important Historical Documents of the Republic of China—The War against Japan*, Volume III, Wartime Diplomacy (1), 350.

5. Young, *China and the Helping Hand*, 146.

6. Ibid., 147.

7. Ibid.

8. Qin Xiaoyi, ed., *The Preliminary Compilation of the Important Historical Documents*, Volume III, 503, 505.

9. Young, *China and the Helping Hand*, 217.

10. Ibid.

11. Qin Xiaoyi, ed., *The Preliminary Compilation of the Important Historical Documents*, Volume III, 324–26.

12. U.S. 89th Congress, Judiciary Committee, United States Senate, *Morgenthau Diaries (China)*, Vol. I, Book 484, 186.

13. Wu Jingping, *A Critical Biography of T. V. Song*, 343.

14. Ibid., 345.

15. Young, *China and the Helping Hand*, 229.

16. Ibid., 350.

17. Ibid., 402.

18. *Morgenthau Diaries (China)*, Vol. II, Book 845, 314–22.

19. Li Shian, *Sino-British Relations in the Pacific War*, 97–109.

20. Cable to FDR from Chiang Kai-shek, Presidential Map Room Files, box 10, folder 2, FDR Library, Hyde Park, New York.

21. For an excellent treatment of this topic, see Li Shian, *Sino-British Relations in the Pacific War*, 16–23.

22. Winston Churchill, "War and International Situation," 28 September 1944, FO 371/41689.F4516.4516/10, PRO; cited in Li Shian, *Sino-British Relations in the Pacific War*, 54.

23. For discussion on this diplomatic crisis, see Li Shian, *Sino-British Relations in the Pacific War*, 54–60.
24. See the People's Liberation Army Special Compilation Committee, ed., *dangdai zhongguo jundui de junshi gongzhuo [China Today: The Military Affairs of the Chinese Army]*, (Beijing: Chinese Social Science Press, 1989), Vol. I., 11.
25. For details on this, see Maochun Yu, *OSS in China-Prelude to Cold War*, chapter 8.
26. Chen Hansheng, *si ge shidai de wo [My Life during Four Eras: A Memoir])* (Beijing: Beijing Culture and History Press, 1988), 68. Chen was a veteran Communist intelligence operative, who was the executive officer of Gung Ho in Hong Kong.
27. Yu Maochun, *OSS in China-Prelude to Cold War*, 187.
28. The best post–Cold War analyses of the wartime Soviet espionage ring in the United States based on internal Soviet Communist Party documents are contained in Allen Weinstein and Alexander Vassiliev's *The Haunted Wood—Soviet Espionage in America, the Stalin Era* (New York: Random House, 1999); and for the most authoritative account on this subject based upon the VENONA decrypts, see Haynes and Klehr's *VENONA—Decoding Soviet Espionage in America*. For the Silvermaster Group, see Weinstein and Vassiliev, 157—71.
29. Haynes and Klehr, *VENONA*, 145.
30. Ibid., 139.
31. Ibid., 138.
32. Ibid., 140.
33. *Morgenthau Diaries (China)*, Vol. II, book 845, 314–22, 9 May 1945, "Gold to China," 1543–48.
34. On Solomon Adler's active role in CPUSA, see Weinstein and Vassiliev, *The Haunted Wood*, 78; on Frank Coe and Adler in the Silvermaster Group, see Weinstein and Vassiliev, *The Haunted Wood*, 158.
35. Young, *China and the Helping Hand*, 399–400.
36. Haynes and Klehr, *VENONA*, 145.
37. Miles, *A Different Kind of War*, 587.

CHAPTER 7
1. Miles, *The Navy Launched a Dragon*, chapter 28, "Unit 9, School of Intelligence and Counter Espionage."
2. Stratton, *The Army-Navy Game*, 98–99.
3. Letter, Miles to Metzel, 10 December 1943, RG 38, *The Milton Miles Papers*, box 1, U.S. National Archives.
4. For Duncan Lee as a Moscow spy, see Haynes and Klehr, *VENONA*, 104–8.

5. Memo, Donovan to Heppner, "Jurisdiction over United States Forces in Foreign Lands," RG 226, entry 146, box 192, folder 2723, U.S. National Archives.
6. Memo, Metzel to Purnell, 29 February 1944, RG 38, *The Milton Miles Papers,* box 2, U.S. National Archives; also Stratton, *The Army-Navy Game,* 147.
7. Stratton, *The Army-Navy Game,* 147.
8. Ibid.
9. Miles, *The Navy Launched a Dragon,* 175.
10. Ibid.
11. Ibid., 177.
12. Ibid.
13. Ibid.
14. Ibid., 182.
15. Ibid., 183.
16. Ibid.
17. Minutes of Meeting Held Wednesday, 16 June 1943, at General Stilwell's Home. Subject: OSS, RG 226, entry 110, box 51, folder 2, U.S. National Archives.
18. FETO Daily Report, 29 February 1944, memo, Hoffman to Stilwell for Coughlin, RG 226, entry 99, box 58, folder 26, U.S. National Archives.
19. FETO Daily Report, 11 March 1944. Subject: Kunjara group, RG 226, entry 99, box 58, folder 26, U.S. National Archives.
20. Miles, *The Navy Launched a Dragon,* 184.
21. Ibid., 189.
22. Ibid., 190.
23. Ibid., 194.
24. Ibid., 191.
25. Ibid., 192.
26. Ibid., 195.
27. Ibid.
28. Ibid., 200.
29. Ibid., 189.
30. Ibid., 197.
31. Ibid., 200.
32. Ibid.
33. Ibid., 203.
34. Ibid.
35. Stratton, *The Army-Navy Game,* 108–9.
36. Ibid., 178.
37. Top Secret cable, Dow to Donovan, 26 October 1944. RG 226, Roll 127, M1642, U.S. National Archives.

38. Report of investigation, Office of Inspector General, China Theater, 5 November 1944, RG 226, Roll 127, M1642, U.S. National Archives.

39. Ibid.

40. Memo, Donovan to Vandegrift, 6 November 1944, RG 226, Roll 127, M1642, U.S. National Archives.

41. Stratton, *The Army-Navy Game*, 179.

42. Ibid., 85.

43. Memo, Miles to Major Hsiao, serial 0303623, 27 March 1942, RG 38, *The Milton Miles Papers*, box 1, folder 3, "Personal," U.S. National Archives.

44. Letter, Donovan to Purnell, 3 November 1943, RG 226, entry 148, box 14, folder 194, U.S. National Archives.

45. Ibid.

46. Memo, Donovan to Hayden, 21 September 1942, RG 226, entry 139, box 267, folder 3934, U.S. National Archives.

47. Memo, Donovan to John King Fairbank, 20 September 1942, RG 226, entry 139, box 267, folder 3934, U.S. National Archives.

48. Memo, Lusey to Donovan, 14 September 1942, RG 226, entry 139, box 267, folder 3934, U.S. National Archives.

49. Ibid.

50. Ibid.

51. Ibid.

52. Letter, Ernest Price to the White House, 8 October 1942, Presidential safe file, "O.S.S.," box 4, folder "O.S.S.," FDR Library, Hyde Park, New York.

53. Ibid.

54. Letter, Miles to Metzel, 2 December 1942, RG 38, *The Milton Miles Papers*, box 1, folder 3, U.S. National Archives.

55. Cable, Hayden to Donovan, 6 October 1942, box 1, folder 9, *The James McHugh Papers*.

56. Memo, Donovan to Heppner, 15 December 1943, RG 226, entry 110, box 51, folder 2, U.S. National Archives.

57. Hoffman's log of tour of duty, 20–21, RG 226, entry 145, box 4, U.S. National Archives.

58. Ibid.

59. Memo, John Coughlin to Donovan, 28 April 1944, RG 226, entry 146, box 82, folder 1167, U.S. National Archives.

60. "The Mansfield Report," RG 226, entry 99, box 67, folder 212, U.S. National Archives.

61. Letter, General Zhu De (Chu The), to Donovan, 23 January 1945, RG 226, entry 190, box 583, folder 435, U.S. National Archives.

62. Memo, Willis Bird to Chief of Staff. Subject: Yenan Trip, 24 January 1945, RG226, entry 148, box 7, folder 103, "Dixie," U.S. National Archives.

63. Memo, Leahy to Marshall, 15 January 1945, RG 218, Leahy files, box 21, folder 136, "Miscellaneous memorandum, 1945–1946, U.S. National Archives.

64. Ivan Yeaton, *Memoirs of Col. Ivan D. Yeaton, USA (RET), 1919–1953,* Unpublished manuscript, The Hoover Institution Archives, 1976, 95–96.

65. Stratton, *The Army-Navy Game,* 134.

66. Ibid.

67. Ibid.

68. Memo, Miles to Metzel, 10 December 1943, RG 38, *The Milton Miles Papers,* box 1, U.S. National Archives.

69. Memo by D. M. Hykes, "Summary of Proceedings at Dinner Party Given by General Tai Li on April 6," 7 April 1944, RG 226, entry 148, box 17, folder 244, U.S. National Archives.

70. Stratton, *The Army-Navy Game,* 105.

71. Memo by Colonel W. H. Bales, FE comment, October 1944, RG 38, entry ONI-China/Malay Desk, box 2, Alusna letters, 1943–1944, U.S. National Archives.

72. Qiao Jiacai, *Weilishi zhuozheng [Witness to History]* (Taipei: Zhongwai Zazhi Publisher, 1985), 384–85.

73. Stratton, *The Army-Navy Game,* 246.

CHAPTER 8

1. Qiao Jiacai, *Selected Writings of Qiao Jiacai, Vol. 2, Daili jiangjun he tade tong-zhi [General Tai Li and His Comrades]* (Taipei, Chongwai Press, 1981), 86.

2. "Note on Conversation with the President on 30 August 1943 from Noon to 1245 PM," box 32, folder "Roosevelt," *The T. V. Soong Papers,* Hoover Institution, Stanford, California.

3. Maochun Yu, *OSS in China,* 36.

4. Wen's decrypts went to only Chiang Kai-shek; T. V. Soong, who was Chiang's foreign minister; and H. H. Kung, who was Chiang's finance minister. For details on this issue, see Ibid., 36–37.

5. For the espionage warfare between the KMT and CCP in the 1920s and 1930s, see Frederic Wakeman, *Policing Shanghai, 1927–1937* (Berkeley: University of California Press, 1995), 131–61; also, Maochun Yu, *OSS in China,* 31–59.

6. Wei Daming, "Ji Gemingjun chuangban wuxiandian shiye zhi jingguo" [The History of Establishing Radios for the Revolutionary Army], *Zhuanji Wenxue [Documentary Biographies]* 41, no. 6: 86, 87n.

7. Ibid.

8. Qiao Jiacai, *Selected Writings of Qiao Jiacai, Vol. 2, General Tai Li and His Comrades,* 76–77.

9. Ibid., 77–78.
10. Wei Daming, "bayisi kongzhan dajie yu qingbao zuoye" [Air Triumph of 14 August and Our Intelligence Operations], *Documentary Biographies* 39, no. 2: 11–17.
11. Ibid.
12. David Kahn, *The Codebreakers: The Story of Secret Writing* (New York: Macmillan, 1967), 368–69.
13. Wei Daming, "Zhenkong qingbao dui fangkong yu kongzhan zhi gongxian" [Air Intelligence's Contribution to Air Defense and Air Battle], *Documentary Biographies* 39, no. 3: 113–14.
14. Ibid.
15. Wei Daming, "Air Intelligence's Contribution to Air Defense and Air Battle," 113.
16. Ibid., 113–14.
17. For more details, see Maochun Yu, *OSS in China*, 38–39.
18. Tang Zong, *My Eight Years as Chiang Kai-shek's Confidential Secretary*, 145.
19. Wei Daming, "zhenkong qingbao duiyu zhongyingmei junshi hezuo zhi gongxian"[Air Intelligence's Contribution to the Military Cooperation among China, Great Britain, and the United States], *Documentary Biographies* 39, no. 4: 104–5.
20. Ibid.
21. Ibid.
22. Ibid.
23. Wei Daming, "Air Intelligence's Contribution to the Military Cooperation among China, Great Britain, and the United States," 103–4.
24. Barbara W. Tuchman, *Stilwell and American Experience in China, 1911–1945* (New York: Bantam Books, 1971), 326.
25. *New York Times,* 1 April 1942.
26. Ni Naibing, "*diliu gongzuo dui mianyin shuoyi*" [Remembrance of Group 6's Work in Burma and India], *Documentary Biographies* 39, no. 5, 90.
27. Wei Daming, "Air Intelligence's Contribution to the Military Cooperation among China, Great Britain, and the United States," 106.
28. Ni Naibing, "Remembrance of Group 6's Work in Burma and India," 91.
29. Wei Daming, "Air Intelligence's Contribution to the Military Cooperation among China, Great Britain, and the United States," 106.
30. Ibid.
31. For more details, see Maochun Yu, *OSS in China*, 48.
32. Memo, Milton Miles to Frank Knox, Subject: SACO Agreement, Article XVIII, 9 December 1943, RG 38, *The Milton Miles Papers*, box 1, U.S. National Archives.

CHAPTER 9

1. Qiao Duofu, "kangzhan chuqi tianjin dixia chuban de kangri kanwu" [Underground Resistance Publications in Tianjin in the Early Stage of the Anti-Japanese War; Shi Fu, "tianjin lunxian hou mimi chuban de jishibao" [The Secretly Published Jishibao after the Fall of Tianjin], in *Tianjin wenshi ziliao xuanji [Selected Documentary Anthology of Tianjin Culture and History]* 39, Tianjin People's Press, April 1987.

2. Chen Sizheng, "kangri zhanzheng he jiefang zhanzheng zhong de kunming guangbo diantai" [Kunming Radio Station during the Anti-Japanese War and the War for Liberation], in *Kunming wenshi ziliao xuanji [Selected Documentary Anthology of Kunming Culture and History]* 11 (August 1988); also, Xiao Zhiyi, "zai guomindang guangbo diantai li de jianwen" [What I Saw and Heard Inside a KMT Radio Station], in *Xian wenshi ziliao [Xian Documents of Culture and History]*, December 1982.

3. Presidential Executive Order, 9 March 1943, cited in Memo, OWI/China to Commanding General, China Theater, 6 December 1944. Record Group 493, box 51, folder "OWI—Army," U.S. National Archives.

4. Leaflet "Warning to the people of Nanchang," Record Group 493, box 52, U.S. National Archives.

5. Leaflet urging puppet troops to desert to the allied side, Record Group 493, box 52, U.S. National Archives.

6. Leaflet requesting local help for downed airmen, Record Group 493, box 52, U.S. National Archives.

7. Memo, Donovan to Joint Psychological Warfare Committee, subject: response to J.W.C. 45/D, forwarded on 31 October 1942 and included as an Enclosure to SECRET, J.P.W.C. 45/1, Record Group 226, U.S. National Archives.

8. Memo, Colonel K. D. Mann, AUS, chief MO, to Lieutenant Commander Reichner, "Typical MO Achievements in ETO, MEDTO & FETO," 4 November 1944, *The Troy Papers*, Record Group 263, box 12, folder 98, U.S. National Archives.

9. Ibid.

10. OSS MO report from Yenan, subject: comments of Japanese Communist leader on American psychological warfare, 29 July 1944, entry 99, box 68, folder 219, Record Group 226, U.S. National Archives.

11. Top secret memo, Colling and Stelle to Hall, subject: APPLE project, entry 148, box 7, folder 103 "Dixie," Record Group 226, U.S. National Archives.

12. Memo, J. M. McHugh, to chief, SI, subject: "Survey of accomplishments of *Shanghai Evening Post and Mercury* enterprise to date," 1 July 1944, *The James McHugh Papers*.

13. McHugh memo, "The Wartime *Shanghai Evening Post and Mercury*—an OSS Project," 1 July 1943. *The James McHugh Papers.*

14. Memo, top secret, The Naval Attaché/China to Chief of Naval Intelligence, subject: "Transportation assistance afforded Chinese Communists by United States Information Service," 29 November 1945. Record Group 38, box 9, U.S. National Archives.

15. Cable, Stilwell to Marshall, Eyes Only, 13 February 1944, Record Group 218, box 21, folder 137, U.S. National Archives.

16. Presidential instruction to Admiral Leahy, 21 February 1944, Record Group 218, box 21, folder 137, U.S. National Archives.

17. Cables, Stilwell to Marshall, Marshall to Leahy, 2 March and 4 March 1944, Record Group 218, box 21, folder 137, U.S. National Archives.

18. Memo, X-2 Branch, New York to Director, X-2, Washington, D.C., 19 October 1943, Record Group 226, entry 92, box 30, folder 18, U.S. National Archives.

19. Memo, Naval Attaché/Chungking to Director of Naval Intelligence, subject: Security, 17 January 1945, Record Group 38, Alusna Letters, ONI-FE-China/Malay Desk, U.S. National Archives.

20. Jingcheng, "jizhongwai jizhe canguantuan fangwen yanan" [Recollections on Chinese and Foreign Correspondents' Visit to Yenan]; also Zhang Keming, "1944 nian zhongwai jizhetuan yanan zhixing" [On the 1944 Visit to Yenan by the Delegation of Chinese and Foreign Correspondents], in *Chongqing wenshi ziliao [Chongqing Documents of Culture and History]* 26 (June 1986).

21. See, for example, Lindsay's report published in *Amerasia* magazine, "North China Front" (March/April 1944).

22. Shen Jianhong, "kangzhan houqi Chongqing de waiguo jizhe" [Foreign Reporters in Chungking in the Latter Years of the Anti-Japanese War], in *Zhuanji wenxue [Biographical Literature]* (Taipei) 46, no. 4.

23. The most glaring example was Pearson's 15 June 1945 "Washington Merry-Go-Round" column in which the Hurley-Wedemeyer dispute was exposed in the public, causing quite a bit of political turmoil.

CHAPTER 10

1. Charles F. Romanus and Riley Sunderland, *Stilwell's Mission to China* (Washington, D.C.: U.S. Department of the Army, 1953), 57–60.

2. "Message to Generalissimo Chiang Kai-shek from the President," 14 July 1942, Map Room File, box 10, folder 1, FDR Library, Hyde Park, New York.

3. Joseph Stilwell, *The Stilwell Papers*, arranged by Theodore White (New York: Sloane Associates, 1948; rpt. New York: Da Capo, 1991), 26.

4. Charles Romanus and Riley Sunderland, *Stilwell's Command Problem* (Washington, D.C.: U.S. Department of the Army, 1956), 381–82.

5. Ren Donglai, *Forever Querulous Partners*, 227.

6. Young, *China and the Helping Hand*, 340.

7. Ren Donglai, *Forever Querulous Partners*, 227–28.

8. Qin Xiaoyi, ed., *The Preliminary Compilation of the Important Historical Documents of the Republic of China—The War against Japan*, Volume III, Wartime Diplomacy (3), 369.

9. Wu Jingping, *A Critical Biography of T. V. Soong*, 269–70.

10. Ibid., 372.

11. Ibid., 373–74.

12. Cable, draft and formal copies, in Map Room Files, box 10, folder 3, FDR Library, Hyde Park, New York.

13. Memo, Cordell Hull to FDR, 28 April 1944, box 10, folder 3, FDR Library, Hyde Park.

14. Cable, Chiang to FDR, 8 July 1944, Map Room Files, box 10, folder 3, FDR Library, Hyde Park, New York.

15. Note for Admiral Leahy from FDR, 13 July 1944, Map Room Files, box 10, folder 2, Hyde Park, New York.

16. Draft cable by the War Department for Generalissimo Chiang from the President, 8 August 1944, Map Room Files, box 10, folder 2, Hyde Park, New York; also Qin Xiaoyi, ed., *The Preliminary Compilation of the Important Historical Documents of the Republic of China—The War against Japan*, Volume III, Wartime Diplomacy (3), 658–59.

17. Wu Jingping, *A Critical Biography of T. V. Soong*, 380.

18. Cable, FDR to Chiang, 5 October 1944, Map Room Files, box 10, folder 3, Hyde Park, New York.

19. Finding Guide to Presidential Files, Map Room Files, box 10, folder 1, FDR library, Hyde Park, New York.

20. Aide Memoir from the Headquarters of the Gissimo, From Chiang to Hurley, 9 October 1944, Map Room Files, box 10, folder 3, Hyde Park, New York.

21. Ibid.

22. Ibid.

23. Ibid.

CHAPTER 11

1. William Leahy, *I Was There: The Personal Story of the Chief of Staff to Presidents Roosevelt and Truman, Based on His Notes and Diaries Made at the Time* (New York: Whittlesey House, McGraw-Hill Book Company, Inc., 1950), 338.

2. Memo, Wedemeyer to Marshall, 12 August 1945, in *The Albert Wedemeyer Papers*, the Hoover Institution, as edited by Keith Eiler in *Wedemeyer On War and Peace*, (Stanford, CA: Hoover Institution Press, 1987), 138. Unless otherwise noted, all Wedemeyer memos in this section are from Eiler's collection.

3. Memo, Wedemeyer to Marshall, 13 August 1945, in *The Albert Wedemeyer Papers*, the Hoover Institution.

4. See, for example, the feisty files regarding removal of General Frank Dorn by Wedemeyer and returning Dorn to the United States "in grade of Colonel for selfishness and failure to cooperate and general unfitness for command." *The Albert Wedemeyer Papers*, box 87, folder 9, the Hoover Institution.

5. Memo, Wedemeyer to Marshall, 13 April 1945.

6. Memo, Wedemeyer to Chennault, 28 April 1945.

7. Chennault, *Way of A Fighter*, 355.

8. Cable, top secret, Wedemeyer to Marshall, 29 December 1944, Record Group 218, box 3, folder 13, "China, Burma, India, 1944," U.S. National Archives.

9. "Amendment I—Agreement to Supplement the SACO Agreement," Exhibit 3, in "OSS-Section V," RG 493, Records of Allied and U.S. Army Commands in the China-Burma-India Theater of Operations (WWII), Records of the China Theater of Operations, U.S. Army(CT), Records of the General Staff, G-5, (Civil Affairs) Section, Formerly Classified Reports—Special Agencies in China, box 61, Suitland Record Center, U.S. National Archives.

10. Memorandum by the commander in chief, U.S. Fleet and chief of Naval Operations to the Joint Chiefs of Staff, top secret, JCS 1290/1, page 5, Special Distribution, FF1/A16, Serial: 00737, 24 March 1945. RG 493, Records of the China Theater of Operations, Records of the Commanding General, box 19, folder "JCS Minutes, 1944–1946, Misc," Suitland Record Center, U.S. National Archives.

11. Cable, top secret, Wedemeyer to War Department, 29 December 1944, Record Group 218, box 3, folder 13, "China, Burma, India, 1944," U.S. National Archives.

12. Memo, Wedemeyer to Brigadier General George Lincoln, 14 May 1995.

13. For an example, see John Singlaub, *Hazardous Duty: An American Soldier in the Twentieth Century* (New York: Summit Books, 1991).

14. Patton never made it to China, because he was killed in a car accident.

15. Memo, Wedemeyer to Marshall, 1 August 1945.

16. Ibid.

17. Wu Tien-wei, "The Chinese Communist Movement," in James Hsiung and Steven Levine, ed. *China's Bitter War* (Westport, CT: M. E. Sharpe, 1997), 79.

18. Cable, Yenan to Chungking, COUSAOS to CGUSFCT, 11 June 1945, Record Group 226, entry 148, box 6, folder 87, U.S. National Archives.

19. Report on Activities of Spaniel Mission, Coolidge to Heppner, 13 September 1945, Record Group 226, entry 148, box 6, folder 87, "Communists," U.S. National Archives.

20. Minutes of meeting held at Ambassador Hurley's home, No. 2 Chialing Village, 7:45 PM, 30 August 1945, box 87, folder 87.6, *The Albert Wedemeyer Papers*, Hoover Institution.

21. Report of Judge Advocate re the death of John Birch, 13 November 1945, box 87, folder 87.2, *The Albert Wedemeyer Papers*, Hoover Institution. Because of fierce American internal politics, archives related to Birch's death became a center of controversy. Ironically, military records on the Birch incident were scheduled to be declassified in 1972 because of a Freedom of Information Act request, but were held up for a period so that their disclosure would not embarrass President Richard Nixon's trip to China.

22. Minutes of Meeting held at Ambassador Hurley's home, 30 August 1945, box 87, folder 87.6, *The Albert Wedemeyer Papers*, Hoover Institution; also Record Group 38, *The Milton Miles Papers*, box 40, folder "Chinese Communists," U.S. National Archives.

23. Ibid.

24. Ibid.

25. Ibid.

26. Urgent cable, Heppner to Halliwell, 10 August 1945, Record Group 226, entry 154, box 192, folder 3285, "OSS Wash/Donovan Trip, August 1945," U.S. National Archives.

27. Top secret memo, Wedemeyer to Marshall, 12 August 1945.

28. Ibid.

29. Cable, top secret, urgent, Wedemeyer to WARCOS, 15 August 1945.

30. Memo, Wedemeyer to Marshall, 1 August 1945.

31. Shi Zhe, *Alongside the Giants in Our Time*, 306–7. Shi Zhe became Mao Zedong's wartime confidential secretary for intelligence and liaison with Stalin after serving as an agent for OGPU (NKVD since 1934) for nine years.

32. Ibid., 308.

33. Ibid., 309.

34. Ibid., 309–10.

35. Don Lohbeck, *Patrick J. Hurley* (Chicago: Henry Regnery Company, 1956), 370–73.

36. Memo, Wedemeyer to Marshall, 13 April 1945.

37. Ibid.

38. Ibid.

39. Memo, urgent, Wedemeyer to WARCOS, 9 August 1945.

40. Memo, Wedemeyer to WARCOS, 20 November 1945.

41. Memo, Donovan to Wedemeyer, 10 August 1945, Record Group 226, entry 154, box 192, folder 3285, "OSS Wash/Donovan Trip, Aug. 1945," U.S. National Archives.

42. Cable, Heppner to Krause, for information Magruder and Shepherdson, 10 August 1945, Record Group 226, entry 90, box 3, folder 30, "Jap Surrender—In and Out, August 1945," U.S. National Archives.

43. Ibid.

44. OSS Report, "Survey of the Mukden Area Situation as It Has Developed from August 16 to September 10, 1945—Team Cardinal," by Major R. Lamar, Record Group 226, entry 148, box 6, folder 87 "Communists," U.S. National Archives.

45. Ibid.

46. Top secret cable, Commanding General, USF CT, Chungking, to War Department, October 5, 1945, Record Group 226, entry 90, box 3, folder 36, "Mission to Mukden," U.S. National Archives.

47. Memo, Wedemeyer to WARCOS, 20 November 1945.

48. Memo, Wedemeyer to WARCOS for Joint Chiefs of Staff, 14 August 1945.

49. Biographical Dossier, Peiping Executive Headquarters, RG 493, box 38, folder "History—Section II-Organization, 13 January–31 March 1946," U.S. National Archives.

50. Robertson's claim to fame on this matter was his 17 October 1945 report to the secretary of state, entitled "U.S. Intelligence Services in China," which was commissioned by the State Department in the hope to catch up with the steps of the Army and Navy's intelligence operations in China. See the Robertson report and the attachment, "Memorandum on Soviet Activities in Shanghai," in RG 263, the CIA files, *The Murphy Collection*, box 18, folder 28.

51. Historical Record of Executive Headquarters-Peiping Headquarters Group-First Quarterly Installment, 10 January 1946–31 March 1946, RG 493, Peiping Executive HQ, box 66, folder "History," U.S. National Archives.

52. RG 493, Records of Allied & U.S. Army Commands in China-Burma-India Theater of Operations, Record of the Executive HQ, Peiping, China, Record of the U.S. Commissioner, Yenan Liaison Group, box 143, folder "Personnel." U.S. National Archives.

53. Ivan Yeaton, *Memoirs*, 125–26.

54. Mark Stoler, *George C. Marshall: Soldier-Statesman of the American Century* (New York: Twayne Publisher, 1989), 147.

55. Chennault, *Way of a Fighter*, xi.

56. Ibid., xiii.

BIBLIOGRAPHY

ARCHIVAL SOURCES

The Claire Lee Chennault Papers, the Hoover Institution, Stanford, California. This is an important collection of papers on and by one of the key figures in foreign operations in wartime China.

Foreign Office files, London. This contains important wartime British documents related to several major issues in military and intelligence operations in China. Especially useful are the cables and memos regarding SOE's China Commando Group efforts in China and the wartime strategic dispute with the Chinese and American military officials with regard to operational turfs in China, Indochina, and other Southeast Asian regions.

Franklin Delano Roosevelt Presidential Library, *Roosevelt—Chiang Kai-shek Wartime Correspondence, Presidential Map Room Files*, Hyde Park, New York. Most of the crucial wartime correspondence between Chiang and Roosevelt can be found in this archival deposit, which provides a "big picture" of the wartime Sino-U.S. relationship.

The James McHugh Papers, the Olin Library, Cornell University, Ithaca, New York. McHugh was the longest-serving U.S. intelligence officer in China, with a total of nineteen years of service as the U.S. naval attaché in China before the Pearl Harbor attacks. His papers have proved very helpful and illuminating for this research, especially on British intelligence activities in wartime China.

The Joseph Stilwell Archival Papers, the Hoover Institution, Stanford, California. This collection was closed until early 1990s. Until then, only a handful of writers, most notably Theodore White and Barbara Tuchman, had been allowed to use the collection. Its opening to the public thus provides good opportunities for scholars to reevaluate the key figure of the Sino-U.S. wartime interactions.

The Lauchlin Currie Papers, the Hoover Institution, Stanford, California. This collection primarily deals with Currie's central role as President Roosevelt's chief handler of China affairs during World War II. Rich in materials on Currie's activities in organizing Lend-Lease materiel to China, securing financial aid packages, and wartime intelligence activities, the Lauchlin Currie Papers contain quite a few revealing documents between Currie and Madame Chiang Kai-shek, James McHugh, T. V. Soong, and other key members of the China aid operations.

The Milton Miles Papers, the Hoover Institutions, Stanford, California. Miles was the chief architect and top representative of SACO during World War II. His complete papers are scattered at Hoover, the Naval War College, and the National Archives in College Park, Maryland. But this one contains much of his China experience during World War II.

Morgenthau Diaries (China), Volumes I and II, ed., U.S. 89th Congress, Committee on the Judiciary, United States Senate, Da Capo Press, New York, 1974. Perhaps the most exhaustive compilation of original documents related to wartime financial and military aid to China, this weighty collection is of crucial importance for the study of this topic.

Qin Xiaoyi, ed. *zhonghua minguo zhongyao shiliao chubian—dui ri kangzhan shiqi [The Preliminary Compilation of the Important Historical Documents of the Republic of China—The War against Japan]*. Taipei, 1980, Volumes I, II, III. This monumental documentary set includes by far the largest number of Chiang Kai-shek's cables, aide-mémoire, conference notes, etc. This compilation is the most comprehensive collection of primary sources on wartime diplomacy and military cooperation in China. It contains rich documents related to military and intelligence operations in wartime China by the USSR, Britain, France, and the United States.

Record Group 38, the Records of US Naval Group/China, U.S. National Archives. This is a central depository on the U.S. side of the SACO files. Extensive, rich, and helpful.

Record Group 226, the Records of the Office of Strategic Services, U.S. National Archives. Mammoth in size, over eight thousand cubic feet of documents, this is the most exhaustive World War II intelligence operations file collection of any kind. First of its kind, this precious set of intelligence operational files have been highly revealing on wartime high politics from an intelligence organization's perspective.

Record Group 493, the Records of AMMISCA from the Magruder Mission to the Wedemeyer Mission, U.S. National Archives. This is the most complete official record of the U.S. Army's World War II missions to China, starting from Brigadier General John Magruder's mission to China between July 1941 and January 1942, to General Joseph Stilwell's mission between January 1942 and October 1944, to Lieutenant General Albert Wedemeyer's mission after Stilwell's mission in China until the war's end.

The T. V. Soong Papers, the Hoover Institution, Stanford, California. As the key Chinese representative in wartime negotiations with Allied nations on military and financial aid to China, Soong held a unique position in Washington and Chungking. These papers provide rare insight on the subject matter of this book.

U.S. Department of State, *United States Relations with China with Special Reference to the Period 1944–1949, (The China White Paper)*, Department of State Publication 3573, Far Eastern Series 30; *Foreign Relations of the United States (FRUS), Diplomatic Papers, 1941 IV; 1942 I; 1942 China; 1943 I; 1943 China; 1944 VI; 1945 VII.* Washington, D.C., Government Printing Office, 1949–1969. The China White Paper was published by the Truman administration to fend off the partisan charge that the Democratic wartime administrations were partly responsible for the "loss of China" to the Communists in 1949. It attempts to show that it was the Nationalist government itself that was solely responsible for this loss. The subsequent volumes of FRUS supplement the main theme contained in the China White Paper.

The Wedemeyer Papers, the Hoover Institution, Stanford, California. This is a highly valuable collection of an American commanding officer in the China theater. It provides useful context to many high dramas in command disputes and policy disagreements among the Chinese, the British, and the Americans.

Wenshi ziliao (Documents of Literature and History). This is a multipart series of memoirs, recollections, and historical documents published at the national, provincial, and local levels of mainland China, where archival files are rarely available for serious historical research. As such, these publications provide the second-best alternative to historical inquiry. Most authors in these publications are captured KMT generals, non-Communist luminaries and ex-KMT agents.

Zhongde waijiao midang, 1927–1949 [Secret Archives in Sino-German Relations, 1927–1949], by the Chinese National Archives II, Guangxi Normal University Press, 1994. This is by far the most comprehensive publication of the Sino-German relationship during China's Republican era.

Zhuanji wenxue [Documentary Biographies]. Published in Taiwan, this has been the most popular and prestigious historical journal devoted to biographical reconstruction of modern Chinese military and political history. A large number of its articles are related to military and intelligence operations of the past.

BOOKS AND MONOGRAPHS

Alvarez, David, ed. *Allied and Axis Signals Intelligence in World War II.* London: Frank Cass & Co. Ltd., 1999. A useful anthology on wartime signal intelligence. Though heavily tilted toward European and North American operations, there are a few articles devoted to the China theater.

Blum, John Moton. *From the Morgenthau Diaries, Years of Crisis, 1928–1938 (1959); From the Morgenthau Diaries, Years of Urgency, 1938–1941 (1965); From the Morgenthau Diaries, Years of War, 1939–1941 (1967).* Boston: Houghton Mifflin Company. *The Morgenthau Diaries (China)* only contains materials originated in 1939. Blum provides good perspective on materials in the preceding years on U.S. military and financial aid to China.

Chen Hansheng. *si ge shidai de wo [My Life during Four Eras: A Memoir].* Beijing: Beijing Culture and History Press, 1988. A high-ranking Chinese Communist Party intelligence officer active overseas during the war, Chen provides precious information on how the Communist intelligence network during World War II functioned, especially concerning foreign aid to the CCP.

Chennault, Claire Lee. *Way of a Fighter—Memoirs of Claire Lee Chennault,"* ed. by Robert Hotz. New York: G. P. Putnam's Sons, 1949. This is the memoir of a key member of America's military support to China. At the center of the great command dispute with General Stilwell and the War Department officials in Washington, Chennault provides candid, often uniquely insightful, albeit bitter, recollections of his wartime exploits, his stormy relationships with General Stilwell and the Washington establishment as a whole, his close collaborations with the Chinese military officials, and his frequently neglected contribution to modern air tactics and joint military operations.

Chuikov, V. I. Memoirs—*My Mission to China,* New Jersey: Eastbridge Publishers, 2003. Before he went on to command the Stalingrad campaign and to gain other glories in European theater, Marshal Chuikov had been the top Soviet military adviser to the Chinese government. This useful and informative memoirs tells the Sino-Soviet military cooperation from a rare source.

Cornelius, Wanda, and Thayne Short. *Ding Hao: America's Air War in China, 1937–1945.* New York: Pelican Publishing Co., 1980. A useful personal account of Chennault's airmen in China during World War II.

Cruickshank, Charles. *SOE in the Far East.* New York: Oxford University Press, 1983. This is an official history commissioned by the British government. It contains many useful archival references.

Dai Houjie, ed. *yangguwen liezhuan [The Biographies of Foreign Advisers in Modern China],* Hebei, China: Hebei People's Press, 2004. This is a collection of biographical sketches of various important foreign advisers to the Chinese government in the twentieth century. It is written by professional historians in mainland China and has a judicious selection of subject matters, although at times its treatment of such figures as Milton Miles is conspicuously politicized.

Eiler, Keith, ed. *Wedemeyer on War and Peace.* Stanford, CA: Hoover Institution Press, 1987. A concise collection of General Wedemeyer's strategic thinking by his wartime aide-de-camp. The documents and comments on China are refreshing and insightful.

Fan Chengkang. *Zhongguo Zhujie Shi [A History of Foreign Concessions in China].* Shanghai: Shanghai Social Sciences Academy Press, 1991. A useful source documenting the general evolution of foreign concessions in the largest "treaty port" of modern China.

Feis, Herbert. *The China Tangle: The American Effort in China from Pearl Harbor to the Marshall Mission.* Princeton, NJ: Princeton University Press, 1953. A detailed semiofficial history of the U.S. involvement in China during World War II; it contains useful sequence of events and important reconstruction of major interactions between Washington and Chungking.

Garver, John. *Chinese-Soviet Relations, 1937–1945—Diplomacy of Chinese Nationalism.* New York: Oxford University Press, 1988. A balanced account of a highly complex subject.

Haynes, John Earl, and Harvey Klehr, *VENONA: Decoding Soviet Espionage in America,* New Haven, CT: Yale University Press, 1999. A path-breaking study and the most authoritative account of Soviet espionage in the United States during World War II, based on the newly declassified decrypts of the KGB's wartime secret cable traffic between Washington and Moscow.

Hotz, Robert B., et al. *With General Chennault: The Story of the Flying Tigers.* New York: Coward-McCann, Inc., 1943. This is an informative early account of experience with the Flying Tigers in wartime China. Many of the tales have become classic lore of the Flying Tigers and have been repeated by many others.

Howard, James. *Roar of the Tiger.* New York: Orion Books, 1991. Another account of the Flying Tiger legend.

Hsiung, James, and Steven Levine, eds. *China's Bitter Victory: The War with Japan, 1937–1945.* New York: M. E. Sharpe, 1997 (reprint). This anthology serves as one of the first post–Cold War efforts to reevaluate the Sino-Japanese war.

Hull, Cordell. *The Memoirs of Cordell Hull.* New York: MacMillan Company, 1948. Useful eyewitness account of World War II diplomacy by America's top foreign policy implementer.

Kahn, David. *The Codebreakers: The Story of Secret Writing.* New York: MacMillan, 1967. The classic of the subject matter by a veteran scholar.

Kirby, William. *Germany and Republic of China.* Stanford, CA: Stanford University Press, 1984. The best-known book outside of China on the subject matter. An informative and useful analysis.

Koo, Wellington. *Gu Weijun huiyilu [The Memoirs of Wellington Koo].* Beijing: Zhonghua Books, 1985. A useful and informative memoir of China's top diplomat in Europe during much of World War II.

Leahy, William. *I Was There: the Personal Story of the Chief of Staff to President Roosevelt and Truman Based on His Notes and Diaries Made at the Time.* New York: Whittlesey House, McGraw-Hill Book Company, Inc., 1950. A candid narrative of the wartime activities of the chairman of the U.S. Joint Chiefs of Staff.

Li Shian. *taipingyang zhanzheng shiqi de zhongying guanxi [Sino-British Relations in the Pacific War].* Beijing: Chinese Social Sciences Press, 1994. This is the best analysis so far of the Sino-British relationship during World War II. Primarily based on wartime Foreign Office and War Office records in the United Kingdom, the author provides useful synopses on the key issues of the troubled relationship during the war.

Li Shushan and Wang Yehong, *zhongguo kongjun zhanshi [A Military History of China's Air Force,* Guangzhou, China: Huaxia Press, 1996. This is the most concise history of Chinese military aviation in the twentieth century, written by two officers of the Chinese People's Liberation Army Air Force.

Liang Jingdun (Liang Chin-tung). *kailuohuiyi yu zhongguo [The Cairo Conference and China].* Hong Kong: The Asia Press, 1962; *shidiwei shijian [The Stilwell Incident].* Hong Kong: The Commercial Press, 1973; *General Stilwell in China, 1942–1944: The Full Story.* New York: St. John's University, 1972. This trilogy, two in Chinese and one in English, comes from the KMT's most respected historian. Liang provides the official views of the KMT government with regard to Stilwell and the Stilwell Incident. The *Stilwell Incident* (1973) is the better known and more influential book.

Liu Zhiqing. *enyuanlijinhou de fansi—zhongsu guanxi qishi nian [Seventy Years of Sino-Soviet Relations—Reflections after Tumultuous Experiences, 1917–1991].* Jinan, Shandong, China: The Yellow River Press, 1998. The author is a People's Liberation Army (PLA) officer whose expertise on the Sino-Soviet relations gives us a rare perspective on wartime interactions between China and the Soviet Union. Much of the book is based on Russian sources, which have been lacking in existing literature.

Lohbeck, Don. *Patrick J. Hurley*. Chicago: Henry Regnery Company, 1956. A sympathetic biography of the controversial general and ambassador, this book puts Hurley's tumultuous China mission in perspective.

Ma Zhendu and Qi Rugao. *dihu? Youhu?—Deguo yu zhongguo kangzhan [Enemy or Friend?—Germany and China's War of Resistance against Japan]*. Guilin, China: Guangxi Normal University Press, 1997. The authors represent China's new professional historians with rare archival access and sophisticated research skills.

Miles, Milton. *A Different Kind of War*. New York: Doubleday, 1967. Miles was the U.S. Navy's top man in China during World War II and was deeply involved in wartime military activities in China and Washington. Although somewhat disorganized, this volume provides valuable inside stories of the key events and key figures in World War II/China.

———. *The Navy Launched a Dragon*. Unpublished manuscript, Naval War College Museum, Newport, Rhode Island. This is another personal account of Miles's wartime experience in China.

Niu Jun. *cong yanan zouxiang shijie [From Yenan to the World]*. Fuzhou, China: Fujian People's Press, 1992. China's official historian looks at the CCP's foreign relations during World War II.

People's Liberation Army Special Compilation Committee, ed. *dangdai zhongguo jundui de junshi gongzhuo [China Today: The Military Affairs of the Chinese Army]*. Beijing: Chinese Social Science Press, 1989, Vol. I. An official history of PLA, this is a volume in a series of books on various branches of the Chinese social, economic, political, and military structures.

Qiao Jiacai. *Selected Writings of Qiao Jiacai*, Vol. 2, *daili jiangjun he tade tongzhi [General Tai Li and His Comrades]*. Taipei: Chongwai Press, 1981; *weilishi zhuozheng [Witness to History]*. Taipei: Zhongwai Zazhi Publisher, 1985. A member and protégé of China's wartime intelligence chief, Major General Tai Li, Qiao has been the most prolific writer on the history and activities of Tai Li during the war. The writing is decidedly sympathetic to Tai Li. Although an overwhelming majority of the narratives can be corroborated by other archival sources, some facts remain misplaced in the text, and the writing can be chatty and disorganized. The primary usefulness of Qiao's writings is in balancing the highly politicized diatribe against Tai Li by the mainland Chinese publications.

Ren Donglai. *zhengchaobuxiu de huoban—meiyuan yu zhongmei kangri tongmeng [Forever Querulous Partners—The American Aid and Sino-U.S. Anti-Japanese Alliance]*. Nanning, China: Guangxi Normal University Press, 1995. This is the most comprehensive analysis on the wartime U.S. military and financial aid to China from a Chinese perspective. This book, based on the author's PhD dissertation, incorporates documents both from China and the United States and weaves them into an intriguing portrait of wartime Sino-U.S. military and financial relationship.

Romanus, Charles F., and Riley Sunderland. *Stilwell's Mission to China* (1953); *Stilwell's Command Problems* (1956); *Time Runs Out in CBI* (1959). Washington, D.C.: U.S. Department of the Army. The standard Army narratives on Stilwell's China mission, this trilogy gives the official War Department's view on the controversial general and his disastrous China mission.

Rossi, Dick. *A Flying Tiger's Story.* Unpublished manuscript, 22 July 2005. A personal account of the author's experience as a Flying Tiger veteran in wartime China.

Schaller, Michael. *The U.S. Crusade in China, 1938–1945.* New York: Columbia University Press, 1979. A widely quoted book by PRC's official historians, this book supplies the standard condemnation of the U.S. and KMT wartime political and military policies. Selective and partisan in using sources, it is nevertheless well written, despite the fact that much of its core argument has been invalidated by the post–Cold War new materials in the United States, China, and the Soviet Union. As a major work on the subject matter, a key drawback is its lack of any meaningful Chinese sources and context.

Shi Zhe. *zai lishi juren shenbian—shi zhe huiyi lu [Alongside the Great Men in History: Memoirs of Shi Zhe].* Beijing: Central Documents Press, 1991. The author was Mao's Russian interpreter in the 1940s and 1950s, and for nine years served in the Soviet intelligence organization. A rare source of historical insights.

Smith, Bradley. *The Shadow Warriors—OSS and the Origins of the CIA.* New York: Basic Books, 1983. Before the release of Record Group 226 at the U.S. National Archives, this was the best account of OSS stories. Although much of it needs revision as a result of the newly available archives, this book has many insights on wartime intelligence still valuable, albeit it is weak on OSS/China.

Stilwell, Joseph Stilwell. *The Stilwell Papers,* arranged by Theodore White. New York: Sloane Associates, 1948; rpt. New York: Da Capo, 1991. A selective collection of Stilwell's wartime records, including his diaries.

Stimson, Henry, and McGeorge Bundy. *On Active Service in Peace and War.* New York: Harper and Brothers, 1947. A useful eyewitness account by America's wartime secretary of war and his aide.

Stoler, Mark. *George C. Marshall: Soldier-Statesman of the American Century.* New York: Twayne Publisher, 1989. A balanced biographical account of Marshall; the part covering the Marshall Mission to China is particularly astute.

Stratton, Roy. *The Army-Navy Game.* Falmouth, MA: Volta Company, 1977. The best nonacademic account of the command rivalry between the Navy and Army in the China theater during the war. Stratton incorporates large amount of archives documents in the text and provides a panoramic look at SACO, OSS, Stilwell, Miles, and other key figures in America's involvement in wartime China.

Tang Zong, ed. *zai jiangjieshi shenbian—sicong shi gaoji muliao tangzong riji [Diaries: My Eight Years as Chiang Kai-shek's Confidential Secretary].* Archives of the Ministry of Public Security, Beijing, Masses Press, 1991. A useful perspective from a high-ranking Chinese intelligence officer working inside Chiang's headquarters.

Thorne, Christopher. *Allies of a Kind: The United States, Britain, and the War against Japan, 1941–1945.* New York: Oxford University Press, 1978. By far the most nuanced study of the wartime Anglo-American relationship.

Tsou Tang. *America's Failure in China, 1941–1950.* Chicago: University of Chicago Press, 1963. An insightful look at U.S. wartime policy toward China. The author is critical of the U.S. wartime policy for its failure to stimulate a workable political solution.

Tuchman, Barbara W. *Stilwell and American Experience in China, 1911–1945.* New York: Bantam Books, 1971. Written at the height of the antiwar movement in the early 1970s, this popular account of Stilwell's wartime experience in China echoes the sentiment of the time, that is, U.S. foreign policy had been based on an unwise policy of supporting unpopular dictators by neglecting the "progressives" who represented the future of the country the United States was involved in. With this approach, this Stilwell biography portrays a temperamental general as a thoughtful, far-sighted progressive fighting against an inept and insensitive Chinese regime. It is fair to say everything that is said about Stilwell in this account is factually sound. Yet, a remarkable amount about Stilwell, which is amply available from the newly opened Stilwell archives, would have made Stilwell a much less sympathetic figure in wartime China, and it is what is not said about Stilwell that is most revealing and renders this hagiographical account in dire need of improvement.

Wakeman, Frederic. *Policing Shanghai, 1927–1937.* Berkeley: University of California Press, 1995; *Spymaster: Dai Li and the Chinese Secret Service.* Berkeley: University of California Press, 2003. Two useful volumes on China's wartime intelligence chief by a prominent American historian of modern Chinese history.

Wang Zheng. *dongdang zhong de tongmeng—kangzhan shiqi de zhongsu guangxi [An Alliance in Turmoil—the Sino-Soviet Relationship during the War of Resistance against Japan].* Guilin, China: Guangxi Normal University Press, 1993. A good analysis of the wartime Sino-Soviet relationship based on informative archive materials available in China.

Wedemeyer, Albert C. *Wedemeyer Reports!* New York: De Capo, 1958. A unique perspective from Stilwell's successor, who is understandably sympathetic to China's many dilemmas.

Weinstein, Allen, and Alexander Vassiliev. *The Haunted Wood—Soviet Espionage in America, the Stalin Era.* New York: Random House, 1999. The most authoritative post–Cold War account on the Soviet espionage in the United States based on newly available Soviet internal party documents. Since its publication, it has decidedly become a classic.

Wu Jingping. *zongziwen pingzhuan [A Critical Biography of T .V. Soong].* Fujian, China: Fujian People's Press, 1992. This scholarly volume provides a good account of Soong's multifaceted lobbying and diplomatic activities in wartime Washington and Chungking.

Yardley, Herbert. *The Chinese Black Chamber—An Adventure in Espionage.* Boston, Houghton Mifflin, 1983. Yardley was the founder of American cryptography and was hired in 1939 by Chinese intelligence to organize a decoding unit in China against the Japanese. This is an account of his exploits in wartime China.

Yeaton, Ivan. *Memoirs of Col. Ivan D. Yeaton, USA (RET), 1919–1953.* Unpublished manuscript, the Hoover Institution Archives, 1976. Perhaps one of the most underrated manuscripts about wartime China by an American high-ranking officer. Yeaton was the top American intelligence officer on the Chinese Communists under General Wedemeyer, first as Wedemeyer's commanding officer in the Army's Observers Group (the Dixie Mission) to Mao's headquarters and then as the head of G-2 for the China theater.

Young, Arthur N. *China and the Helping Hand, 1937–1945* (1963); *China's Wartime Finance and Inflation, 1937–1945* (1965). Cambridge, MA: Harvard University Press. The author was China's wartime chief foreign financial adviser and was an important participant in military, and especially financial, aid to China. The first volume is particularly detailed on America's failure to sufficiently carry out its promises to China for aid. The author also spares no punches at the KMT for mismanagement of the American aid. On a whole, however, Young was methodic and highly critical of U.S. military aid to China.

Yu, Maochun. *OSS in China—Prelude to Cold War.* New Haven, CT: Yale University Press, 1997. A study of one single American intelligence organization and its wartime policies and activities in China, based on the newly opened archival files.

Yue, Qianhou. *guweijin yu zhanshi waijiao [Wellington Koo and Wartime Diplomacy].* Hebei, China: Hebei People's Press, 1998. A useful biography of China's wartime ambassador to France and England.

INDEX

Page numbers followed by the letter f indicate a figure on that page; those in italics indicate a photograph on that page.

Adler, Solomon, 101, 102
aid programs. *See* Lend-Lease program; loan packages; military aid
air combat tactics: Chennault's development of, 25–26; Japanese, 32, 37–38
Air Force. *See* Chinese Air Force
Air Force Day, 146
Air Ground Aid Service (AGAS), 181
Air and Ground Forces Resources and Technical Staff (AFGRTS), 121
Air Intelligence Group, 149
air-warning ground intelligence system, 26, 30, 38
aircraft manufacturing facility, 16, 20
airpower strategy: bomber-centric, 25; Chennault on, 42; fighters *vs.* bombers in, 24–25; Madame Chiang's interest in, 28; *vs.* Burma Road focus, 166–67; weapons acquisition for, 13
Alsop, Joseph, 162
Amerasia case, 163
American Black Chamber, The (Yardley), 147
American Military Mission to China, 41
American Volunteers Group (AVG). *See* Flying Tigers
AMMISCA, 90
amphibious operations: in Burma, Chiang's support for, 171, 173; U.S. coordination of future, 70, 80
Anti-Comintern Pact, 4

Arcadia Conference, 92
arms movement: by Britain, 49; passing rights for, 5–6; Russian refusal to allow, 8–9; from Soviet Union to China, 16; Tibet-India highway proposed for, 7–8; by United States, to China, 42
Army. *See* U.S. Army
Army Military Intelligence (G-2), 71
Arnold, Henry H. "Hap," 25, 26
assassination, in wartime, 55–56
Atkinson, Brooks, 163
aviation: downed pilot rescue leaflet, *135*, *136*, 158; Soviet support for, 15–16, 194. *See also* airpower strategy

Barbarossa, 23
Barrett, David, *129*
Battle of China, 1
Beijing Tax Academy, 144
Beldon, Jack, 162
Birch, John, 183–84, 192
Bird, Willis, 123
Bissell, Clayton, 25, 43
"black" propaganda, 157, 159
blood chit, *135*, *136*, 158
Blücher, Vasily Konstantinovich, 11
Boelcke, Oswald von, 25
Bogomoloff, Dimitri, 12
bomber generals, 25
bombers, *vs.* fighter planes, 24–25
bombing warning leaflets, *136*, 158
Borodin, Mikhail, 11, 55

Bowley, A. J., 40
Britain: appeasement of Japan by, 9, 47; Chiang on Far East policy of, 47; China policy of, vs. American, 180–81; Chinese assistance refused by, 59; colonial interests of, 46, 180–81; Japan's challenge to, 48; Lend-Lease material totals, 94f; loss of Asian empire by, 60; objections of, to Thai operation, 110; in passing rights decision, 5; in pilfering of Lend-Lease material, 59, 165; in signal intelligence cooperation, 149–51; on Tibet-India highway issue, 8
Brooke-Popham, Robert, 51
Buck, Pearl S., 60
Bureau of Investigation and Statistics (BIS), 149, 156
Burma: British plans to liberate, 59–60; Chinese interests in, 49; Flying Tigers in, 39; signal intelligence in, 152
Burma Road, 134; alternatives to, 5; British closing of, 48–49; passing rights on, 6; proposed joint Allied operations to reopen, 96; strategic focus on, vs. air power priority, 166–67; U.S. Army's focus on, 167
Byroade, Henry, 192

Cairo Conference, 96, 170
"cash and carry" loan regulation, 89
CCP. See Chinese Communist Party (CCP)
Chamberlain, Neville, 47
Champe, Joseph E., 78
Chan Chak, 64
Chen Mingshu, 143
Chen Yibai, 150
Cheng Xi-geng, 48
Chennault, Claire Lee: in acquisition of P-40B, 32; on air combat strategy, 25–26; in air defense strategy, 166–67; with Chiang Kai-shek, 133; on fighters vs. bombers, 24–25; on Flying Tigers, 45; growing fame of, 39; image building by, 162; lobbying efforts of, 31; on Marshall Mission, 193;

in OSS independent operations, 120–22; pilot recruitment by, 35–36; promotion of, 43; retirement of, 178; and The Role of Defensive Pursuit, 26; on Stilwell appointment, 41; on William Henry Donald, 29. See also Flying Tigers
Cherepanov, Ivanovich, 15
Chi Ch'ao-ting, 101
Chiang Kai-shek, 130; air power priority of, vs. Burma Road focus, 166–67; on British Far East Policy, 47; Communist purge by, 11; as head of Whampoa Military Academy, 10; Indian independence supported by, 7, 61; in Japanese surrender, 184–85; kidnapping of, 12; in KMT-CCP peace talks, 186; on Lend-Lease material distribution, 175; with Stilwell, 132; in Stilwell recall, 172–75; with Tai Li, 133; on Tibet-India highway, 7; use of German military advisers by, 2–3; in warlord pacification, 143–44; with Wendell Wilkie, 141
China Commando Group: Chinese lessons learned and, 67; Chinese suspicions concerning, 57, 63–64, 195–96; command structure of, 58; Dennys on need for, 50–51; disbanding of, 65–66; expanding operations of, 63; failure of, 66; formation of, 52; initial support for, 56; Kerr's proposal for, 53–54; SOE role in, 57–58
China Defense Supplies, Inc., 31, 89
"China Theater Reorganization Plan," 170
Chinese Air Force: American volunteers in, 32; Chennault's attempted reform of, 30; inadequate training of, 29; in signal intelligence, 146, 149
Chinese Central Military Academy, 2
"Chinese Code-Breakers, 1927-1945" (Yu), ix
Chinese Communist Party (CCP): cash-for-weapons business of, 99; and Dixie Mission, 122–25,

172; establishment of, 10; foreign military aid to, 98–100; in Fuping Incident, 182–83, 184; international network of, 99–100; on Japanese surrender, 185; Lauchlin Currie support for, 34; media control by, 155–56; media partisanship and, 160–61, 162–63; in murder of John Birch, 183–84, 192; Nazi-Soviet Pact supported by, 18; and New Fourth Army incident, 20; in peace talks with KMT, 186; post-Yalta agenda of, 182–83; radio surveillance of, 145; relationship with Japanese in North China, 99; war-time growth of, 182

Chinese Eastern Railway, 11

Chinese government. See Kuomintang (KMT) government

Chinese nationalism: as counter to CCP, 10; following Paris Conference, 2; foreign operations' impact on, 196–97; OSS insensitivity to, 115–16; SACO's response to, 114–15

Chuikov, Vasily Ivanovich, 15, 130

Chungking, Japanese bombing of, 147–48

Churchill, Winston: Burma Road closed by, 48; on "excessive" aid to China, 98; on SOE purpose, 52; in Tibetan affairs, 7

civil war in China: Marshall Mission in settlement of, 189, 190–93; occupation to preclude, 185–86; as Soviet-U.S. power struggle, 186

code breaking. See signal intelligence

Coe, Frank, 101, 102

Colling, John, 123

colonialism, 46, 180–81

communication channels, of White House, 174–75

Communist purge, 11

Communists. See Chinese Communist Party (CCP)

Coughlin, John, 121

Cromley, Raymond, 123, 159

currency stabilization measures, 94, 96, 102

Currie, Lauchlin, 141; in Flying Tiger approval, 34–35; in Flying Tiger induction into Army Air Corps, 43–44; in Lend-Lease management, 89; pro-Communist bias of, 34

Curtiss P-40B, 32

Davies, John Paton: in Dixie Mission, 122; pro-CCP bias of, 100

De Gaulle, Charles, 111

De Wiart, Adrian Carton, 97

Dennys, L. E.: on Britain's expectations for Chinese assistance, 62–63; guerrilla team proposed by, 50–51; in mutual assistance talks, 49

Detachment 204, 51

Dimitrov, Georgi, 101

dive-bombers, 4

Dixie Mission, 122–25, 129, 172, 192

Dkatwin, M. I., 15

Dolan, Brooke, 8, 75, 123

Donald, William Henry, 28, 29

Donovan, James, 105

Donovan, William J., 60, 71, 138; apology of, for Miller incident, 117; on "black" propaganda, 159; on Chinese signal intelligence, 153; clash with SACO on OSS involvement, 104–6; intelligence philosophy of, 118; propaganda mission of, 156; on Soviets in Manchuria, 188

Douhet, Giulio, 25

Douhet Theory, 25

Dow, Arden, 104

"Dragon Plan," 74–75

Drum, Hugh, 164

Du Yuming, 50

Duff, Arthur, 74

Durdan, Tilman, 163

Eifler, Carl, 74

8th Route Army, 183

Embick, Stanley, 187

Epstein, Israel, 163

espionage: in military aid disposition, 100–102. See also intelligence operations

"Europe First, Asia Second," 92–93

Falkenhausen, Alexander von, 3, *129*
fascism, 11
Father Bec, 113, 114
Feng Yuxiang, 143
financial loans. See loan packages
Finland, Soviet invasion of, 21
Fitzgerald, Oscar P., 127–28
Flying Tigers: as aid recipients, 97; in air
    defense strategy, 166; in Burma, 39,
    59–60; Chinese assessment of, 45;
    combat record of, 44–45; emblem of,
    141; foreign policy implications of,
    33; Madame Chiang as patron of,
    28, 40; military control over, 43; in
    OSS independent operations, 120–
    22; P-40, 131; pilot recruitment
    for, 35–36; signal intelligence and,
    152; squadrons of, 38; success of,
    38–39; training of, 37–38; U.S.
    pursuit fighter planes for, 89. *See also*
    Chennault, Claire Lee
Flying Trapeze, 24
Foreman, Harrison, 163
14th Air Force, 44. See also Flying
    Tigers
France: appeasement of Japan by, 9;
    Lend-Lease material totals, 94*f*; in
    passing rights decision, 5
Free French resistance: British-Vichy
    agreement concerning, 52; De
    Gaulle's mission to Chungking,
    111–12; factionalism within,
    196; Meynier group in, 112–14;
    objections of, to Indochina
    operation, 111, 113
French Indochina: Britain in restoration
    of colonialism in, 180–81; British-
    Vichy agreement concerning, 52;
    Japanese control of, 48; Vietnamese
    intelligence net in, 181. *See also*
    Indochina
"Friendship Project," 72
Fu Tso-yi, 64
Fujiwara Iwaichi, 61
Fuping Incident, 182–83, 184

Gandhi, Mahatma, 7
Gauss, Clarence, 73
Germany: arms imports from, 1, 3;

declared neutrality of, in Sino-
    Japanese confrontations, 3; ties with
    China cut by, 4–5; trade deals with
    China by, 4
Giraud, Henri, 112
Gleason, Frank A., 104
gold shipments: in currency stabilization,
    94, 96; sabotage of, 101–2
Gordon-Bernard-Tam Team, 181
Gorky, Maxim, 112
Group 6, 152
Group 8, 150
Gu Zhutong, 64
guerrilla forces: SACO training of, 104,
    126–27; Tai Li on U.S. training of,
    80–81
"gung ho," 99–100

Hainan Island, 48, 69
Hao Peng-ju, 183
Hayden, Joseph, 74, 120
Haynes, John, 101
Heppner, Richard, 105, 179, 184, 188
Ho Chi Minh, 181
Ho Yin-chin, 62
Hoffman, Carl, 121
Holbrook, Roy, 27
Hong Kong: bombing of, 150–51;
    British plans to liberate, 59;
    Japanese threat to, 46; signals
    intelligence in, 150
Hope, Victor Alexander John, 62
Hopkins, Harry, 73, 170
Hornbeck, Stanley, 90
Horne, Frederick J., 71
Hu Zongnan, 145
Hull, Cordell, 91
Hump airlift totals, 169
Hurley, Patrick: on Dixie Mission's
    impact, 124; in halting OSS
    weapons transfer, 100; in KMT-
    CCP peace talks, 186; in Stilwell
    recall, 174–75I

Ichigo campaign, 171
"In God We Trusted, In China We
    Busted—The China Commando
    Group of the British SOE" (Yu), ix
India, signal intelligence in, 152–53

Indian independence movement: China's support for, 7, 61; Japan's support of, 61

Indian National Army, 61

Indochina: Japanese control in, 111; SACO operation in, 111–14. *See also* French Indochina

industrial capabilities, 16

Industrial Cooperative, 99

inflation spiral, 90–91, 102

Inner Mongolia, 64

Inspection and Decoding Office of the Secret Telegrams, 144

Institute of International Relations (IIR), 66

intelligence operations: allied, reorganization of, 179; British, in French Indochina, 181; and China Commando Group lessons learned, 67; impact of, on Chinese nationalism, 196–97; independent, of OSS, 118–20; during Marshall Mission, CCP and KMT, 191–92; during Marshall Mission, U.S., 190; newspapers used in, 160; SACO disputes with OSS concerning, 104–6; Tai Li's suspicion's concerning, 74–76; in Thailand, 107–11; U.S., keys to success in, 75–76. *See also* signal intelligence

interagency competition, 177–78

International Longshoremen's Union, 101

"Iron and Blood" unification, 2

Japan: attrition policy of, in China, 3; British attitudes toward, 46; conquest of Manchuria by, 11; in Indochina, 111; naval blockade by, 5; passing right challenged by, 6; signal intelligence against, 147; Soviet neutrality pact with, 21; surrender of, 184; in Thailand, 107–8; Western appeasement of, 9

Jiang Renjian, 146

JianQiao, Battle of, 30

Johnston, Charlie, 104

Jones, Jessie, 91

Kachanov, K. M., 15

Kendall, F. W., 65

Kerr, Clark: on aid to China, 47, 97; on China Commando Group, 53–54

Keswick, John: background of, 56; in China Commando group takeover, 57–58; destabilizing actions of, 63–64

Kharb Kunjara, 109, 111

Killery, Valentine, 52

King, Ernest J.: Pacific strategy of, 70; on SACO approval, 84; on SACO command and control, 180

Klehr, Harvey, 101

Klein, Hans, 4

Knox, Frank, 35, 72

Koo, Wellington, 6

Kung, H. H., 5

Kuomintang (KMT) government, 10, 182; invited to join Communist underground's Industrial Cooperative, 99–100; media ventures of, 156; in peace talks with CCP, 186; propaganda in fall of, 155–56, 162–63; in Revival Society, 55

Language, Art, and Leaflets Unit, 157

Larson, Robert, 113

Lattimore, Owen, 34, 36

leaflet drops, *135*, *136*, 157–58

League of Nations, 21

Leahy, William, 161; on aid failures, 103; on China theater, 177; on SACO approval, 86–87

Lee, Duncan, 105

Lee, Willis "Ching," 69, 70

Lend-Lease program: airpower vs. Burma strategy in allocation of, 167; British pilfering of, 59, 165; China's yearly percentage of, 93*f*; delivery problems in, 95; military oversight mission to China, 90; Stilwell control of, 41, 164–66, 175; totals, by country, 94*f*; totals for 1941, 90; totals for 1942, 92; totals for 1945, 92. *See also* military aid, U.S.

Lenin, Vladimir, 10

Li Jisheng, 143

Li Kenong, 191

Li Zongren, 143
Lin Wei, 50
Lindsay, Michael, 163
Linlithgow, Second Marquess of, 62
Liu, Eddie, 65
Liu Zhiqing, 15
loan packages: from British, 91, 96–97; from Soviets, 13–14, 194
loan packages, U.S.: cash-and-carry, 89; compared with Soviet, 88; for currency stabilization, 94; delivery problems with, 95; interest rates on, 13; for military salaries, 91; Roosevelt support for, 89
Loyal Patriotic Army, 127
Lung Yun, 64, 184–85
Luo Ruiqing, 191
Lusey, Alghan, 73, 118

MacArthur, Douglas, 187
MacDonald, Billy, 24
MacDonald, Elizabeth, 159
Madame Chiang Kai-shek: and Air Force Academy, 146; on British lack of fighting spirit, 60; with Eleanor Roosevelt, 137; and Flying Tigers, 28, 40; with Stilwell, 132; support of Stilwell by, 170; with Wendell Wilkie, 141
Madame Meynier, 112–13
Madame Sun Yat-sen, 74
Magruder, John, 40–41
Manchukuo, 4, 18
Manchuria: American withdrawal from, 189; Cold War activities in, 188–89; Soviet involvement in, 186–87
Manchuria Incident, 3, vii
Mansfield, Walter, 122
Mao Bangchu, 24, 148
Mao Zedong, 10, 129, 140; in cash-for-weapons business, 99; with George Marshall, 131; in KMT-CCP peace talks, 186; Polish partition supported by, 18; post-Yalta agenda of, 182–83
Marco Polo Bridge Incident, 12, 30, vii
Marshall, George C.: on airpower vs. ground forces strategy, 167;

"command unity" policy of, 42–43; with Mao Zedong, 131; military mission and, 40; as prestigious mediator, 190; in SACO approval, 83, 85, 86; in Stilwell assignment, 164
Marshall Mission, 131, 189–93
MASH (television series), 95
McHugh, James, 72, 73
"Measures to Stop the Submission of Misleading Reports," 191–92
media: faulty intelligence gathering by, 161–62; infighting revealed by, 162; pro-Communist bias of, 160–61, 162–63; security breeches by, 162. See also propaganda
Metzel, Jeffrey C., 71, 106, 114
Meynier, Robert, 112
Meynier group, 112–14
Miles, Milton Edward "Mary": agent recruitment by, 76; clash with OSS on SACO mission, 104–6; early career of, 68–69; on French intransigence, 114; on guerrilla training plan, 80–81; on horses in Thai operation, 109; on Old China Hands, 77; as OSS coordinator, 75, 125; respect of, for Chinese, 78, 114–15; Tai Li's suspicions of, 74–76
military advisers: American, 15; German, 2–3; Soviet, 15–16
military aid: British, 48; to Chinese Communists, 98–100; Communist espionage in disposition of, 100–101; as "excessive," 98; Soviet, 12–14, 194. See also weapons transportation
military aid, U.S., 42; 1941 totals, 90; Hump airlift totals in, 169; inadequacy of, 97–98; pursuit fighter planes in, 89; Stilwell's impact on, 165. See also Lend-Lease program
military dogs, 139
military reconstruction program, 2–3
Miller, Lyle H., 115
Miller racism incident, 115–17
Ministry of Economic Warfare, 56, 57

Minter, Mary Miles, 69
Morale Operation (MO) branch, 159
Morganthau, Henry: Communist
    spies' influence on, 101; in loan
    disbursement solution, 91; T. V.
    Soong's friendship with, 35
Moscow-Tokyo Neutrality Pact, 23
Mountbatten, Louis, 110, 170, 180–81

Nagumo, Chuichi, 37
National Broadcasting Company
    (NBC), 156
nationalism: Indian, 7, 61. *See also*
    Chinese nationalism
naval blockade, by Japan, 5
Naval Group China, 179–80
naval intelligence, in "Friendship
    Project," 71
Navy. See U.S. Navy
Nazi-Soviet Nonaggression Pact, 14, 18,
    195
Nehru, Motilal, 7
New Fourth Army incident, 20
Ni Naibing, 152
Nimitz, Chester, 187
Nomonhan, Battle of, 19
Northern Expedition, 2
Nyholm, Erik, 57, 63

occupation policy, 185–86
Office of Strategic Services (OSS):
    agent recruitment for, 76; "black"
    propaganda by, 157, 159; in Dixie
    Mission, 122–25; Flying Tigers in
    operations of, 120–22; independent
    SI operations of, 118–20; "Mary"
    Miles as coordinator of, 75; origin
    of, 156; and proposed CCP weapons
    deal, 100; racism within, 115–16;
    SACO guerrilla camps run by, 104
Office of Technological Research, 149
Office of the Coordinator of
    Information (COI), 71, 73; "Dragon
    Plan" of, 74–75
Office of War Information (OWI):
    mission of, 157; origin of, 156;
    "white" propaganda by, 157
oil fields, 16, 20

Okano Susumu, 159
Okinawa campaign, 187
"Old China Hands": Chinese
    resentment of, 76–77; SACO policy
    on, 114–15
Operation Barbarossa, 23
Oriental Mission, 52, 56
Orville, Howard T., 71
OSS. *See* Office of Strategic Services
Outer Mongolia, 19

P-40, *131; vs.* Japanese Zeros, 148–49
Panay, 69
Paris Conference, 2
passing rights, 5–6
Patton, George, 181
Pearl Harbor attack: China's reaction to,
    59; Flying Tigers' response to, 36;
    lack of intelligence on, 71
Pearson, Drew, 162, 163
Pechkoff, Zenovi, 111–12
Percival, A. E., 52
Petropavlosky, Vladimir, 57
pilot rescue leaflet, *135, 136,* 158
Poland, partition of, 18
police training school, 104
Popular Front, 11
Potsdam Declaration, 181, 184
Price, Ernest, 119–20
Prince of Wales (Britain), 37, 151
prisoners of war, 188
propaganda: American use of, 156;
    Communist control of, 155–56;
    in fall of Kuomintang, 156; leaflet
    drops in, *135, 136,* 157–58; pro-
    Communist media bias and, 160–
    61; "white" *vs.* "black," 157.
    See also media
psychological warfare leaflets, 157–58
Public Law Number 422, 91
Purnell, W. R., 106, 125
Putzell, Edwin, 105

Qinghua University, 144
Quebec Conference, 110

racism incident, 115–17
radio stations, 156, 157

Rangoon defense, 39
raw materials trade, 4, 17
Repulse (Britain), 37, 151
resistance movement. *See* Free French resistance
Resources Investigation Institute (RII), 66
Revival Society: in signal intelligence, 146; Tai Li's use of, 54–55
Robertson, Walter, 190
Role of Defensive Pursuit, The (Chennault), 26
Roosevelt, Eleanor, with Madame Chiang, *137*
Roosevelt, Franklin D.: on aid to China, 89; on Burma campaign, 171; failure of attention by, 95, 98, 103; Flying Tigers supported by, 35; on media-caused misunderstandings, 161
Rossi, John "Dick," 35, 36
Royal Patriotic Army, 56
Russia. *See* Soviet Union

SACO. *See* Sino-American Special Technical Cooperative Organization
Sanzo Nozaka, 159
Second Division, Military Operations Department, 149
Seeckt, Hans von, 3
Seymour, Horace: China aid supported by, 97; on Tibetan issue, 7
Shang Zhen, 50, 150
Shanghai, Battle of, 3, 30
Shanghai Evening Post and Mercury, 160
Shanghai Pilot Association, 145–46
Sheng Shicai, 19
signal intelligence: British cooperation in, 149–51; British pilfering of, 152–53; in Burma, 152; as Chiang family monopoly, 144–45; in Hong Kong, 150–51; ignored, in sinking of British warships, 151; in India, 152–53; interservice rivalry in, 149, 153; in Japanese defeat, 146; Japanese military code broken by, 147–48; SACO use of, 149, 153; Tai Li in creating program for, 145; training program for, 145–46; T. V. Soong's role in, 143; in warlord

pacification, 144
Silvermaster Group, 100–102
Simpson, William, 181
Singapore, 60; signal intelligence in, 151; surrender of, 151–52
Singh, Mohan, 61
Sino-American Special Technical Cooperative Organization (SACO), 67; approval of, 86; Chinese nationalism and, 114–15; command and control disputes within, 104–6, 117–18, 179–80; George Marshall's objections to, 84–85; guerrilla training camps run by, 104, 126–27; Indochina operation of, 111–14; initial drafting of, 82; Naval Group China in, 179–80; origins of, 68–69, 80–81; OSS circumvention of, 118–20; in signal intelligence activities, 149, 153; Stilwell's comments on, 85–86; successes of, 128; in Thailand operation, 107–11
Sino-Soviet Nonaggression Pact, 12, 21
Smedley, Agnes, 163
Smith, William, 159
Snow, Edgar, 69
Soderbaum, George, 57, 64
Somervell, Brehon B., 170
Song, Qingling. *See* Madame Sun Yat-sun
Soong, Mayling. *See* Madame Chiang Kai-shek
Soong, T. V.: Flying Tigers and, 31, 45; as Lend-Lease intermediary, 89; in SACO treaty approval, 83; signal intelligence role of, 143; in Stilwell control of Lend-Lease material, 165; in Stilwell's recall, 169, 173; in unification of China, 143
Southeast Asia Command, 110
Soviet-Japanese Neutrality Pact, 8, 195
Soviet Union: in air defense strategy, 166; aircraft plant built by, 16; arms shipment routes refused by, 8–9; aviation support from, 15–16, 194; in CCP establishment, 10; diplomatic cover for, 17; expulsion of, from League of Nations, 21; fascism resisted by, 11–12; financial

loans from, 13–14; financial loans from, compared with U.S., 88; invasion of Finland by, 21; Japan neutrality pact with, 21; Lend-Lease material totals, 94*f;* in Manchuria, 186–87; military aid from, 12–13; military training support from, 10–11, 16; post-Yalta agenda of, 186–87; strategic minerals trade with, 17; strategic motivations of, 21–22, 34; territorial issues with, 18–20

Spanish Civil War, 11

Special Operations Army, 56

Special Operations Executive (SOE): creation of, 52; in rescue of Madame Meynier, 112; role in China Commando Group, 57–58; role in Yugoslavian Communists' success against Germans, 122

Stalin, Joseph, 8

Stankevich, Kavqun, 189

Stapler, Jack, 69

Starr, C. V., 74, 160

Stein, Gunther, 163

Stelle, Charles, 123

Stilwell, Joseph, 15, 40; Burma Road as focus of, 167; with the Chiangs, *132;* Chiang Kai-shek's charges against, 175; in ending Thai operation, 110; forced appointment of, 164; in Lend-Lease coordination, 92; public relations savvy of, 41, 162; recall of, 96, 172–75; on SACO draft, 85–86; terms of appointment of, 165; T.V. Soong in recall of, 169; with Yang Xuanchen, *135*

Stilwell incident, 172–75

Stoler, Mark, 193

strategic minerals trade, 4, 17

Stratemeyer, George, 178

Stratton, Roy, 76, 83

Strong, Anna Louise, 163

Suess, Ilona Ralf, 163

Sun Fo, 74

Sun Yat-sen, 10

Tai Li, 8; on American assistance, 67; antipathy toward British, 56, 57, 63; British attack on, 66; with Chiang Kai-shek, *133;* in China Commando Group enforcement, 54–55; in disbanding of Commando Group, 65; on guerrilla force development, 80–81; resentment of Old China Hands by, 76–77; on SACO approval, 87; in SACO command structure, 117–18; in signal intelligence program creation, 145

Taierzhuang: Battle of, 17; campaign, 15

Ten Men Group, 145

10th Air Force, 178

territorial issues, Chiang Kai-Shek's with Soviet Union, 18–20

Thailand operation, 107–11

Tibet-India highway, 7–8

Timberman, T. S., 192

Ting, Hollington, 66

Tito, Josip Broz, 122

Tolstoy, Ilia, 8, 75, 115

Tong, Hollington, 162

Treasury Department, U.S., Communist espionage ring in, 100–102

Tulsa incident, 59, 165

23rd Fighter Group, 43

two-plane team combat, 25–26, 38

United Front, 10, 20

United States: agencies of, in China, 177–78, 196; China policy of, *vs.* British, 180–81; in decisive attack on Japanese homeland, 187; financial loans from, 13; as potential source of aid, 9; presidential communication channels in, 174–75

U.S. Army: Burma Road strategic focus of, 167; in Dixie Mission, 122; Flying Tigers envied by, 40; SACO treaty role of, 84; on wartime aid programs to China, 89–90; in White House communication channels, 174

U.S. Army Air Corps: fighters *vs.* bombers in, 24–25; Flying Tigers' induction in, 43

U.S. Army Observer Group. *See* Dixie Mission

U.S. Naval Weather Service, 71

U.S. Navy: Pacific strategy of, 70–71; in presidential communication channels, 174–75; in SACO, 80–81, 179–80

Versailles Treaty, 1, 2
Vietnamese intelligence net, in French Indochina, 181
Voroshilov, K. E., 21
Votaw, Maurice, 163

Wang Huimin, 150
Wang Jingwei, 75
Wang Pengsheng, 66, 156
Wang Shijie, 73
War of 194-, The (Douhet), 25
war propaganda. *See* propaganda
warlord revolts, 143, 184
Wavell, Archibald, 59
weapons movement. See arms movement
weapons sales, Sino-German, 4. *See also* military aid
weather intelligence, 70–71, 104, 108
Wedemeyer, Albert, 123, *133;* on Birch murder, 184; on China policy, 180–81; on China theater, 177; command consolidation by, 178; on Communist expansion, 182; on occupation policy, 185
Wei Daming, 145, 161
Wen Yuqing, 144, 149
Wetzell, Georg, 2
Whampoa Military Academy, 10, 54
"what the hell" pennant, 69
White, Harry Dexter, 100–102
White, Theodore, 161–62
White House communication channels, 174–75
"white" propaganda, 157
Wight, David, 79
Wilkie, Wendell, *141*
Williamson, John "Luke," 24
working dogs, *139*

Wuhan campaign, 15

"X" forces, 167
Xian Incident, 12
Xiao Bo: on American infighting, 126; in SACO creation, 69, 84; signal intelligence activities of, 147
Xinjiang, 19
Xu Yongchang, 190

"Y" forces, 167
Yalta Conference: CCP policy changes following, 182; Manchuria secret deal in, 187
Yan Xishan, 143
Yang Jie, 6, 12
Yang Xuanchen, *135,* 149
Yardley, Herbert: on assassination, 55–56; in breaking of Japanese military code, 147–48
Ye Jianying, 191
Yeaton, Ivan, 125, 192
Young, Arthur N.: on failure of U.S. aid, 94, 169; on gold shipment sabotage, 102; on inflation spiral, 90
Young, James, 163
Yugoslavia, 122
Yunnan Expeditionary Forces, 175

Z Force, 65
Zeros, *vs.* P-40s, 148–49
Zhang Chun, 190
Zhang Gu Feng Peak, 18, 19
Zhang Xueliang, 28
Zhang Zhizhong, 190
Zheng Jieman, 60, 150, 191
Zhongtong, 145, 149
Zhou Enlai, *142;* in CCP-KMT peace talks, 190; Nazi-Soviet Pact supported by, 18
Zhou Weilong, 56, 65
Zhou Zhirou, 146
Zhu De, 99, *129,* 185

ABOUT THE AUTHOR

MAOCHUN YU is an associate professor of East Asia and Military History at the United States Naval Academy in Annapolis, Maryland. He holds a doctoral degree from the University of California at Berkeley (1994), a master's degree from Swarthmore College (1987), and a bachelor's degree from Nankai University (1983). Dr. Yu is the author of *OSS in China: Prelude to Cold War* (Yale University Press, 1997) and numerous articles on the history of military and intelligence operations during World War II and the Cold War.